Michael Tanner was ⋯ ⋯ ⋯ ⋯ ⋯ ⋯ ⋯ ⋯ ⋯ ⋯ After attending a local grammar school he went up to St Edmund Hall, Oxford, where besides gaining a degree in geography he represented the university on the rugby field.

A schoolmaster for eighteen years, he began writing about racing in 1982 with a memoir of a personal favourite, the steeplechaser Spanish Steps. Eight more racing books have followed, including *The Champion Hurdle*; *Dessie: A Year in the Life of Desert Orchid*; *The Major: The Biography of Dick Hern*; and *Great Jockeys of the Flat*.

He is married, with two daughters, and lives in Lincolnshire.

Michael Roberts

A Champion's Story

**Michael Roberts
and Michael Tanner**

HEADLINE

First published in 1994 by
HEADLINE BOOK PUBLISHING

First published in paperback in 1995 by
HEADLINE BOOK PUBLISHING

10 9 8 7 6 5 4 3 2 1

ISBN 0 7472 4257 7

Typeset by Avon Dataset Ltd., Bidford-on-Avon, B50 4JH

Printed and bound in Great Britain by
Cox & Wyman Ltd, Reading, Berks

HEADLINE BOOK PUBLISHING
A division of Hodder Headline PLC
338 Euston Road,
London NW1 3BH

Contents

To Verna, Melanie and Carolyn,
whose sacrifices have been
greater than mine.

Acknowledgements

In helping me bring this project to fruition, Michael Roberts spent many hours talking into a tape recorder with infinite grace and good humour when the pressures of the moment – the contrasting autumns of 1992 and 1993 – could have excused any number of less charitable reactions. Racegoers everywhere have come to respect Michael's presence in the saddle: they can take it from me that his bearing out of the saddle is to be equally admired.

Besides Michael – and Verna – Roberts there are several individuals I must thank for their co-operation and their contribution. Catherine Jenkinson, Herman Brown, Fred Rickaby, Brian Cherry, Lew Tankel, Trevor Denman and Robbyn Ramsay provided fond memories of Michael's South African career; Eric Denman produced the accurate list of Michael's wins per season. I should particularly like to single out Robbyn Ramsay: without her unflagging assistance, the problem of gathering South African information at long range might well have become insuperable.

The following gentlemen ensured that Michael's UK career received coverage of similar depth: Gavin Hunter, Alec Stewart, Dick Denney, Ron Boss, Clive Brittain,

Graham Rock, John Gosden, Anthony Stroud, Luca Cumani, Michael Stoute, Henry Cecil, Peter O'Sullevan and Graham Goode. Lastly, I salute the skills of all the photographers, but especially Ken Wilkins, Gerry Cranham, John Crofts, Trevor Jones and George Selwyn, who expended considerable energy on my behalf.

Michael Tanner
Sleaford, Lincolnshire
May 1994

Foreword

If my Mum could see me now! Mum was not keen on racing, yet here I am writing the foreword to a book which would never have come about but for racing.

It came as quite a surprise when Michael Tanner told me (in August 1992) that someone was interested in publishing a book about me. What with the championship and double century in 1992 and riding for Sheikh Mohammed in 1993, this biography applies the finishing touches to an extremely eventful two years. I am very grateful to everyone who has helped me reach this point in my career, they know who they are. But it's at times like this that I remember and value those who were especially supportive during my initial British seasons when I was fighting hard to establish myself. Thank you, Alec and Clive; and Dick Denney. Also I mustn't forget Gavin Hunter, who asked me to come over from South Africa in the first place.

I really believe it is an honour to have a book written about you, particularly because I don't think a South African jockey has ever been the subject of one before; which reminds me I would not be where I am today were it not for a number of people back home. Cyril Buckham and Jock

Sproule, both sadly deceased, set me on the right road at the Jockeys' Academy and Herman Brown, who taught me so much when I was apprenticed to him.

I have dedicated this book to my wife, Verna, and my daughters, Melanie and Carolyn. They have had to suffer the sacrifices imposed by having a husband and father away from home so often. The encouragement they have provided has been the cornerstone of my career. I thank them from the bottom of my heart.

Finally, I would like to thank Michael Tanner for the considerable time and meticulous research that he has put into this book.

Newmarket
England,
May 1994

1 200 Up

5.15 a.m., Wednesday, 21 October 1992. In a darkened room, an alarm clock shatters the stillness, shortly followed by two rings of a telephone wake-up call. The back-up proves unnecessary. At the first sound a shadowy but patently slight figure automatically rises and, padding deftly lest the warm slumber of the bed's other occupant be disturbed, heads for the bathroom. Although the face greeting him in the mirror belongs to a 38-year-old man, its tanned and vaguely elfin features suggest someone younger.

Within ten minutes the eyes are straining through the windscreen of a white BMW cleaving the pre-dawn gloom of a dank autumnal morning. The car noses along a high street deprived of its vitality. No worm need yet fear an early bird; newsboys are still abed and precious few milkmen are stirring. But there are signs of activity, for this is Newmarket, home to 2,000 thoroughbred racehorses that must be tended and exercised. For grooms and assorted stable staff the working day has commenced; for work riders and jockeys it is just about to. For one jockey in particular, a day begun like oh so many others since he set out twenty-four years ago to climb the greasy pole which defends the summit of his chosen profession will end like no other. He will enter the history books. The driver of the BMW is Michael Roberts, eleven times champion jockey of his native South Africa, now champion-elect of Britain and at this moment one victory away from becoming only the fifth jockey ever to ride 200 winners in a British Flat racing season.

Many miles and many landmarks separate the training grounds of South Africa's Summerveld and England's Newmarket Heath, but they share the common denominators of frisky youngsters and wily veterans – both the four- and the two-legged variety. Awaiting Roberts on the Long Hill gallops is Clive Brittain, a renowned early riser among the Newmarket training fraternity.

'Morning, Guv'nor.'

Everyone in racing calls Clive Brittain by his first name except, it seems, Michael Roberts, who still addresses him as Mr Brittain or Guv'nor. The jockey listens intently to the trainer's instructions, snaps secure the chin-strap of his crash hat, hiding beneath its royal blue bobble covering, zips up his grey jacket in anticipation of the forthcoming battle with the elements and thrusts his fingers deep into a pair of white riding gloves. The trainer grabs a shiny boot and legs his jockey into the saddle.

The animal is an old comrade-in-arms, the five-year-old Shambo, who has a date at Newbury three days hence. Off they go. The muffled thud of the centaur, man and horse in perfect unison. How many times has Roberts watched the early morning dew glisten on a thoroughbred's hooves? Shambo's one-mile spin completed, Roberts vaults on to the two-year-old filly Love Of Silver for a routine blow over seven furlongs. Love Of Silver is bound for the Breeders' Cup at Gulfstream Park in Florida, a hot and humid destination far removed from the chill of an East Anglian morning.

After a restorative cup of coffee at Brittain's Carlburg Stables, Roberts recrosses town to rendezvous with Alec Stewart, his number one retainer, on Racecourse Side. Brittain and Stewart are two sides of the same coin – consummate professionalism – but whereas Brittain is an outgoing former stable lad who made it big, ultimately, Stewart is a reserved former public schoolboy and City gent who made it big quickly. The reason was simple: within five years of taking out a full licence Stewart found himself training a champion. Its name was Mtoto; its jockey was Roberts. Neither man had looked back since and the bond between them was water-tight. This coming afternoon Roberts would sport the Mtoto colours on a three-year-old filly called Jasoorah in the Heswall Graduation Stakes at Chester. The two men compare notes. Although Roberts's three mounts for Brittain hold chances, Jasoorah is the banker. If all else fails she will bring up the 200.

However, Roberts was well aware that all manner of things could go wrong – not just in the race itself, but between now and 3.50 p.m. He kept reminding himself of the hard-luck stories which riddle all sports and bedevil all sportsmen, be they jockeys or cricketers. One fall at this late stage of the season is tantamount to a batsman being run out on 99. The jitters were inescapable as he returned to Long Hill to put Stewart's Jdaayel through her paces. Back in August a fall from one of Brittain's juveniles had left him in agony with injuries to his neck and back that cried out for three weeks' rest. They got four days. Roberts was not about to let slip the lead of twenty-six he held over Pat Eddery in the jockeys' table. Eddery was another fierce competitor, quite capable of closing the gap given half a chance. British champion nine times, he had himself achieved Roberts's immediate goal by registering 209 winners in 1990 to become the first double centurion since Gordon Richards in 1952.

Jdaayel is on her best behaviour, thereby eliminating one potential source of disaster, but others await; later on Roberts must endure the fifty-minute ordeal of the journey to Chester by light aeroplane, a combination of conveyance and course which had nearly proved terminal earlier in the year. When attempting the return leg of the journey, Roberts's aircraft failed to lift off properly, ploughed through a hedge and wound up in a drainage ditch. The very next day Roberts was airborne again. He had to get back in the saddle; so he had to get back in the air. There could be no let-up in the quest for a slice of racing history.

Body and soul would be sustained through the rigours of yet another gut-wrenching take-off and the six rides in prospect at Chester by a cup of tea and a slice of toast. At around 8.30 both taste pretty good. One of today's sextet demands his minimum weight and Roberts will not eat again until this evening. The racing papers remind him that until Iota's success yesterday he had gone twenty-nine rides without a win, his longest losing sequence of the season. Besides being win number 199, the filly had been his 1,007th domestic ride of the season, already a record in its own right. Richards alone had previously managed 1,000, and then only with the very last race on the very last card. The thought is a timely cue for a call to his agent, journalist Graham Rock, without whose form-book acumen, numerous contacts and powers of telephonic persuasion Roberts would not be on the brink of making further history. Yes, Jasoorah was a good thing. If all else fails, Jasoorah would bring up the 200.

A benevolent smile from Lady Luck would not come amiss, all the same, and Roberts goes to the wardrobe and picks out the navy-blue double-breasted sports jacket that had always brought good fortune back in South Africa. It could do no harm to wear all the lucky items of clothing today. His wife Verna and younger daughter Carolyn, home from school with a nasty bout of asthma, nod in agreement. They kiss him goodbye and Roberts heads for the July Course and the aircraft which will ferry him and fellow jockeys George Duffield and Richard Hills to Hawarden Airport, two miles from Chester racecourse. A fifteen-minute taxi ride will complete the journey. The little Cessna soars into the air with Roberts holding on for dear life. Landings he can tolerate, but take-offs . . . what can you do if something goes wrong? There's no safety net, is there? Thankfully, apart from discussing the previous afternoon's innovative jump jockeys versus Flat jockeys race over hurdles at Chepstow, the flight involves nothing more eventful than another flip through the papers and a cat-nap. On arrival at Chester's historic Roodee – the oldest track in England – Roberts makes directly for the weighing-room; having raced here yesterday he sees no need to walk the

5

course again. The welcome is pleasantly boisterous. All the top jockeys are here bar Pat Eddery. Cauthen, Carson, Dettori, Swinburn and Cochrane are adamant: hurry up and get the 200 so we can open the champagne.

Chester has good as well as bad memories. In 1987 the Stewart–Roberts partnership got off to a cracking start when Just David won the Chester Cup. Roberts chooses a peg and changes into the colours he will wear in the first, the blue and yellow silks which his valet Paul Kingsley has laid out ready for him. He does not profess to be a superstitious man but he decides to give his whip a thorough cleaning nevertheless. He did this by chance prior to the 1988 Geoffrey Freer Stakes and his mount Top Class, the 20–1 outsider of six, proceeded to beat three Classic winners. Every little helps.

Having confirmed he is carrying the correct weight on the check-scale he waits for the bell telling jockeys their presence is required outside. Roberts's horse in this race is a small brown gelding trained by Richard Hannon, the champion trainer elect, who has already contributed twenty-nine winners to his total, most notably five courtesy of the season's sensational two-year-old flying machine Lyric Fantasy, nicknamed the Pocket Rocket by her adoring public. Top Pet is no Lyric Fantasy, and although he ran well on the soft last time he can't get through this heavy ground made heavier by each drop of afternoon rain. The writing is on the wall some way from the finish and Top Pet trails home last. Nor can Range Rider, first of the Brittain trio, handle the surface any better in the next, betraying his discomfort by hanging to the left in the straight.

Colossus engenders far greater optimism. He ran creditably here in the spring and hinted at a return to form at Newmarket a week ago. But Roberts has a nettle to grasp. He is drawn in the middle of the fourteen runners. If he elects to stay towards the outside on a tight circuit like Chester he will effectively convert this seven-and-a-half-furlong race into a mile, and it was the final half mile that found out Colossus back in May. No, he must miss the kick and go up the inner. As Causley breaks from the stalls into the lead Roberts sticks to his guns and the rail. Rounding the top turn Colossus is moving with such assurance that some of it inevitably travels up the reins to his jockey's hands, heart and head. At the two-furlong pole Colossus strikes the front, still on the bridle. In the split second it takes for Roberts the icy pro to suppress the excitement rising within Roberts the ordinary mortal, Colossus begins to labour. Once again those last 110 yards are his nemesis. Half an hour later Roberts is left with a feeling of *déjà vu*. The third Carlburg representative also leads into the final furlong; a stride or two of hope, however, is rudely dashed as Lost Reputation comes by with a wet sail to win comfortably by three lengths.

Roberts drags the saddle from a heaving Major's Law and provides an instant post-mortem for John Spouse, Brittain's travelling head lad, standing in for the trainer who is back at Carlburg. In another part of Newmarket Verna and Carolyn Roberts have the *Racing Post* spread out in front of the television, which is tuned to Teletext. Between games of pinball they have been methodically ticking off the races. They turn their attention to the fifth and prepare

7

to dial the Racecall telephone commentary. Come on, Michael! Come on, Dad! Come on, Jasoorah! Michael has always believed it was just a matter of time. Not if, but when. Will the minutes never tick away? Has the clock stopped or will it never reach 3.50? Mother and daughter play yet another game of pinball.

In the Chester weighing-room Roberts's highly developed sang-froid is under siege. There's no use denying it. He can detect the same surge of extra adrenalin he used to feel in '87 and '88 whenever he donned Sheikh Ahmed Al-Maktoum's yellow jacket with the black epaulets. Mtoto's colours; the colours Jasoorah will carry. Would that she *were* Mtoto; the champagne could be uncorked now. Just half of Mtoto's ability would surely suffice?

For what seems the hundredth time Roberts goes down the list of five opponents and runs the race through in his mind. They've got the beating of Shahaamh on the evidence of their York clash in which Jasoorah prevailed by three and a half lengths, easing down. Barahin, Anchorage and Faugeron? Surely they are moderate animals compared to Jasoorah. The lightly-raced El Cortes could be the dark horse. Trainer Peter Chapple-Hyam once considered this colt superior to both Rodrigo de Triano and Dr Devious, with whom he subsequently won three Classics. But, Roberts assures himself, the colt injured his knees in the Dante Stakes and has not run for five months; he could not possibly be sufficiently match-fit to upset Jasoorah in this heavy going. She'll love this ground. Barring accidents, she's got to be a certainty.

There's the bell. It's time to go. No more dreaming: there's a job to be done.

Roberts was not alone in his opinion of Jasoorah's chances. A dozen punters backed their judgement with four-figure wagers and the best you could find on the boards at the off was 11–10. The one-mile four-and-a-half-furlong start of the Heswall Graduation Stakes, 'for three-year-olds only, which, at starting, have not won more than two races', lay on the far side of the Roodee adjacent to the River Dee itself, set against the picture-postcard backdrop of Grosvenor Bridge. The distance of the race demanded one and a half circuits of the dead-flat track which is not only the oldest in the country but also the sharpest. On this very site they ran for a 'bell of sylver' worth 111 shillings 111 pence on Shrove Tuesday 1540. At one time or another described variously as a Circus, Cockpit and Hippodrome, this tricky little course was loathed by even Fred Archer, who thought nothing of tearing down Epsom's treacherous Tattenham Hill with complete disregard for his own preservation. Not that his hatred of the Roodee prevented him from riding half the eighteen winners at the Spring Meeting of 1881. The Roodee requires its jockeys to be brave and, above all else, quick-witted. Jasoorah was most definitely in safe hands.

One hundred and eighty miles to the south-east, Alec Stewart switches on SIS coverage to see the six runners circling in front of the stalls. Walter Swinburn, unhappy with Faugeron, is calling for the vet. The horse's breathing is giving cause for some concern and Faugeron is withdrawn. That's one less for you to worry about, Swinburn tells Roberts as he leads the horse away. Roberts clucks his filly

9

into stall three, between Willie Carson on Barahin and Richard Hills on Shahaamh; John Reid (El Cortes) and Steve Cauthen (Anchorage) are on the outside. This is it, this is the one, Muis, they chorus. Verna Roberts punches out Racecall's number for the fifth time and cradles the receiver between herself and her daughter. Come on, Michael! Come on, Dad! Come on, Jasoorah!

Four minutes later than advertised, starter John Mangles presses the button. Stewart has instructed his jockey to make the pace if no one else is so inclined, but Roberts's belief that Shahaamh would accept the task as she had in their previous encounter is immediately vindicated. Barahin comes next, followed by Jasoorah and Anchorage, with El Cortes held up in rear. This suits Roberts fine. He feels his filly was left in front too long at York and wishes to avoid dictating affairs if he can. A sudden rush of sound from the County Stand is acoustic confirmation of the mounting tension and bids to accelerate their progress. The crowd has come to witness history, to be able to claim: 'I was there.'

Experienced Roberts-watchers realise how easily Jasoorah is travelling. The rhythmic rocking motion of the jockey's head is the tell-tale sign to look out for, and today Roberts's cap is nodding like a yellow metronome. Then, passing the six marker, Jasoorah drops her bit and momentarily gives her partner the impression she is losing her action. Roberts instantly makes the transition from rider to jockey. To most onlookers there is no difference; but those who know about these matters say otherwise. What makes a great jockey, according to master trainers of yore like Charles Morton and Richard Marsh, is brains: brains and the priceless attribute of using them at the right moment. If the ground is inconveniencing his filly, Roberts wants to know while he still has time to kid her and her opponents that this is not necessarily the case. Better to throw up a smokescreen now than discover in the shadow of the winning-post that Jasoorah cannot deliver what is required. One tap down the shoulder will tell him what she is thinking. One, two, three – tap. Whoosh! The power is there, all right, just longing to be unleashed. Were it not for the enormity of the circumstances her jockey would already be calculating his winning percentage.

The binoculars trained on Jasoorah tell the same story. With three furlongs to run, Shahaamh is finished. It's a long haul to the winning-post in ground as heavy as this, but Roberts has no qualms about Jasoorah's stamina: he knows she will stay two miles. It's time to move. He changes his hands and shortens her up a bit to make her race, to summon up that different level of effort signified by the irritating but strikingly appropriate motoring metaphor 'a change of gear'. The bay filly responds to order and leaves her rivals toiling like ants in treacle.

Cutting the final corner, Roberts makes for the centre of the track and the best ground. The pumping elbows have stoked up a fine head of steam now: he and Jasoorah are really rolling. The Roberts style has its detractors, but horses do run for him. Just two words are all these critics must eat: Gordon Richards. His style was likewise not so easy on the eye as some, but he too made horses want to run their hearts out. Jasoorah is enjoying every stride. She is revelling in the conditions, stretching out and using herself superbly. There is no call for the characteristic Roberts finish: the inimitable short, chopping whip action as, with shins clamped almost vertical and torso tilted at an angle of sixty degrees, he becomes a dead ringer for Richards – or Steve Donoghue . . . two more words for detractors to choke on. Steve Donoghue: English racing's Dr Dolittle, a man whose rapport with all God's creatures found no deeper expression than in his almost telepathic understanding with thoroughbreds. It is a gift bestowed on precious few, but once grandfather Roberts gave him his first cow when he was six years old it was all too obviously a gift with which Michael Roberts had been similarly blessed. The best of Richards and Donoghue makes a potent blend which can elicit fits of pique from less talented rivals. Many a foe would contemplate selling his soul for half the ability.

No such thoughts are allowed to penetrate Roberts's concentration, however. There may be under 200 yards to negotiate; the course commentator's voice, shouting words to the effect that this is the 200th, may just be discerned above the din redolent of Derby day; there may be similarly inclined voices willing him on back in Newmarket – but Roberts remains the cool, collected professional consumed by tunnel vision. There will be no flamboyant salute to the crowd, no standing up in the irons, no waving of the whip. He has seen too many animals change legs or jink and dislodge their riders in mid-celebration. It's tempting to do so in these circumstances but preferable to desist. It's unprofessional. Why abandon the habits of a lifetime?

The winning-post comes and goes for the 200th time in

1992 just as swiftly as it did for the previous 199. The winning horse receives three grateful pats down the neck capped by a playful swipe across the mane; the winning jockey tries desperately hard not to appear any different from normal. The hunched shoulders signify understandable exhaustion but also betray a rising tide of emotion. Behind the goggles are closed eyes filling with tears and the elated spirit of a man thanking the Lord for his success. The loss of control is short-lived and even if the lump in his throat shows no sign of subsiding it is invisible to the serried ranks of well-wishers who enthusiastically swamp victorious horse and jockey. In acknowledgement the right hand is raised in the 'papal wave' which has become the trademark of any Roberts victory celebration.

On dismounting, the significance of this particular success is soon corroborated by scenes which will lodge only as a blur of euphoric images in Roberts's personal memory bank. Posing for photographers at Jasoorah's head; being pursued up the weighing-room steps by a posse of reporters eager to snatch those 'what-does-it-feel-like' quotes; the warm congratulations of those waiting inside. If the truth be told, Michael Roberts feels so springheeled he could jump high in the air and touch the ceiling. Before the notion can be tested he is called outside for the presentation of two bottles of champagne. More photos, surrounded by fellow jockeys, and yet more questions. Yes, it was a relief to have finally done it; yes, it was pleasing to have done it on one of Alec Stewart's because he was a man who always had faith in him; one of Clive Brittain's or Richard Hannon's would have been nice, too, as they had contributed enormously to the score, but he and Alec went back a long way.

So much has been happening that Roberts is in danger of failing to weigh out in time for the last race. Nor has he yet managed to catch the replay of win number 200. Pausing only to organise a crate of bubbly for thirsty colleagues, he scampers out to ride Don't Forget Marie in the nursery. He endures a terrible ride. The filly is squeezed leaving the stalls and nearly comes down, for a few strides she actually straddles another runner's backside. With the race already as good as lost, Roberts suffers the added indignity of having mud and clods of earth kicked up into his face as Don't Forget Marie tracks the bunch. What a way to treat a champion. Jeez, these buggers are getting even with me now!

By 5.25 the captains and the kings are departing. Roberts slips into the navy-blue talisman which has worked the oracle once more and reaches for his camel-hair overcoat. The track he must cross has been reduced to a quagmire; he puts two plastic bags over his shoes and fastens them around his ankles with elastic bands. No point ruining a decent pair of shoes. The presence on the plane of two further bottles does nothing to pacify the customary butterflies as the Cessna leaves terra firma, but once aloft he and George Duffield soon fall to discussing the momentous seasons they have enjoyed. The likeable Duffield, for so long considered a mere journeyman of the minor tracks, has notched up not only his first century but also his first Classics – on User Friendly, who but for a twist of fate would have been partnered by Roberts. There were numerous landmarks of his own for the South African to ponder: the most rides ever taken during a British season; now the double hundred. Nothing new there, it was true, but seldom had a jockey ridden 200 in two different countries as he had. And still to come was the jockeys' championship itself; the first South African to lift the title. Not only a champion in two countries, which is a rare enough occurrence, but a champion in two hemispheres, which is rare to the point of being unheard-of.

However, this is no time to savour statistics. This is a moment to share with his wife and daughter; so, cruising high above middle England, he calls home. The telephone at Roberts's flat has in fact been taking a pounding since Racecall informed Verna and Carolyn Roberts that Jasoorah had safely crossed the line. When all the screaming, shouting, clapping and jumping had abated, the good tidings were promptly relayed to elder daughter Melanie, at school in Natal, and other family and friends in South Africa. Then a conversation with Alec Stewart; over the wall at Carlburg Clive Brittain had also ridden every furlong with an imaginary whip cracking fit to snap. He rushed into the yard to inform his lads, who let out a spontaneous whoop of genuine delight for a man who has quickly won their utmost respect. In a neat Moulton bungalow on the far side of Warren Hill a dapper 76-year-old is equally ecstatic. Fred Rickaby was responsible for polishing Michael Roberts's natural talent: it was he who had provided him with the first great horse, the mighty Sledgehammer. Now 'Mr Rick' had returned to his Newmarket roots. Verna Roberts was struck by a sense of relief that was almost tangible. She too had been haunted by the nightmare scenario of injury or fate conspiring to divert the course of justice. No cause for concern any more, thank goodness. Put some champagne in the fridge. Yes, she mustn't forget that. Mother and daughter then set about making a poster to hang over the front door: 'Well Done, Champ,' it declares.

It's getting on for 7.00 p.m. when the 'Champ' in question rests weary eyes on this touching personal affirmation of his achievement. The unconfined joy which engulfs the Roberts household is marred only by the absence of Melanie – but friend and neighbour George Geen downs a few glasses and helps fill the void in an intimate family celebration. They speak of the past; the knock-backs and the triumphs, to which today's great deeds must henceforth be added.

Having eaten nothing since 8.30 a.m., the 'Champ' is more than ready for his steak, though soon afterwards staggering to bed becomes the only sensible option. Briefly, he indulges a mind now satisfyingly at peace with itself. All this excitement, he reflects, would have reduced his mum to a nervous wreck. Sleep quickly claims him. By 10.00 p.m., Wednesday, 21 October 1992 is over.

2 The Electric Bump

Magdalena Van Wyk would have preferred her first-born to have entered the priesthood, of that he is pretty certain. However, besides being a devout member of the Dutch Reformed Church, Magdalena Roberts, as she became, was a tiny woman who bequeathed Michael Leonard a jockey's frame. Furthermore, she was to imbue the child who entered the world on 17 May 1954 in Cape Town's Groote Schuur Hospital with traditional Afrikaner strengths, such as profound respect for teachers, elders and all persons in authority and strict adherence to a disciplined lifestyle. Unwittingly, Mrs Roberts had equipped her son for stoic acceptance of the spartan physical and mental regimen necessarily endured by the jockey.

ROBERTS: Mum was only five feet one or five feet two. She was very strict and a perfectionist in everything she did. For example, if it was raining shoes had to be left outside the door and we always had to eat on time, all together, and grace had to be said. And it was Sunday School, without fail. Everything was well ordered. We had to play in the garden – and needed permission to go to friends. Mum was very protective, but, saying that, most South African families were like that. Yes, Mum was very strict; more so than my dad – but then again, he was away working a lot. If we got out of hand, though, he wore the belt!

Magdalena Roberts fulfilled the role of sheet anchor to her budding champion jockey and his three brothers Gerhardus, James and Charles (also destined to become a jockey) while husband Leonard coped with the demands of working shifts on the railway; further demands on her resulted from the Roberts family being uprooted from Cape Town to Despatch, a dormitory town of Port Elizabeth in the Eastern Province, before finally settling in Oudtshoorn, 200 miles or so further west.

ROBERTS: Dad started as a signalman, I think, and rose to the rank of station master by the time he retired. He was transferred to Port Elizabeth for a few years and we lived in Despatch, which is quite a big place. I can remember going fishing with my dad, off the rocks. I attended the Susanna Fourie Primary School; accountancy was my best subject – I was good at figures. But Dad always wanted to go back to where he was born and he took the farm outside Oudtshoorn, up the George road, before he retired. I went to the local school until I was twelve and then Oudtshoorn High School as a weekly boarder. I used to play a bit of rugby, scrum half, believe it or not, and ran cross-country: nothing great, just school sports really, because I was so tiny.

Oudtshoorn is located in the arid and blisteringly hot region known as the Little Karroo and grew up where the River

Grobbelaars cuts a fertile gap between the Swarteberg and Outinqua mountain ranges. Its two halves are still linked by a fine old suspension bridge and the heart of the town is pleasantly laid out with jacaranda-lined streets that feature several elegant Victorian buildings. Apart from Philip Blaiberg, the first person to survive a year with a transplanted heart, and Langenhoven, the composer of *Die Stem*, the Afrikaner anthem, Oudtshoorn has produced few famous sons. The scorched badlands surrounding Oudtshoorn are renowned for their ostrich farms (originally to provide hat feathers; nowadays for biltong – dried meat for chewing), but most local farmers concentrate on more conventional livestock. One such individual was Roberts's grandfather Michael Henry Roberts, the South African-born son of a Welsh hill farmer.

ROBERTS: I was always in love with animals and I couldn't wait for the next holidays so we could get down to the farm: my brothers wanted the seaside but I wanted the farm. My grandfather gave me my first cow – a Jersey – when I was six or seven and I soon had a little herd which I used to milk before going to school. I used to just live for my granny and grandpa. They lived on what we called a proper farm where they used to make their own bread in the morning and grind their own coffee. They had three or four hundred acres and got their income from milk; I remember they had no electricity for many a year and used candles, which as kids we used to love. Grandad preferred traditional methods. He never had a driver's licence; he did most of his ploughing with horses and donkeys until my dad's younger brother took over. He would rather prepare his own manure than buy fertiliser in a bag; he used to chase the reps off the farm! But his way was the right way.

The first time I actually sat on an animal was a donkey. We'd ride them bareback with old bridles and later on we got on to a few horses. But not proper riding, you understand, bareback, no saddle. All I wanted to do was get on a horse's back. The first mention of me becoming a jockey that I can remember was one day in school when the teacher told me to stand up in class – and I was already standing up! She said, 'Michael, you should be a jockey.' The person that actually got me interested in racing was my dad's uncle, who was a stud manager down in the Cape. Every year people had a flutter on the July Handicap – England has the Derby, South Africa has the 'July' – and he used to say to my dad that I'd be a jockey some day. It began to stick in the back of my mind and it became all I ever wanted to do. I used to cut out pictures of horses and keep them in a scrapbook. I was probably only seven or eight then and, of course, you couldn't go to the Jockeys' Academy until you were fourteen. When I was eleven or twelve I thought about becoming a vet, but then I saw an article in a magazine about the Academy and the desire to become a jockey came back quite strongly. I said to my old man: 'I'd like to do that.' I collected pictures of the top racehorses like Colorado King and Sea Cottage – who was the nation's favourite. I'll never forget when he got shot on the beach before the July.

Mum was very much against the idea – it was gambling and so on. Then she got very sick with leukaemia. Things happened so quickly. The doctors virtually told us to the day how long she had to live: six months. She prepared us for her death. My dad was shattered.

There can be no question that Magdalena Roberts's twelve-year-old son was shattered. However, one family was about to be replaced by another. On 1 June 1968 Michael Roberts entered the South African Jockeys' Academy at Marianhill, about fifteen miles outside Durban. 'It was just like starting from scratch again. My mum had passed away and I left the family. It was like a new chapter all of a sudden.'

The Jockey Club of South Africa had launched its innovative Academy in 1958 as an experimental school for apprentice jockeys, with a view to increasing the supply and elevating the status of a profession which had not always presented a squeaky-clean image. The location selected was Durban, one of the country's three principal racing centres, and with financial assistance from the Natal Provincial Council the institution was established at Hamilton Lodge, Marianhill, at a total cost of £34,000. (In 1972 the Academy was moved to its present site on the Summerveld complex at Shongweni.) In 1968 the Academy catered for up to thirty apprentices at a time, boys who normally entered between the ages of fourteen and eighteen. Demand for places far exceeded availability and only one in five applicants was accepted. The reasons were all too apparent. Hamilton Lodge was run on the lines of a private boarding school: apart from the tuition in jockeyship, stable management, elementary veterinary science and the Rules of Racing, all the apprentices received a comprehensive academic education up to Standard 8 or matriculation, while the strictest attention was paid to developing good manners, deportment, speech, tasteful attire and a rigid sense of honesty and loyalty. Quite simply, the Academy's aim was to turn out gentlemen as well as first-class jockeys; and at no cost to parents apart from nominal outlay on clothing and equipment.

ROBERTS: I went to Port Elizabeth for my first interview because Oudtshoorn fell under the Eastern Province Racing Authority; after two years in Durban all the apprentices are then returned to their own province. You had to be the right age, fit, and have reached at least Standard 6; and they measure your legs to see if you're going to grow too much and put on too much weight. I was four feet four inches and weighed fifty-eight pounds – four stone two! I tell you, at high school I was a mascot! They passed me and sent me to the main board in Durban.

They prefer people that haven't ridden before so they can teach them from scratch. I could sit on a horse and not fall off, but I had no idea about proper trotting or cantering. A couple of months before I went to the Academy my uncle said he'd better teach me to ride properly. Anyway, this horse he put me on ran with me; we were going through dongas – dry ravines – under trees and I was hanging on to the saddle for dear life: I'd let go of the reins! My uncle was trying to keep up with us but he couldn't. I thought we were going to go straight through the fences and on to the road so I grabbed the one rein and we started heading up this hill. It was going to kill me, the way this horse was galloping because the veld was rough, all rocks, like desert.

When the horse stopped and I got off my legs just crumpled. I was absolutely legless!

The regime awaiting Roberts was far removed from the carefree rustic idyll he favoured and savoured on his grandparents' farm. This was more Borstal than Butlins; Greyfriars with more than a hint of Dotheboys Hall. Every day was a test of endurance. Whoever's turn it was to act as 'coffee boy' was abroad at 4 a.m. to rouse his fellows. The first-year students took riding lessons until 6.30 a.m. while others were bussed to the tracks in order to ride work for trainers. School began at 10.15 a.m. and continued to 2.45 p.m., with just half an hour for lunch. From 3 to 4 p.m. the juniors had more riding lessons while the seniors were taught animal and stable management. Supper was at 5.50: the boys' diet, naturally, was strictly controlled and consisted of meat, fish, eggs and salad, with no potatoes or rice, and just toast in the mornings. After that there was a final school session, and then equipment would be cleaned and polished for the next day. Only when that was completed could the apprentices relax until bed at 8.15 p.m.

ROBERTS: The Academy regime came very easily to me really because I'd been a weekly boarder at Oudtshoorn after Mum had died, which did me a lot of good. It was hard, tiring work, though: mucking out boxes; chaffing a bale of lucerne between two of you; grooming the horses. There were only eighteen there when I arrived and I was the only intake of that June. There were a couple three or four months ahead of me and I can assure you that all the work got passed down and down. They did eventually change to a 1 January intake but when I started it was whenever you turned fourteen; my birthday was 17 May, so I started in June. Mr Curran was headmaster then – Mr O'Connor came later – and Mr Buckham was the Riding Master.

I got pushed around a bit to begin with by the seniors but in general they were a pretty good bunch. Getting up at 4 a.m. and going to work was no joke at the age of fourteen and you'd often fall asleep in class, which got you a clip round the ear! Towards the end I worked at bookkeeping for an hour every night too, because I thought it might help if I went into business. It was much tougher than the boarding school in Oudtshoorn. The seniors did give you a rough time. I was so tiny, which was how I got the name 'Muis'. Everyone had a nickname – Slug, Flipper – but I'd not had one before. Usually they disappear in time but somehow mine stuck. I've tried to put people off using it; I don't mind Muis but I don't like being called Mouse.

One lifelong friendship initiated hereabouts involved Trevor Denman, eventually to find fame as a racecaller both in South Africa and in the USA.

DENMAN: Michael was a first-year apprentice at the Academy when we met. I wasn't at the Academy but I lived around the Greyville track and mixed with the apprentices. The Academy wouldn't take me: I was four feet six and sixty-six pounds. I was about sixteen, I suppose. Michael only spoke broken English at the time, just enough to make himself understood, although he had no trouble understanding what you were talking about. The Academy was a hell place, six days a week. You only had Saturday night free but there was no wild night life for them – or any of us for that matter. There was a local ice rink; two or three discos. But you could never have got in and the drinking laws were so strict.

The task of overseeing the daily welfare of the apprentices fell to the matron, Catherine Jenkinson. The Dublin-born, Glasgow-trained nurse, known to the boys as 'Miss Jinks', was, in effect, a surrogate mother to them all, a view exemplified by the light she sheds on the tortuous rites of passage negotiated by Roberts en route to manhood.

JENKINSON: I found Michael very quiet and in my opinion he was bullied into cleaning kit and fetching and carrying. Some of the older boys terrorised the younger ones. The 'I walked into a door, Miss Jinks' or 'a horse kicked me, Miss Jinks' didn't work with me and I soon put a stop to it all when I took over. They said I would make the boys grow 'soft' but I would have none of it.

When it came to riding horses, however, the teenage Roberts encountered scarcely a hitch.

ROBERTS: I couldn't believe how quickly I became proficient and progressed from the slowest ponies through really strong horses to the ex-racehorses. One or two were so strong that if you could control them you were considered ready. I just seemed to have the knack; I'd get my hands right on them and they used to drop their heads for me. Then the next boy would get on and it would race round the track with him. I arrived on a Thursday and on the Saturday I saw my first race at Scottsville, the local Pietermaritzburg track. The apprentices go to every meeting in the Academy uniform of grey 'longs' and black blazer with the horseshoe badge, and every Thursday evening they'd get the cine films and play back all the races to show us what was good or bad, or which jockeys had made mistakes. You couldn't ride on a track until you had been there a year. I could have ridden in ten months, so I wasted two months really. Anyway, I was sent to the Summerveld training centre after two months; usually it was six. You could ride twenty horses a morning, like in America. Summerveld was a twenty-minute bus ride away and is a bit like a smaller version of Newmarket – only minus the town. John Jacobs was the first trainer to help me out, and then Joey Joseph. I'd ride work in the morning but I couldn't ride in races; as I could ride all the horses in the string I was getting very frustrated.

Jacobs had no hesitation in advising the Riding Master that the Academy's latest prodigy was ready to compete in races. Arthur Gorton, the first holder of this vital post (and uncle of crack jockey John) had been succeeded by Cyril Buckham, himself no mean artist in the saddle. Buckham had twice won the July Handicap at Durban's Greyville, on Monasterevan in 1948 and Spey Bridge in 1956. He recognised the spark of greatness when he saw it and soon appreciated the God-given qualities bestowed upon his latest fledgling. When the media eventually came calling he told them: 'When he came he was very small – tiny – and those are the boys we look for. But it doesn't mean if they're small they're going to make it. Michael had the ability and the size. The first time I ever put him on a horse he just belonged there, as if that's where he should be. When I was teaching him everything I taught him he did exactly as I wanted. It was absolute magic. He was always looking for the edge on every little thing he did. He was a great competitor; he always tries, like Clive Rice in cricket or Gary Player in golf. They have a term in racing called the electric bump: when the rider gets up they just want to run. He's got it; and he's got enough ability to capitalise on it. You can't really define it. Great sportsmen have it. It's born in them. I was just lucky enough to be the one there to teach him. I've had other boys who were very good as well but not as good as him. He has it all and then some more.'

Jacobs's persistence paid off and towards the end of the 1968–9 season it was agreed Roberts should ride a horse named Galley Lad in the mile-and-a-half Pietermaritzburg Stayers Handicap, the fifth race on Scottsville's card of 28 June, a month after Michael's fifteenth birthday. Jacobs reckoned the colt was a cert. Just to ease the pressure on the youngster, Joey Joseph arranged for him to make his debut on the filly Dartmoor in a seven-furlong juvenile plate earlier in the afternoon. The future champion and his first partner beat two of their thirteen opponents. Everything was set for Galley Lad three races later.

ROBERTS: John had taken me to the track one morning,

put me on Galley Lad and led us on another animal called Knockwatch. He told me exactly how to ride the horse as we were going along, the different pace and so on – when to step up the tempo instead of just jumping out and bowling along. Anyway, I beat him ten lengths and he said I'd as good as won the race already. The big day came and I weighed out and then sat down in the weighing-room, waiting to be called out. Then in walks the stipendiary steward, Mr John Otto, and he says to me: 'Roberts, I'm afraid you can't ride in this race. The rules state you're not yet qualified.' In those days you had to have twelve qualifying rides – six down the straight and six around a turn – before you could be considered experienced and they must have thought a race over a mile and a half was going to be too much for me. John Jacobs went mad and I went up into the stands to watch the race. Another apprentice, 'Snowy' Reid, took my place and the further he and Galley Lad went the further they went ahead. They bolted up! And I was so cut up. 'This game's no bloody good!', I was thinking to myself.

Fortunately, I didn't have too long a wait for my first winner, which was Smyrna six races later. She was a little bay filly, full of character. She used to buck and kick and fly-leap before she'd settle. She always went well in gallops but she was still a maiden; John Jacobs trained her. She scooted up. I think we virtually made all but I can't remember too much about it. Apparently, I went past the post patting this poor horse and kept patting her right to the weighing-room – and then I gave her a pick of grass. No one had seen such an emotional jockey before!

* * *

Smyrna's race – a fillies' maiden plate over six furlongs worth R1,200 – was seventh on the Scottsville card of Saturday, 30 August 1969; an hour earlier Roberts had seen dear old Galley Lad unplaced in the big event, the Azalea Stakes. Mr and Mrs H. J. Ennever's three-year-old bay filly possessed a smidgeon of form. She had only just been caught in an earlier outing on the same track, and last time up had been the unfortunate victim of some squeezing at Greyville. At 9–2 she was not unfancied to beat her seven rivals. The 6–4 favourite was Stage Beauty, ridden by the Academy's current apprentice sensation 'Tickey' Carr, who had won the opening race of the day to make it seven winners for him from three meetings. History fails to record whether Carr was miffed at seeing one of his younger and 'inferior' schoolmates beat him by a cosy two and a quarter lengths, but he proceeded to lodge an objection. Had it proved successful, goodness knows how Smyrna's partner would have coped.

Once the Academy's apprentices have satisfied the Riding Master as to their capabilities, circulars are distributed among selected trainers inviting applications to have an apprentice placed with them on a first-claim basis. By rights Roberts should have been returned to Port Elizabeth and his home authority of Eastern Province to complete the five years of his indentures, but Cyril Buckham had other ideas.

ROBERTS: Kids were taken from each province and then sent back, so each one could have two or three apprentices

coming through. But one day Cyril Buckham told me he
intended to keep me in Durban and he wondered if my dad
would be happy with that. He explained all the advantages
of such a decision; so they exchanged me for a Durban boy
who went to Port Elizabeth. All the trainers see you riding
work in the mornings so they know who the good apprentices
are. I had five applications; they put them all in a hat and
draw them out. I was lucky enough to go to Herman Brown.
He was a chap who liked to give apprentices a chance, and
he was very much a father figure at a time when I was
starting out again. He looked after me and would invite me
to his home. We used to get one rand a week pocket money
(fifty pence then), but he would give a bit extra for carrying
the saddles and the weight-cloths for him when he went out
to saddle a horse; or sometimes I might ride one around the
paddock to keep its back down if it was excitable. Everything
considered, he was fantastic to me. He had a nice string of
horses – thirty in those days – and everything went just
right. He was such a good master. If I was beaten on a
favourite and the owners moaned he'd always stand by me.
I remember one day I rode a real terrible race, everything
went wrong, and I thought he's got to moan now. The owner
didn't look too impressed but Mr Brown just patted me on
the back and said: 'Better luck next time.' On Monday
mornings he'd take me into the office and go through any
problems. 'It's no good me shouting and screaming. We
can't change anything. It's history.' One day he did give
me a right rollicking. I rode a little filly for some really
good owners and coming back after she'd run fourth or fifth
I said to them: 'She's no good.' The owner must have

complained and he gave me hell. 'You can tell me they're useless but never tell the owner – it's like you are talking about their children.' He taught me a lot about talking to owners and how to treat them properly. He would teach you how to treat the different sorts of owner in the right way.

BROWN: Michael looked a natural; there was nothing to him but his eyes glared with ambition. His build was perfect. I'd had a lot of top jockeys through my hands, like David Payne for example, so I had experience of what was needed. I always like to give my apprentices every possible chance. Few people realise the strain these boys are under when they start their riding careers and it is understandable that while learning they don't always do the right thing in a race. I've always made it a strict rule never to bawl these boys out for their mistakes but instead build up their confidence. You're always disappointed when a boy doesn't come up to scratch but it is absolutely useless upsetting a youngster and making him nervous. Michael possessed a natural jockey's make-up, very raw but very keen; and when he sat on a horse you could see he was a natural. He also had a real riding brain. He'd be prepared to bounce out and then take a pull, having read the race within a hundred yards of the start and realising how the race was going to be run. This is a very important facet of a jockey's art. One race he'd make all; the next he'd be last all the way until the final fifty yards.

Muis was a bit of a loner, something of a Lester Piggott, but he had a sharp sense of humour. In fact, he was a real little farm boy and spoke little English; my wife used to take him for elocution lessons in Pinetown twice a week. Inside three months he spoke pretty good English; he cottoned on very quickly. One thing that really struck me was his love of animals. When he started with me he came to me and asked whether I'd mind if he kept some pets. I said it would be all right and the next thing he's brought down a pig, then a goat, and then it was some sheep. The goat, Barney, used to butt everybody; you really had to run from that fellow! Eventually the pig, Matilda, had a litter of thirteen piglets! So the whole yard was cluttered up with animals: goats, pigs, sheep, rabbits, bantams . . . Eventually, the manager of the Summerveld centre came to me and told me to clear the lot out because it was getting out of hand. And that was Michael! He was just a natural with animals.

ROBERTS: I found this little runt of a pig and thought it was bound to die. So, I took it in, fed it and she grew massive. I managed to find a boar and she had thirteen piglets – I couldn't believe it when they just kept coming out! Fred Rickaby's yard was next door to Mr Brown's. It was absolutely immaculate, with lawns and rose bushes. My pigs used to get through into his yard and dig up his roses; they got reported and were thrown out!

Although hindsight undoubtedly allows embryonic champions to be pinpointed with unerring accuracy by each and every one of us, Buckham and Brown had read the signs at source. Within four years of Smyrna passing Scottsville's winning-post Roberts was champion jockey while still an apprentice, an almost unheard-of achievement. The Academy had justified its foundation by producing a young rider to rank alongside John Gorton and David Payne and, more importantly, one who represented an impeccable role model for all who followed – Robbie Sham, Basil Marcus, Felix Coetzee, Jeff Lloyd – in what was becoming a world of rapidly changing values. However, Roberts cast a long shadow, as the Academy's headmaster, Paddy O'Connor, observed on his departure: 'Michael was one of those boys with whom it was a pleasure to deal. Right from his second year he had all the makings of a champion jockey. Generally speaking, once boys begin to ride winners and earn money their interest in school goes down and down and down; some of them even begin to resent being at school. That wasn't the way with Michael. He had his head screwed on. He did his work well and neatly and carried it on till Standard 10 successfully; he was a very good student. And in other ways he was a chap you could depend upon in every way, in the dorms or dining room – everywhere. He set an example and you could really be proud of him.'

By the same token, the Academy could be proud of the job it had done in moulding this gauche young man into an upright citizen. Nor would instant celebrity succeed in turning his head; by thought and deed Roberts continually demonstrated he had not forsaken his roots or lost his generosity of spirit.

JENKINSON: Michael's heart is bigger than himself. Once he won a race for an owner who was a wholesaler in menswear and part of the 'present' for winning was any suit Michael cared to choose. The black grooms adored Michael because he was decent to them, unlike most. Anyway, one of the grooms was to be married so Michael took him and had the prize of the suit made for the groom instead of himself; and then he bought the shirt, tie and shoes for him. This groom had never owned a pair of trousers in his life! As usual, Michael swore him to silence.

I had an old car, which I had bought for eighty rand. Michael was very disturbed about this car because he thought the wheels were all over the place. He took the car away to have them aligned properly. I didn't see hide nor hair of the car for six weeks. Eventually I asked him when he was bringing my car back. 'I'm sorry, they took the wheels off and the car collapsed. You can't get it back; it was all rusty. I'll give you your eighty rand back.' On Christmas morning he came in loaded down with presents for everybody; you couldn't see him for presents. He took me outside and there was my car. She had yellow wheels, new tyres, she was painted a beautiful shade of white with a narrow yellow stripe down her side and a wonderful yellow interior. That was my Christmas present!

When Michael became champion the Jockey Club was determined to give him something substantial as a mark of his achievement. Michael asked if the money could instead be given to St Augustine's Hospital in Durban for a dialysis machine. But the Jockey Club wouldn't make the donation; I think they ended up giving Michael some candlesticks.

It is very hard to get to understand Michael because he is a very private person. He does not possess a mean bone in his body – though he detests hypocrisy in any shape or form – yet anyone who underestimates Michael Roberts is in for a shock. Like every champion he has the killer instinct. Yes, he gives the impression of an easy-going person, but hurt him or slight him and the steel backbone emerges. The fact that Michael became an upright and honourable young man was none of our doing. The Academy put the polish on, but the innate goodness and moral standards were already bred in the lad: his attention to personal appearance; never loud or boastful; always a 'thank you' card to owners. They say staying power comes from the dam: his mother must have been a very great lady.

3 The Apprentice with the
Golden Touch

Michael Roberts's march towards the South African jockeys' championship proved nothing short of relentless. In his debut season of 1969–70, when Gerald Turner took the title with a score of 104, he rode seventeen winners; in 1970–71 he totalled fifty-nine (which included his first four-timer, at Greyville in April) to claim twelfth place in the national standings behind Raymond Rhodes on 122 and in so doing beat Johnny McCreedy for the Natal championship – not only a record total by a Natal apprentice, but also the first occasion an indentured rider had won the title.

Life, however, had its ups and downs. On 2 December 1970 Roberts enjoyed a less than friendly encounter with a snake while walking through some long grass near the Summerveld stables. Although the incident was over in a matter of seconds, the angry reptile had time to wrap itself round his left leg and bite him on the ankle. Instinctively Roberts lashed out with his foot and sent the serpent flying. A tourniquet was applied and Roberts was rushed to hospital where snake-bite serum was administered. His action of kicking the snake off his leg undoubtedly saved him from a worse fate. Then, seven weeks later to the day, he experienced his first race-riding accident when his right boot struck a running rail and he broke a toe.

The following season of 1971–2 saw Roberts increase his tally to seventy-four, taking him into fifth (equal) place as Turner regained his title with 102 winners. He also won his first major event, the Smirnoff Plate, on Brown's two-year-old Glenever, one of a Scottsville five-timer on 13 May. A futher twelve months' progress pushed his return up to 121 to secure the South African title by fifteen over Rhodes. This rare distinction for an apprentice (Turner had been the first apprentice champion for forty-two years) almost took Roberts by surprise.

ROBERTS: Racing tended to be kept separate in each province. Once a month there was a national roll; but we had a little book called *Duff's Turf Guide* which gave details of each province and I remember looking at it one day and I was in front! Mr Brown told me not to look at another list and just get on with it; he didn't want me worrying.

Roberts, naturally, was parading his talents on the tracks of Durban (Greyville and Clairwood) and Pietermaritzburg (Scottsville) while continuing to hone his technique on the exercise grounds of the Summerveld training centre at Shongweni, twenty-five miles north of Durban and some 2,000 feet above sea level. The 450 acre site was opened in the mid-1960s to accommodate two dozen trainers, 500 or so grooms (mainly Zulus) and up to 1,200 horses. Three sand tracks and three grass tracks were meticulously laid out and fenced with posts and rails; farriers, general stores, a cinema and a restaurant 'clubhouse' overlooking the training tracks completed the purpose-built complex. Herman Brown was among the training fraternity, as was an expat named Frederick Arthur Rickaby, who had come to South Africa in 1947.

Rickaby is a name requiring little introduction to any student of the English Turf. Fred Rickaby's brother Bill won English Classics on Privy Councillor and Sweet Solera in the 1960s; their father Frederick Lester won five of his own; grandfather Frederick collected another three; great-grandfather Frederick was a steeplechase jockey; and four generations back, great-great-grandfather Frederick trained Wild Dayrell to win the 1855 Derby. Finally, there was the not inconsequential decision of Fred's Aunt Iris to marry jump jockey Keith Piggott: Fred Rickaby and Lester Piggott are cousins. The pair have much common ground: both were champion apprentices; both riding careers were plagued by the tyranny of the scales; and both are hard of hearing. However, while Piggott's fling with hurdle racing was short-lived and transitory, Rickaby ultimately concentrated on racing over timber (he once rode Champion Hurdler National Spirit to a winner), while his partial deafness resulted from high altitude met-climbs in the cockpit of a Spitfire during the Second World War which gained him the Air Force Cross and Bar. After a brief flirtation with running a pub, The Wheatsheaf at Alwalton, near Peterborough, he decided to strike out for greener pastures. A chance meeting with South African champion jockey Harold 'Tiger' Wright, who was riding in England during the summer of 1947, provided just the incentive he had been seeking. 'You train 'em and I'll ride 'em,' Wright had said to him.

* * *

RICKABY: I battled like hell to start with, I don't mind telling you. I modelled myself on Syd Garrett, who was different from all the other South African trainers. He'd been a good jockey until he got too heavy. He was the leading trainer in Cape Town and was different class; he was always very kind to me. He'd win the big races in preference to the little ones. He'd keep a horse and give it a chance to mature; he didn't want to win the early two-year-old races and burn his horse up. The horse had to tell him when it was ready before he'd exploit it. I used English methods to start with but I had to adapt – the climate, the black boys looking after the horses. I preferred the longer races. I liked my horses to settle down in the early stages and, about two from home, to pick up and finish. I never watched my horses work from the winning-post like most trainers in South Africa, looking through their glasses. I used to sit two furlongs out and instruct the riders to sit in behind until they reached me and only then gently pull the horse out, get it balanced and, when it's balanced, let the horse go so that it would hit the front a hundred yards from home. That's how I trained and Michael used to do it perfectly.

Once Rickaby had adjusted to his new surroundings and a workforce which was a far cry from that of Newmarket the winners began to roll in. Beau Sabreur became the first of eight Natal Derby winners in 1955; Aztec annexed the Cape Derby three years later; Savonarola inflicted one of the great Sea Cottage's four defeats in the 1966 Cape Guineas; Jollify (dead-heating with Sea Cottage in 1967) and Naval Escort (1969) both landed the coveted July. Even rival trainer Theo de Klerk was obliged to concede: 'There is nobody in the game quite like Fred. In my opinion he is the best trainer in the land and the one with the best "feel" for horses.' Of greater significance to Michael Roberts was the fact that Rickaby's yard, named 'The Severals' in homage to Newmarket, was right next door to Herman Brown's.

RICKABY: Michael was always a farmer at heart; he had rabbits, pigs and chickens and every other kind of animal you can imagine running round Herman Brown's yard. You could walk through from his yard to mine; actually, we had a communal loo. I'd been a jockey and I'd got a pretty good eye for a boy and I could see this kid was a cut above the rest. My intention was to get him under my control and mould him, to keep him straight before grafters got hold of him and taught him the wrong ideas. He would have been a sitting target for the racecourse sharks who would offer 'readies' for tips – or worse. I hadn't got a jockey at the time. I'd had John Gorton, who'd come over to England and won the Oaks, and I had an apprentice, 'Snowy' Reid, who won the July for me but he got into trouble. I was dying to get Michael Roberts. I thought, whenever I've got a horse with a low weight I'm going to try to use him. One year I needed a jockey in Cape Town and as it was out of season in Durban I got Herman Brown to lend Michael Roberts to me and I got the Academy's permission to take him down to Cape Town. He had to stay at the Academy in the Cape but I used to pick him up every morning and take him back at night. He was still only a kid of fifteen or sixteen and was like a son to me; I remember buying him his first surfboard on a trip to the beach. So, although he was apprenticed to Herman Brown, I was more or less his boss. Herman had never ridden and I had been a jockey, so I think I can take some credit for helping Michael on. I put him right in one or two ways but he really was a natural.

He had the classic jockey's build, intelligence and was exceptionally sharp – sharp about everything! He was always shrewd about money. We used to tease him about being jealous of Lester's reputation for meanness and love of cash. He'd come into my office even as a kid to discuss his money and we'd be working it out and he'd suddenly say: 'Give me the pencil, it's this,' and he'd write it out in a flash. He also had Lester's intuition for taking the best rides and coming back after a race and telling you exactly what had happened – which is so rare in South Africa.

His principal asset, though, was balance; when he starts pushing a horse he's in balance and he never stops. If you watch him he's nodding his head – you can pick him out in a field of twenty runners because his head will be the one that's nodding. And then he starts to push and his head doesn't nod so much, so you know he's coming off the bridle and he's coming under pressure – he's stopped nodding because he's now pushing with his arms. Once he starts doing that he never stops.

ROBERTS: Rickaby was very professional and it was a pleasure to work with his horses. Seven meant seven in the morning and when his string arrived for work it was as if everyone else had to get out of the way. They all wore the same rugs and all the boys wore the same overalls with a red beret. His yard was a showpiece; foreign visitors always visited his yard when they came to Summerveld. At evening stables there would always be a carrot wedged in the bolt bracket of each box which he could give the horse. One boy would then turn the horse so he could inspect both sides and there'd be another boy with him pulling a little trolley carrying all his syringes, tooth rasps, liniments and medicines. The boys used to call him 'Mr Jollygood' because each inspection always ended with him saying it.

You never saw Rickaby horses go out on the gallops in anything other than a straight line, with the good horses leading the way. You'd canter for a furlong, pull up, walk for a furlong, and then the gallop would start. When I came to England I could see where he'd got it all from; that's why his horses were always so relaxed and well schooled. Mr Brown trained more the South African way, and he was more of an easy-going person, whereas Mr Rickaby was very particular. Mr Brown went for short, sharp work and was easy on his horses; Rickaby would gallop them like they do in England where they are much fitter.

Rickaby helped me in all sorts of ways. I was always fascinated by Lester and he had all the books about him. I tried to copy Lester, though not to riding so short because it felt uncomfortable. And then Lester started coming out to South Africa. I remember him coming out and winning this fillies' Guineas on Dark Elf. First he was on the outside of five horses as we approached the turn and the next moment he was on the rails. This filly usually pulled but Lester was riding her on a long rein and had her so relaxed that he slowed the pace to half-speed and had us racing outside him. Just when I thought she must be tiring Lester shook Dark Elf up and they shot forward to catch the rest of us napping.

The one thing they taught us at the Academy was to keep our hands level with the pommel of the saddle. Being small I used to pull up my irons because the shorter I was sitting the more strength I had. Most South African jockeys used to grab the horse's head like the Australians; at work they only used to canter and the horses would pull like stink. I changed all that. I was getting a better result dropping my hands on the horse's neck, riding with a bit longer rein, and it would drop its head. I didn't see many riding like me apart from Johnny McCreedy. I based myself on him and Bert Abercrombie. Both were taught by Henry Eatwell. McCreedy was a great man to watch in a finish; he had brilliant rhythm and fantastic hands. South African horses are more highly strung than those over in England – probably because they're trained on the track – but if they began to mess around with this man, rear up in the air or something, he'd just sit on them; not with short reins, but at the end of the buckle. The man was unbelievable! I've never seen a horseman like him. We called him Mr McCreedy because he was the senior jockey. He didn't say much; if you asked him something he'd tell you and that was that. And if you did something wrong in a race he'd grab you and quickly tell you. To compete against him was fantastic, especially if you could beat him. He was one of the few South African jockeys I've seen who after each finish you could say the horse had nothing left; the horse gave him everything.

Then I developed my own style. I don't believe you can copy everything because you've got to be comfortable. I've seen so many jocks try to fit styles. They try to look pretty in a finish yet come a close one I see them getting beat. They're trying to look pretty instead of getting on with the job. The speed you're going, you haven't time to adjust yourself to look fancy with your whip or things like that; your horse could change its legs and you've lost on the nod.

Cyril Buckham monitored his protégé's development with the critical gaze expected of teacher and mentor. The quasi-'Piggott perch' did not please the Buckham eye but the swiftly evolving Piggott racing brain most certainly met with approval.

BUCKHAM: After Piggott has been over here all my boys start riding with their knees around their ears. It takes me a month to get them to drop their leathers back down. But long before Michael ever rode in a race I said in my personal reports on the various apprentices that if he did not turn out a champion I would resign my job. He was a natural right from the time he got up on his first horse. Everything I told him he did, and whenever we discussed race riding and tactics he knew exactly what I meant. Michael had any amount of self-confidence and really believed in himself. The game was made for him and right from the outset his mind worked like that of a top jockey. I remember one race at Clairwood where he was boxed in and it looked hopeless, he wasn't going to get a run. All of a sudden he got a run, came through and won. When the race was over the chief stipe said: 'You were lucky to get a run there.' Michael said nothing. Then as he walked with me to the jockeys' room he turned and said: 'I wasn't lucky. I've ridden that horse who was in front and I know if you hit him with the right hand he shifts in. I also know that the jockey riding him is not keen on changing his whip into his left hand. So I knew if I settled in behind him and the jockey hit him with the right hand he would shift in and I'd get my run.' That's how Michael rides a race; his brain is going all the time.

Little wonder an article in the *Daily News* was headed 'The apprentice with the golden touch'. As his apprenticeship drew to a close, Roberts took steps to confirm his new-found status by enrolling for driving lessons prior to purchasing his very first car. All that he now needed was a champion equine conveyance upon which to exhibit the skills of a young master. Just such a vehicle happened along in the shape of Sentinel, trained not by Brown or Rickaby but by one of Roberts's early benefactors, Joey Joseph. Roberts had won the 1971 Gold Cup for Brown on Rain Storm but Sentinel was the first Classic horse he had got on.

The southern hemisphere season runs from 1 August and due to the vagaries of distance, climate and altitude the South African racing calendar had developed a highly regionalised character. The thirteen leading tracks are spread among three major centres which are many miles apart:

from Johannesburg to Durban is 400 miles; from Jo'burg to Cape Town is 1,000 miles, as is Durban to the Cape. To this logistical hindrance are added tremendous variations of climate and altitude. During the summer months of November to March Durban is stifled by sub-tropical heat and humidity whereas Johannesburg, on the same latitude, has the Rand's 6,000 feet altitude to soften the impact. By contrast, the Cape's mild Mediterranean summer comes as close as can be to ideal racing weather. In winter, however, the Cape is wet and miserable while the Rand can be prone to dull, bleak and frosty conditions; at this time Natal thrives in weather that is positively spring-like.

There are lesser centres – Port Elizabeth, Bloemfontein – but the upshot of the aforementioned geography is a racing calendar directed towards Natal's Durban and Pietermaritzburg in August, Johannesburg and Pretoria in the Transvaal in November and December, and Cape Town between January and March – building up to a seasonal climax back in Natal for the July Handicap. The preeminence of Natal is reflected in the lion's share (60 per cent) of the country's graded races topped by the 'July', long regarded as the premier event on the South African Turf and one annually drawing a crowd in excess of 55,000. However, the July – like its Australian counterpart the Melbourne Cup – is a handicap and typified a Pattern in which the status of Classic races was diluted by the separatist policy of each centre insisting on holding its own Guineas, Derby and Oaks. Further complication arose from one province's Derby, for example Natal's, being run before the Guineas of another, for example the Cape's, which made it impracticable for a trainer to teach his horse to settle in order to see out a mile and a half and then re-educate the horse to use its speed over a shorter trip. In open competition, the weight-for-age equivalents of an Eclipse or Queen Elizabeth II Stakes, for instance, were the Champion Stakes at Greyville (Durban) in August and the Queen's Plate at Kenilworth (Cape Town) in January, and, later on, the Schweppes Challenge at Durban's second track, Clairwood, in June. The emphasis was on speed: the vast majority of prize money was to be won at around a mile. There was no equivalent at twelve furlongs of the King George VI and Queen Elizabeth Diamond Stakes. In summary, there was still some way to go before the semblance of a unified South African Pattern was established.

The really lucrative prizes were the handicaps and weight-for-age races involving penalties, such as the Metropolitan, run over ten furlongs at Kenilworth in January; the Holiday Inns (originally the Johannesburg Summer Handicap), over ten furlongs at Turffontein (Johannesburg) in May; and, of course, Greyville's July Handicap, which began life in 1897 as the Durban Winter Handicap over a mile, becoming eleven furlongs in 1970. Sponsorship was the key to this imbalance. The richest of them all was the Holiday Inns which dated from 1972, having commenced sponsored life as the Castle Summer Tankard in 1962; the first July to be supported by Rothmans was Colorado King's race of 1963; and the 1964 'Met.' was run as the State Express 555 Metropolitan Handicap. By comparison the various 'Classics' and weight-for-age events struggled to find sponsors, and when they did the names changed with bewildering frequency.

ROBERTS: The Classics aren't the most important races to us but the best of the Classic horses will always run in the Cape Guineas: it's our best Classic. The altitude puts a lot of people off the Transvaal Classics. Sentinel was a massive horse but straightforward to ride. He was a sprinter actually, but as a three-year-old he had to go for the Cape Guineas.

Sentinel's 1971–2 Classic campaign involved a succession of duels – seven in all – with Natal's other star colt In Full Flight. Sentinel was a good horse but not a great one; In Full Flight was a great horse, which made Sentinel's performance in the 1972 Cape Guineas and South African Guineas all the more meritorious. Sentinel ran out a comfortable winner of the Natal Guineas in October 1971 before his initial clash with In Full Flight in the Summerveld Free Handicap: despite receiving three pounds Sentinel went under by a length and a half. The rivals met twice more prior to the Cape Guineas and on each occasion Sentinel fared no better. He could only finish third to In Full Flight and the Roberts-partnered Transvaal champion Elevation in the Bull Brand Jockeys' International at Scottsville (in which mounts were decided by lot) and in the Swazi Spa 'Holiday Inn' Stakes, a trial for the Cape Guineas run over seven furlongs at Kenilworth on 26 January, he and his regular partner were touched off by a short head. Ten days later the two Natal protagonists lined up on a typically breezy afternoon at Milnerton for the richest (R38,200) sponsored race of the season.

ROBERTS: I always thought we could turn the tables in the Guineas because it was a different track. Milnerton is sharper than Kenilworth and you must have speed. We had a lovely run up the inner after coming into the straight and hit the front about two furlongs out just as In Full Flight passed the leader on his outside. We were neck and neck all the way to the line. Personally, I still think we won. Sentinel had a big white nose and in the actual print of the finish I think you can see his nose broke the line first.

The judge called it a dead heat. There was no doubt about the time, however: 1:37.2, a record for the Guineas and only 0.2 seconds outside the track's best ever. As the season wended its way back to the Natal coast In Full Flight tightened his stranglehold on Sentinel until the score read 5–1 in his favour, with one draw. Sentinel's solitary outright victory came in the South African Guineas at Greyville in June when the pair were separated by Elevation: either side of that reverse In Full Flight twice humbled Sentinel in prestigious events – the Queen's Plate and the Woolavington Cup. The South African Guineas was In Full Flight's only defeat in ten starts during a season which culminated in a truly historic victory in the 1972 July. The pundits had given him no chance: he would not stay the eleven furlongs and no three-year-old – not even Colorado King – had won with as much weight since 1903. Sadly, In Full Flight – known to his stable, for obvious reasons, as 'the Breadwinner' – collapsed and died of a ruptured lung shortly after running third in the 1973 Met. He had won sixteen of his twenty races.

Sentinel himself just kept on going and had accumulated twenty-nine wins from fifty-six starts by the time he retired after winning a second Woolavington Cup on 19 July 1975, at the age of six. Roberts had won thirteen races on him but was cruelly denied that successful swansong owing to the after-effects of a fall three days earlier: he suffered concussion and severe bruising to his chest and, more vitally, to a finger which impaired control of the reins.

It seemed inconceivable that Michael Roberts could find a more consistent or more popular partner with whom to announce his arrival at the top of the tree. Yet he did. Two of the 121 successes that had presented him with his first South African jockeys' championship in 1972–3 came courtesy of a big two-year-old colt trained by Fred Rickaby. The colt's name was Sledgehammer.

4 Sing a Song of Sledge

'See what you think of this colt.' The time: early February, 1973. The place: the saddling boxes at Kenilworth racecourse, Cape Town, set amid the pine and oak trees wherein the squirrels were bounding and the doves cooing. The interested party: Fred Rickaby.

In all honesty the gloriously tranquil surroundings were failing miserably to still Rickaby's anxiety. He was more than a mite interested in his jockey's reaction, because this unraced New Zealand-bred juvenile had for some time been the apple of his eye. Despite the passage of twenty years, Michael Roberts's automatic response to the recollection of that morning and the precise moment he first clapped eyes on Sledgehammer remains both immediate and evocative.

ROBERTS: 'Jeez!' was all I could say. He was a striking-looking individual, a tall rangy horse, and particularly as he was a liver chestnut which you don't get often. He had a beautiful neck like a stallion's but he was actually a little weak behind the saddle; quite narrow but with a beautifully arched neck. He was very intelligent, very sweet and possessed a lot of charm – he would always stick his tongue out and give you a lick – and used to present himself extraordinarily well.

Sledgehammer was by the New Zealand-based stallion Stunning, once a mediocre racehorse back in England: Lester Piggott had won on him as a two-year-old in 1957, but by the age of six he was being ridden unsuccessfully over hurdles by that future trainer of speedsters, Jack Berry. However, in Stunning's favour was the fact that he belonged to the prepotent male line of Hyperion; his sire Stardust won the 1940 Champion Stakes (only to be disqualified) before getting Star Kingdom, a leading sire in Australia. Sledgehammer's bottom line was no less distinguished. His dam Fair Isle, though unraced herself, had produced nothing but winners; she was a daughter of champion broodmare sire Fair's Fair and her half-brother Second Earl had won Group I races in Australia.

The colt belonged to Cyril Hurwitz, South Africa's very own cattle baron, who had acquired him while on a cattle-buying expedition in New Zealand. The red and grey check colours of Cyril and Peggy Hurwitz were first seen during the 1947–8 season; the size of their string subsequently kept pace with their burgeoning interest and invariably put them high in the list of leading owners.

ROBERTS: Mr Hurwitz was fantastic for South African racing. He loved every single one of his horses, as did his wife Peggy; they weren't just numbers to them. He was a big, flamboyant man, always with a fat cigar, and you felt his presence as soon as he walked into the room. He was very generous and a big punter. He had A, B or C investments: a chance; a big chance; and past the post. It used to be worrying sometimes to know he'd got twenty thousand rand on your mount; that was a lot of money in the mid-1970s.

In 1968 Hurwitz had sent his horses to Fred Rickaby. Hurwitz could not stay for those New Zealand yearling sales of 1971 but he left strict instructions with his trainer to buy the Stunning colt at whatever cost. NZ$15,000 was as high as Rickaby had to go: the consensus of opinion around the ring insisted the yearling's knees were far too bad.

RICKABY: When I saw him his hocks were in the next parish but I never bother too much about this blemish so long as the actual hock joints are strong and powerful. He had such presence! When I was picking horses I had a list of priorities and presence was top of my list. They've got to look like a racehorse. You can pull them to pieces afterwards but you've got to say first of all: 'Does he look like a racehorse?' Sledgehammer turned out to be the greatest thing that's ever been in my life. He was such a wonderful horse; we used to talk to each other. He was a great big horse and I intended to give him all the time in the world but he wouldn't let me. 'Let me run, guv! Let me run! I've only got to canter down and canter back!' He was easy to train, without a single vice. But he had to lead the string in the morning. Usually some old horse does the job, but like a pack of wild animals tends to be led by the dominant male, he wanted to lead; he knew he was the dominant male and wanted to lead the herd. If he was in behind he grew restless, he'd jig-jog and try to pull his way to the front. One day we were working on the track at Summerveld: half the string had worked but not Sledgehammer. It looked like rain was due so I told my head groom to send the first lot home. Five minutes later I noticed they were still circling. 'I thought I told you to send those home!' I shouted to him. And he said: 'I can't! Sledge hasn't finished yet. He gets upset if he doesn't lead the string back.' Sledgehammer had even got the stable staff frightened!

As the Natal summer is hot and humid Rickaby liked to take his best horses down to the Cape, particularly the promising youngsters. As a result of this policy Sledgehammer's initial racecourse experience was scheduled for Kenilworth in February 1973. He ran twice within the space of eleven days before shipping back to Natal. He won the first race, the Inverthorn Plate, by five lengths, in the hands of Herbie Lasker as Roberts was unavailable; the second, the Festival Juvenile Handicap carrying top weight, by three and a quarter lengths in a hack canter with Roberts aboard. The clock stated the time was a track record – but, possibly swayed by the consummate ease of Sledgehammer's display, the officials believed the mechanism must have been faulty and overruled it. Scottsville's Smirnoff Plate, a Grade III event over six furlongs on 19 May, was the next target. Here Sledgehammer was bound to clash with a second New Zealand-bred and Natal-trained juvenile, Sun Monarch, who was unbeaten in five starts. Herein lurked a conflict of interest for Roberts, because Sun Monarch was trained by Herman Brown.

ROBERTS: I was still apprenticed to Mr Brown but I thought Sledgehammer was the better horse. You could sit behind on him whereas Sun Monarch went from the start. I told Mr Brown I thought Sledgehammer was the better of the two and asked if I could ride him instead of Sun Monarch in the Smirnoff. He went absolutely mad. 'This is the best horse you'll ever ride!' He refused to let me off Sun Monarch.

Marty Schoeman replaced Roberts on Sledgehammer who, despite receiving eleven pounds from Sun Monarch, was second best in the market. The two principals raced each other hammer and tongs over the first three furlongs (which undoubtedly contributed to the new juvenile track record) before the favourite blew up. Sledgehammer beat him three and a half lengths into third: 'Kiwi colt hammers them all,' was the verdict of the *Daily News*. The next round was due in Greyville's Champion Nursery, over a furlong longer distance.

ROBERTS: Once again I asked Mr Brown to let me ride Sledgehammer and once again he refused. I was furious! Mr Rickaby was putting pressure on me because Schoeman had been claimed to ride another one in the race which was meant to be the business. Sun Monarch was a tearaway and I'd got no chance with Sledgehammer if I led. I decided to jump out and sit last just to see what happened. I missed the break deliberately. Sledgehammer had to be kept relaxed and allowed to build himself up. They all thought I was going to go like the clappers and they weren't going to let me get away – so they'd all geed up their horses. Anyway, Sun Monarch dropped his bit and Sledgehammer had been set alight; his rider is looking everywhere for me and I'm at the back. Sledgehammer quickened up in the straight but I had so much horse under me I was able to get up on the line and beat him three-quarters of a length. Mr Brown was so pleased!

The two arch-rivals thus completed their first season having each inflicted one defeat upon the other – the single blot in their respective copybooks. There would be further confrontation, and as the 1973–4 season opened it was not long in materialising. Thanks to sponsorship from Hurwitz's Bull Brand firm, Scottsville had since 1969 been staging an invitation event featuring a cast of jockeys drawn from all over the world. A dozen hand-picked three-year-olds representing the cream of South African talent were then allocated to the jockeys by lot. In 1973 the equine contingent naturally included Sledgehammer and Sun Monarch, plus the highly regarded Jamaican Music, referred to by the press as 'The Cape's Grey Bomber'. Sledgehammer, with Roberts in the plate, duly won the seven-furlong 'trial' on 27 October in a track record time; but who would draw his coveted number for the race proper on 17 November? The names in the hat were Willie Carson, Joe Mercer and Lester Piggott from the UK; Johnny Sellers and Chilean-born Fernando

Toro (who had won the previous two runnings on In Full Flight and Yataghan) aiming to uphold American prowess; Alfred Gibert (France); Sergio Fancera (Italy); Robin Platts (Canada); Tony Murray (Ireland); and David Peake (New Zealand), while Messrs McCreedy and Roberts flew the flag for the home side. In a cut-throat contest like this one promised to be Rickaby understandably wanted his cousin's name to be paired with Sledgehammer's, although he was confident Roberts would be no disadvantage. Cyril Hurwitz exercised the sponsor's prerogative by drawing the names. Piggott drew Sun Monarch; to partner Sledgehammer . . . Michael Roberts.

RICKABY: We wanted to get Lester, naturally, but if we couldn't get him we wanted Michael because he knew the horse so well. And when he won the race barely out of his apprenticeship and beating all those imported jockeys it showed he was international class. It put him on the map.

Indeed, as the headline in the following morning's *Sunday Tribune* declared: 'Roberts Whips World's Best On Super Sledge.' The afternoon had been swelteringly hot. Between riding a double on Rickaby's fine sprinter Abbey Boy in the opener and Sunburst in the fifth, Piggott sweated off four pounds! Joint favourites for the big race at 16–10 were Sledgehammer and Jamaican Music, who would surely benefit from the invaluable assistance of Toro. The race was preceded by a parade of the twelve jockeys – each wearing the colours of his country rather than those of his mount's owner – and the ceremonial raising of the national flags, after which Alan Snijman, chairman of the South African Jockey Club, presented Roberts with his trophy – silver candlesticks – for winning the jockeys' championship of 1972–3. Adding to the international flavour was the presence of Peter O'Sullevan at the Scottsville microphone. The race he called was plain sailing. Frantic Chief (Tony Murray) and Cool Million (Johnny Sellers) led a cracking gallop round the right-hand bend into the straight, whereupon Totem Pole (Robin Platts) took over. Roberts had Sledgehammer in the centre of the field until just above the furlong marker. One flick of the whip was sufficient: Sledgehammer burst clear up the middle of the track and effortlessly withstood Jamaican Music's fast finish. The winning margin was two and a half lengths; Sun Monarch was a further three and a quarter lengths adrift. The clock registered 1:35.88 for the one mile, Sledgehammer's third track record in six races. The victorious combination thoroughly deserved the plaudits which came their way. Even Piggott was moved to say: 'That is a real good horse and it won't be long before Michael Roberts comes over to England.'

O'SULLEVAN: I formed an immensely favourable impression of Michael and in a piece shortly afterwards I predicted he'd get a European contract. Two features especially impressed me. Firstly, there was his obvious skill in the saddle; second, there was the engaging, quiet and self-deprecating manner and total dedication. I also think it was quite significant that when two stalls failed to open for the last race Michael was the only rider to pull up his horse

– the other eleven kept going. It was an indication of how disciplined he was.

ROBERTS: It was just unbelievable luck that I drew Sledgehammer. But I was there; they had three bags – one for the horses, one for the jockeys and one for the draw – and out I came! I was nervous beforehand because all the big names were there but, saying that, we had all been staying together in a Durban hotel for a few days which eased the tension a lot. As far as the other horses were concerned Sun Monarch was one of my rides so I knew all about him; my main concern, the only 'dark' horse, was Jamaican Music, because he was up from the Cape and they were very bullish about him. Fernando Toro rode him work and said he was better than In Full Flight. More worrying was the possibility of the American jockeys going off at a hundred miles an hour, which they had done in the past. Our horses were just not used to that. Fred never gave me many orders. His favourite instruction was: 'Jockey, go read a book in the first half of the race!' You couldn't rush Sledgehammer, anyway. He'd go to post very short, a very choppy action, and he'd be the same in a race. Once he broke from the stalls you never had to pull him back, he'd do it himself. Then, when he'd warmed up, about halfway through a race, you could start to creep up on him. That's exactly what happened in the Bull Brand. Johnny Sellers went off like a scalded cat and my biggest job was to hold on to Sledge for as long as possible because he had a short one- or one-and-a-half-furlong run on him. The leaders going so fast suited him as they were bound to come back to us

61

and so I didn't need to rush him. It was quite emotional coming back into the winner's enclosure. Mr Hurwitz's two daughters led Sledgehammer in; and of course, it was Mr Hurwitz's race and he and his wife treated Sledge like a son; he was their big baby.

Three more races fell to Sledgehammer and his nineteen-year-old accomplice during the remainder of the 1973–4 season; but the two that mattered most were not among them. The first setback came next time up, in the Benoni Guineas at Gosforth Park, Germiston. Sledgehammer was a 3–1 on favourite to lift this Transvaal Classic, only to be thwarted by a sudden change in the weather.

ROBERTS: Gosforth Park is the most difficult track to ride. It's very sharp with a straight of only two and a half furlongs and has never been one of my favourites. The draw is very important because you have to be up there in the first three or four coming into the straight. If you're drawn wide you're always losing ground on the turns. Early pace is essential; very few horses come from behind to win there. If you miss the kick you're gone. It's one of those tracks where you see a lot of good horses get beat because of the track more than the opposition. Sledgehammer wasn't a horse who liked being bustled early on, but I was drawn well and had to keep my position by forcing him. We'd also had a tremendous thunderstorm as we were going into the stalls and the ground was bottomless, which didn't suit his low action; he didn't like it one bit and didn't produce his usual finishing kick.

* * *

In the circumstances victory appropriately went to a 33–1 outsider, Kanaka, who beat Sledgehammer by four lengths. Sledgehammer was ineligible for the Cape Guineas (won by Jamaican Music, who then added the Cape Derby) because he was New Zealand-bred (the rule was lifted in 1975), so it was doubly unfortunate that his only other Classic venture also proved disappointing – almost disastrously so. On 8 June he entered the Greyville stalls as a 5–4 on favourite (even with Jamaican Music in the field) to win the South African Guineas.

ROBERTS: We were brought down. The horse in front of us, Frantic Chief, snapped a leg; we tried to jump over him but were hit from behind and came down. Then another fell over us. There was only a furlong or so to run. Sledgehammer was cut and he pulled a muscle in his back as well. I woke up in St Augustine's Hospital with a face like a football not knowing what had happened. It could have been a lot worse.

Discharged within forty-eight hours of this three-horse pile-up, Roberts was promptly readmitted the next day suffering from a raging headache – 'the worst I've ever had in my life' – and high temperature, having succumbed to the flu bug that was sweeping through Summerveld. Roberts's tribulations this season were not yet over. On returning to race riding only the speedy reaction of fellow jockey Dana Siegenberg prevented him being throttled in a horrendous accident at Clairwood on 17 July. While the field was awaiting the start of the Umtata Handicap, Roberts's mount Magic Square got its head trapped under the front of its stall, dragging the jockey's hands underneath in the process. More dangerously, Roberts's head was being pressed hard against the gate, causing him to choke; he began to turn blue. Siegenberg quickly leant over from the adjacent berth and held him back in an effort to relieve the pressure on his neck. Roberts was fortunate indeed to escape with just a sore chest and scraped hands.

Sledgehammer's own injuries put paid to Rickaby's aspirations of a tilt at the July; ten days after the Greyville crash Sledgehammer was scratched. However, the best of Sledgehammer was yet to come: 1974–5 was known in South African racing as 'The Year of The Sledge'. He won eight of his ten races, including five of the country's most important weight-for-age events in the course of which he defeated stars like Jamaican Music, Yataghan, Elevation, Sabre and Foreign Agent, and set two more track records. One of the latter came on his seasonal debut at Greyville over seven furlongs, after which he was sent north for the Transvaal Champion Stakes at Gosforth Park on 31 August. Awaiting him was the darling of the Rand, the six-year-old Elevation, winner of the 1972 South African Derby, twice a winner of the Holiday Inns and the greatest stakes winner in South African history.

Sledgehammer's journey to Germiston proved a nightmare.

RICKABY: Sledgehammer travelled up in a trailer with Fitzgerald, another runner in the race. At some point he became frightened and went berserk. He cut his forelegs and there was blood coming out of his nostrils – he had struck his head on an iron bar. When I came upon the trailer the two horses were stood on a grass verge between the road and a railway line. I couldn't administer antibiotics or sedatives because of the proximity of the race; I just dressed and bandaged him. It should have been a ten-hour trip but it took thirteen. Elevation beat him by a neck, but he had hung across Sledgehammer and was subsequently disqualified. When we returned to Transvaal in December for the Holiday Inns – at Turffontein – I went in the trailer with Sledgehammer; that's how close I was to him. I loved that horse; he needed me after he'd had that terrible fright, and I discovered that he disliked travelling 'across' the direction of travel – he wanted to face forward. Things hadn't gone smoothly leading up to the race, either. One day he locked his stifle; his near hind leg was sticking right out and I had to push it back in with the aid of two grooms. Then we were advised by the police he was going to be got at; he had two police guards once he arrived at the racecourse stables. And I was always concerned about the distance of the race because he'd never gone ten furlongs before.

If that was not enough to be going on with, the Holiday Inns – befitting the lure of its sponsor's promise to provide South Africa's richest race (R50,000 to the victor) – had attracted a superlative collection of thoroughbreds. The weights were headed by Yataghan (nine stone nine pounds), a five-year-old whom Syd Laird had trained to win a Benoni Guineas, a Bull Brand, a Met. and a July. He was set to give Elevation two pounds. After the Transvaal Champion, George Azzie's chestnut suffered another reverse in the Hawaii Stakes in which Jamaican Music beat him by a short head; of more concern was the fact that the six-year-old entire had tried to bite the grey during the frantic closing stages. This day the 'Grey Bomber' carried eight stone twelve pounds; Sabre, on whom Roberts had won the 1973 South African Guineas, had eight stone five – four pounds more than Sledgehammer, who was the 5–2 favourite. Elevation was a 7–1 shot. Nothing, however, was going to stop the Transvaal champion on his own patch and in his favourite race. He and Sledgehammer came through the field as if tied together, but the Natal champion could not sustain his effort and dropped away to finish third, five and three-quarter lengths in arrears; softish ground and that extra quarter mile seemed the culprits.

If revenge was to be exacted it would have to be in the Grade I Met. on 18 January, since this was designated Elevation's final race prior to commencing stud duties. It seemed a tall order. Elevation was thirteen pounds better off at the weights and the distance was again a mile and a quarter. On the positive side for supporters of Sledgehammer was the knowledge that he had settled handily to win his slowly run prep race, the Grade I weight-for-age Somerset Plate, very impressively. Perhaps he could be restrained to better effect on this occasion. Nevertheless, Elevation was always liable to be preferred to him, especially once the race day had brought forth a typically strong Cape south-easter which would be against the runners up the straight and would consequently test Sledgehammer's stamina to the very limit. The wind failed to deter 25,000 people from filing into Kenilworth and they were to witness a sensational start to the race when Sledgehammer's gate refused to open properly. This sluggish break may well have worked to his advantage. The blinkered Ballyhoo set a scorching pace and was still fully eight lengths clear coming into the straight. For most of the way Sledgehammer had only a couple of horses behind him, but by the time Jamaican Music seized the lead with two to run Roberts had Sledge glued to Elevation's tail ready to match any move he might make. The two horses launched simultaneous thrusts either side of Jamaican Music.

ROBERTS: Kenilworth is a beautiful track; it's very like an English track and riders rate it one of the best in the world. You've got to ride it with a lot of patience, though; it has a long straight and stamina comes into play. When the gate finally opened properly Sledgehammer was a bit sluggish hitting his stride but, quite honestly, I knew the race was in the bag because they went off like hell. I started to ride a race from the seven and by the time we came into the straight I was cantering behind Elevation and went past him as if he was standing still. And he wasn't a bad horse!

RICKABY: Michael rode a very intelligent race because after losing ground at the start when his gate opened tardily he was right at the back. Then, in the straight, he had to make a split-second decision to make his run on the outside of Jamaican Music. Sledgehammer became slightly unbalanced as he brought him round the grey, who was tiring, but he kept his head and got Sledge going again in great style.

'Sing a song of Sledge,' enthused the *Sunday Times*; 'Slick Sledge slams that Elevation hoodoo,' opined the *Cape Times* on the subject of Sledgehammer's two-length victory alongside a photo of him contentedly munching oats and carrots from the Met. trophy under the admiring gaze of trainer and rider. This impromptu banquet made up for his absence from the official Met. dinner, where Alan Snijman had said: 'It is all very well proposing the toast to the horse in absentia but I feel that the hero of the whole show should be accommodated somewhere at our dinner.' Another speaker observed: 'It takes a good horse to win the July, a very good horse to win the Holiday Inns and a great horse to win the Met!'

The July was still six months away, however, with valuable prizes aplenty en route. Sledgehammer soon showed he had acquired the taste. While exercising at Kenilworth in preparation for the Queen's Plate he threw his rider passing the Met. start and ran right round the track and past the winning-post before halting at the entrance to the winner's enclosure; and there he waited! He duly won the Queen's Plate (Grade I) to become the first horse to complete the 'Cape Treble' initiated by the Somerset; toiling in his wake were Foreign Agent (the beneficiary of his fall in the 1974 South African Guineas), Sword Dancer (the 1973 Cape Derby winner and the previous year's winner of the Queen's Plate), Sentinel and Yataghan. Sledgehammer positively toyed with them all, lying way out of his ground until Roberts elected to move at the distance. The papers went wild: 'The inimitable Sledge does it again' (*Cape Times*); 'Sledge slays 'em – again' (*Sunday Times*); 'The field bows to Sledge' (*Weekend Argus*). Following that scintillating display he twice more trounced Yataghan in the Drill Hall Stakes and Clairwood Champion Stakes (Grade I): 5 July, it appeared, could not dawn soon enough.

The spell had to break. Two weeks before the race coughing struck Rickaby's yard. Sledgehammer was secretly moved into one of the dope boxes at Greyville – secret, that is, until Rickaby was spotted buying carrots in a nearby supermarket. Sledgehammer had already earned R88,010 during the 1974–5 season, raising his career total to R157,030; another R54,225 would push his earnings through the R200,000 barrier to within touching distance of Elevation's South African stakes record of R238,465. No rider counts his chickens as far as the July is concerned, but Roberts could be excused for thinking that he would never have a better chance of realising every South African jockey's dream. Sledgehammer (56.5 kg) was a 2–1 favourite, despite the eleven furlongs of the race dragging him ever deeper into uncharted waters and an array of talent in opposition which included familiar adversaries in Yataghan and Jamaican Music as well as young bloods such as the Cape Guineas winner Gatecrasher (trained by Herman Brown, and ridden that day by Roberts), the Cape Derby winner Arion and the South African Derby winner Distinctly.

The conclusion of the 1975 July turned out to be one of the most dramatic on record, but to Roberts's profound disappointment it did not involve Sledgehammer. Gatecrasher (49.5 kg) beat Principal Boy and Distinctly by a head and a neck. Unfortunately the winner had badly interfered with Distinctly, his only challenger on the stands side, and thus had to be placed behind him; consequently, Principal Boy (49 kg), racing in isolation on the far side, became a lucky winner. Sledgehammer finished twelfth of the seventeen runners – and very distressed. He'd been struck into from behind and thrown off balance, causing him to sprain a muscle above his hock. He would not run again for six months.

ROBERTS: He got very badly chopped on the top turn; they all came over and then eased up. I didn't know the extent of the damage but I felt something gallop into us. It wasn't the Sledge we knew: he'd been training well at home. He never came three or four furlongs out, which is what he usually did. I eased him out, gave him some daylight but there was nothing there, so I just left him alone. The next day he was terribly lame.

Roberts, too, ended the 1974–5 season in the wars. The finger injury sustained on 16 July that was to cost him the ride in Sentinel's last race succeeded in bringing the season to a premature conclusion. He embarked on his first trip outside South Africa: a holiday in Switzerland, France and England, highlighted by a visit to Ascot for the King George VI and Queen Elizabeth Diamond Stakes in which Grundy and Bustino ran what was for some the race of the century.

Roberts had missed out on Natal's greatest prize in 1975

but even during Sledgehammer's enforced absence he still managed to plunder the Transvaal's on another inmate of The Severals. This was Majestic Crown, also in the ownership of Cyril Hurwitz. Aided by Roberts, this colt had toppled Jamaican Music to win the Natal Derby in 1974 (Verna Oliver's first visit to a racecourse) before a hairline fracture to a cannon bone appeared to have brought an end to his career. The horse was confined to his box for two months with the leg in plaster, and it was a further seven before he moved out of a walk. By some miracle Rickaby got Majestic Crown back on the track in September 1975 after a fourteen-month layoff. Amazingly, the horse – now a five-year-old – pulled up sound, and four weeks later he won the Michaelmas Handicap to prove he was fit and ready to run for his life in December's Holiday Inns, which had always been the object of the exercise. That Majestic Crown was able to win the Holiday Inns paid a handsome tribute to Rickaby's uncanny veterinary skills and owed not a little to an inspired ride from Roberts. First of all the jockey had to hold his mount together after receiving a hefty bump from a tiring rival; having done so, Roberts then found himself shut in.

ROBERTS: Turffontein is a tough track, with a climb from the seven-furlong pole into the straight which is a long one. You can't use a horse up that incline or you won't get home. It is a very testing track but Majestic Crown was a true mile-and-a-half horse, a big robust animal. Luckily I spotted an opening but I remember thinking to myself at the time I went for it: 'I'll either fall or I'll win!' Majestic Crown

71

would have been another Gatecrasher if he'd not been in
the same year as Sledgehammer; he was overshadowed by
Sledgehammer, being in the same ownership and stable.
But he was a lovely brown horse, beautiful looking, not as
tall as Sledgehammer but there was more of him. Like
Sledgehammer he used to lag behind in his races – a bit
like Mtoto would later on – and he was a very placid
individual, a real gentleman's ride. Actually, he only ran
against Sledgehammer once: the 1976 Met. I chose
Sledgehammer and we beat him, but Gatecrasher beat the
both of us. Gatecrasher definitely stayed better than
Sledgehammer, though we were conceding weight in both
the July and the Met. He was a year younger than
Sledgehammer but they couldn't avoid taking each other
on which meant I only won the Cape Guineas on him. He
was a real galloper and we made all. He was a massive
seventeen hands chestnut with four white socks and he wore
a hood; all that and his style of running reminded a lot of
people of Secretariat.

Sledgehammer made his eagerly anticipated comeback at
Kenilworth on the first day of 1976 in the Somerset Plate.
At seven furlongs his reputation remained unsullied, and
opposition was growing distinctly thin on the ground. The
race was reduced to a farce. 'This was an insult – wake up
Cape Town trainers and jockeys,' boomed the *Cape Times*.
'A damned disgrace. Anyone who watched this travesty of
horseracing – if it can be described as racing – must have
wondered whether Cape Town's trainers and jockeys have
just thrown in the sponge and given up all hope against

Sledgehammer and Muis Roberts. They wound their way slowly round the turn with the restrained dignity of a funeral cortege and came into the straight as if each stride was bringing them closer to the open grave.' The *Argus* warmed to the same theme: 'Sledgehammer stuns Somerset field: after winning the race by two and a half lengths he would not have blown out a candle, which was hardly surprising for the race was run at such a slow pace that Roberts faced a major dilemma of what to do with the big horse.'

Rickaby knew precisely 'what to do with the big horse': Sledgehammer would try for a second Met., but the July was ruled out; henceforth the weight-for-age races were to constitute Sledgehammer's staple diet. Not entirely unexpectedly, Gatecrasher proved two lengths too good for him over the Met.'s ten furlongs on terms four pounds worse than weight-for-age – though he was not helped by running into Majestic Crown's heels on the bend. A second Queen's Plate, however, posed no problem whatsoever, before Rickaby broke with precedent and sent him to Port Elizabeth for the one-mile Fairview Autumn Stakes, the richest prize in the Eastern Province. Sledgehammer won (at 10–1 on), but at some cost: he overstretched himself, and Rickaby noted a certain stiffness after each of his next two races. Gatecrasher got the better of him for the third time in the Administrator's Champion Stakes after once again capitalising on greater luck in running; Brown's colt found room along the rails to steal first run while Roberts was preoccupied with reorganising Sledgehammer, who had to pull round a beaten horse. Things returned to normal in the Woolavington Provincial Cup where Sledgehammer could afford to trail Brer Rabbit by eight lengths entering the Greyville straight yet still smother him with speed.

His first outing as a six-year-old, the Champion Stakes, concluded less happily and spelt the beginning of the end. Rickaby discovered a swelling on the inside of a check ligament after his champion had failed to reach the frame for only the fourth occasion in twenty-nine races. It was decided to rest the horse, give him a season at stud with the Birch brothers and bring him back in the new year. This novel change of occupation clearly revitalised Sledgehammer: indeed, he was so exuberant on being returned to training that he rapped the old injury. However, once he had won Greyville's Daventry Handicap on 16 April 1977, at his leisure, it appeared that the audacious strategy might just conceivably pay off. The horse was only R12,595 short of Elevation's stakes record which Rickaby was determined he should surpass. Sadly it proved a classic case of a horse being taken to the well once too often; there was to be no happy ending to this particular fairy tale. The great horse went to post for the thirty-first and final time at Clairwood on 11 June 1977 for the Administrator's Champion Stakes; always struggling, he could finish only fourth, earning just R900.

Sledgehammer's twenty-one victories (numbering six Grade Is and six track records) and five places had netted R226,770; on sixteen of those occasions Michael Roberts was in the saddle. The South African press quickly, and justly, paid fulsome tribute. One devotee wrote: 'Dear Sledgehammer: I am writing to you on behalf of the South African public to thank you for all the glamour, excitement and colour you have brought into our sport. You are beyond doubt the equal in merit, courage and soundness of the legendary Sea Cottage. He was one hell of a horse and so too are you. As brilliantly as Fred has trained you, Michael has ridden you. As a jockey Michael has everything – kind hands, superb balance, a cool head, split-second timing and a tremendous drive in a finish.' Space was provided for Sledgehammer's 'reply': 'Thank you Michael for the manner in which you have ridden me, both at home on the training track and out on the racetrack itself. Your superb balance and kind hands make you a tremendous partner – a great 'elp and never an 'indrance.' Sledgehammer was installed at his owner's Riverholm Stud, near Mooi River in the Natal Midlands. Later on he moved to the nearby Oakwood Stud, where he was eventually put to sleep on 8 November 1989 after suffering a particularly severe bout of colic.

RICKABY: Sledgehammer's life at stud was doomed before it started because Cyril Hurwitz imagined he could run his stud career himself. But he only had a few mares. The Birch brothers offered to buy the horse but he insisted on keeping 51 per cent of the shares for himself. What he had not realised was that no stud owner was going to send its top mares to a stallion they did not own outright. It would not have been good business to make Sledge a leading stallion for the benefit of Cyril Hurwitz. So he was given only moderate mares. After two wasted seasons the penny dropped and Cyril bought back the 49 per cent of the shares, but then he went bust. Sledgehammer had to be sold with the mares and all the other stock. This was the last time I saw Sledge and I nearly cried. He had been left in his own box next to the covering yard which was being used as the sale ring. Naturally, he went mad every time a broodmare went into the ring so I sat with him for the rest of the sale to calm him down. He was something different; and I don't mind admitting I shed a tear or two when I heard of his death.

ROBERTS: From the jockey's point of view the Bull Brand gave me the greatest feeling personally because I was riding against the best jockeys in the world. But the Met. was his own greatest triumph. He was at his peak as a four-year-old, even though he got a bit 'shouldery' and developed muscle problems as he got older. He always had quite a scratchy action going down to the start, he looked like a real cripple, but, I promise you, halfway through a race all you had to do was guide him to the right position and he'd come through. I didn't have to ride him: I just had to pilot him, steer him and he'd do the rest like a machine. He was just a freak; he is the best horse I've ridden in South Africa – better than Sentinel, Wolf Power, Bold Tropic, Gatecrasher, or Elevation, who I rode in a Bull Brand – and definitely the best miler I've ridden anywhere. Sledgehammer would not have disgraced himself in a European Group I race like the Queen Elizabeth II Stakes or the Prix du Moulin, for instance.

The last time I saw him was up at the Riverholm Stud. As a racehorse he'd been very lean and narrow behind the saddle; in front of the saddle he had this great depth through the girth and a long neck which he used to stretch up and out; he always carried himself well. But as a stallion he was a majestic-looking horse, with a real crest to his neck. I'd always been able to stand outside his box at Summerveld and he'd put his head over my shoulder and actually fall asleep on me. Or he'd stick his old tongue out for me to stroke. And he was still like that at stud. I rode quite a few of his progeny but there was never any chance of them becoming another Sledgehammer. He was unique.

5 'There were times when I wondered how long it would take'

While basking in the afterglow of Sledgehammer's headline-grabbing victory in the 1973 Bull Brand, Roberts was quick to confirm riding in England as his greatest ambition. However, although regularly pitting his wits against the world's best in subsequent Bull Brands and also the innovative series of International Jockeys' Tests begun at Gosforth Park in February 1976, his only experience of riding outside his homeland had come in Mauritius and Zimbabwe: invitations to Australia and Japan had floundered in a sea of red tape. Both Lester Piggott and Fred Rickaby had made it crystal clear that in their opinion Roberts was good enough. The opportunity was bound to come sooner or later; it finally materialised in October 1977 in the form of an offer from Berkshire trainer Gavin Hunter.

Based at Kennet House, East Ilsley, the 37-year-old Indian-born and Clifton College-educated Hunter was regarded as one of the most promising young trainers in England. On professional pedigree alone his chances had to be a cut above the rest; time spent in acknowledged training academies like those of Ryan Price and Tom Jones stated as much. On performance Hunter also seemed to be making progress; in 1975 Super Cavalier and Western Jewel won him his first Pattern races and two years later Shangamuzo won the Doncaster Cup. By 1977 Hunter's string approached fifty horses and on the promised patronage of leading French owner Daniel Wildenstein for the following season he began searching for a retained jockey.

HUNTER: My owners were beginning to want a regular jockey. It was expensive to retain a jockey and they insisted on someone who wasn't just anybody. They wanted Paul Cook but he wished to stay freelance. I said there's a guy in South Africa, I don't know him very well but there's a chance he might come over for six months. My grandparents had gone to South Africa after the war and my sister is married to a South African, and I used to go out there regularly for holidays. Des Scott, for instance, became one of my best friends eventually and I bought Spanish Pool for him. I remembered Michael as a very good apprentice and then Fred Rickaby signing him up. One doesn't really take that much notice on holiday. I'd go racing twice a week but I was more interested in having fun than watching the racing intently – but I quickly saw this guy was different class to everyone else. South Africa was having a trying financial time, so it was an opportunity for a young man. A lot of people were trying to get money out illegally: it was a chance for Michael to do it legally. If South Africa hit trouble he'd have money in England. The fact that I'd got horses coming from Wildenstein and some from Antonio Blasco, a leading owner in Spain, was enough to persuade him to come.

Even before Roberts, accompanied by his wife Verna and

baby daughter Melanie, boarded the Heathrow flight on 7 March 1978, the *Sporting Life* had announced his impending arrival with an extravagant fanfare. Roberts and Michael Cave had recently won the third Jockeys' International, relegating the 'Brits' to runners-up. 'Hide, Starkey roasted by British-bound "Muis" Roberts,' blared the headline. One millstone thus hung around Roberts's neck before he had even swung a leg over an English horse.

The glorious sunbaked afternoon Roberts remembered from 1975 was a world away from the scene which met his eyes as he prepared to make his English debut on Hunter's Super Symphony in the Queen's Prize over two miles at Kempton Park on Saturday 25 March.

ROBERTS: The first thing that really shocked me were the conditions. I've never been so wet in my life; it was like standing in the showers. My boots were full of water. Peter O'Sullevan commentated on the race for television and he said he felt sorry for me because it was actually snowing and hailing during the racing. As soon as the jocks see a raindrop back home they usually want to postpone the meeting. What shocked me most was the amount of roads we had to cross. I walked the track with Gavin and I just couldn't believe it. Another thing that struck me was how clean the race was. You didn't see much interference and the horses ran wide round the turns. It was very gentlemanly out there and it made race riding appear easy.

Super Symphony weakened in the soft ground, finishing eighth of the eleven runners, while Roberts soon discovered

81

just how *un*gentlemanly some of his new colleagues could be if they had a mind. 'When you go up north you do get knocked about a bit,' he says, ruefully. In 1978 he had to go 'up north' rather a lot – indeed, all over the place, because the class of animal he found himself riding turned out to be less than top class. To Hunter's chagrin, 'my geese were geese not swans.' All aspirations to the giddy heights of the Pattern race circuit were quickly replaced by a necessarily rapid introduction to the delights of the 'gaff' tracks. Of the country's thirty-four Flat tracks, Roberts was to encounter thirty-one by the time he returned to South Africa in October. Therefore it was quite apt that the first winner should have come 'up north' on 3 April. Those initial eight racing days encompassing the Queen's Prize and Ayr's Auchans Stakes passed in a blur of strange towns and motorways as Roberts travelled the length and breadth of the country and experienced – though 'endured' would be more accurate – a crash course in the quantity and quality of British racetracks. After that Kempton debut on the Saturday his itinerary read Newcastle (Monday; three mounts), Warwick (Tuesday; one), Folkestone (Wednesday; one), Newmarket (Saturday; two) and, finally, Ayr (Monday). 'Roberts off the mark by a whisker,' said the *Sporting Life* after he had forced the previously unraced Wildenstein filly Pakeha up in the last stride. The winning jockey gave the first of many post-race appraisals to the British press: 'Pakeha ran a little green in the early stages but she soon settled. Generally, the horses and jockeys are better class over here compared to South Africa. It all depends how I go with Mr Hunter whether I return in 1979 – I certainly would like to.'

This first British winner – his own 901st – may have taken just nine rides but they had involved travelling some 1,200 miles. Roberts was going to need help; in obtaining outside rides and in finding his way around. Enter the not unsubstantial form of Dick Denney.

DENNEY: I lived in East Ilsley and used the same pub – The Swan in Compton – as Gavin Hunter. He asked me to look after Michael, show him the ropes, take him to the tracks and book his rides. I knew nothing about him. Gavin had told me he was brilliant and was going places. It was an awful job because virtually nobody knew anything about him; he was just a big fish in a little pond in South Africa. To me he was like a little boy: I'm twenty-odd stone! I was always tempted to hold his hand and help him across the road. The first sign of promise to me was on Mrs Trotter at Warwick, the second outside ride I'd booked for him. It was bucketing with rain. He was drawn on the outside and I told him to take care on the bend because it gets like a bog. She was sprawling all the way and Michael brought her wide into the middle and she flew to finish fourth. I was very impressed with that. It was good for Michael that he had Verna with him, but I don't think she was very happy. She was alone all day with a young baby and it was difficult for her to integrate, living on the edge of Chilton.

Roberts and Verna Lesley Oliver had been married at Kloof Methodist Church on 18 January 1977, when he was twenty-one and she nineteen. The petite, dark-haired Miss Oliver hailed – appropriately enough – from Horseshoe Road, Everton, near Durban, and boasted a Scottish grandfather to counteract the Welsh forefather of her future husband. 'A bonny filly for the "Muis" ' was how the *Natal Mercury* made the announcement. An avid horsewoman in her own right, she had excelled on the Natal junior eventing and showjumping scene (especially in speed classes aboard her favourite grey horse South West) and had won selection for the province. However, she began part-time work in Summerveld's saddlery and supply store with stern words of maternal warning ringing in her ears.

VERNA ROBERTS: My mom said: 'Don't ever bring a jockey home.' Perhaps that gave me the impression they weren't very nice people. But I found there were exceptions to the rule! So it was definitely not a case of setting my cap at the champion jockey. I didn't know anything about Michael apart from seeing his photo in the racing pages. I'd never been on a racetrack; the first time was when Majestic Crown beat Jamaican Music in the Clairwood Derby. I used to work my horses in the morning and then help out in the store, on the phone and doing the accounts. My boss owned racehorses and he wanted to introduce me to Michael: he was trying to be the matchmaker. He was keener on me than I was on him to start with. The first time he asked me out was to go and see a movie and I told him it was my grandmother's birthday and I had to visit her. The girl I was working with got to hear of this and told him I was telling fibs! He would pick me up after work and it simply took off from there. I found him a very warm person, very genuine and down to earth. Melanie came with us to England in 1978, and was baptised at Chilton; Carolyn was born on 4 August 1979, and there's quite a story attached to that because it was Durban Gold Cup day. The maternity hospital was opposite the entrance to Greyville and Michael dropped me off. The car park was chained-off at the front and the guard wouldn't let us in because he thought we were just after a parking space for the racing. So I'm pointing to my big stomach saying: 'Look! We don't want the track, we want to go in here!' Mom rang the track later to tell Michael the birth was imminent and he was allowed to miss the second race to be present. He put a jacket over his silks and ran across – there was a front-page cartoon of him holding a baby in the next day's paper! When Michael missed the second race people wondered what on earth was wrong with him, so Trevor made a special announcement over the track loudspeakers.

DENMAN: It was the only announcement of its kind I've ever done in twenty-two years: usually I make a point of avoiding that sort of thing. I don't think I'd have bet on his horses that day because his mind was not on the job! After the announcement a great cheer went up and although he failed to win the Gold Cup he did win the fourth race. I also acted as Michael's best man, which had its funny side. We had to take waltzing lessons down in Cape Town in readiness for the reception because neither of us could dance a step. And, of course, everywhere we went in Cape Town Michael was pottering around with this big, black businessman's bag containing all his papers; you could not help but be amused at the sight. But he's got a good sense of humour and is a subtle fun-poker himself. He sees the funny side of everything and takes no interest in a sour face. He can also laugh at himself. In my best man's speech I said that I knew I must be a good friend of his because he lent me his car and he was devoted to his Mercedes. 'He doesn't lend his car to anyone,' I said, and some wag shouted out: 'Or his money!' Michael's not tight but he saw the joke!

Roberts was not the first South African jockey to try his luck in Britain. In addition to 'Tiger' Wright's sortie of 1947 he could also draw inspiration from the exploits of Ike Strydom who rode three winners at Royal Ascot in 1920–1; Cecil Ray, fifth in the 1929 table; and 'Bunky' Buckham – father of Cyril – who won three prestigious races at the Royal meeting, in 1933, before his death in a car crash a month later. Lastly, there was Roberts's predecessor at Rickaby's and another product of the Academy, John Gorton, who after riding five winners on a lightning 1966 visit returned to ride 321 more between 1969 and 1974, including Sleeping Partner to win the 1969 Oaks. Gorton maintained that a top jockey should win races anywhere if he was intelligent enough to adapt. Roberts had no problem on that score: but it would not be easy. Few people knew much about South African racing or its champion jockey – not even racing professionals. 'Do you race on dirt?' 'Do you race thoroughbreds?' Roberts was asked. For himself, he knuckled down to the onerous task of learning not only how to ride the plethora of British tracks but also how to ride Hunter's downland gallops.

* * *

ROBERTS: Downland was a shock to the system but Rickaby had told me what to expect and I came over in 1975 and stayed with Joe Mercer; he took me down to Ian Balding's. The Heath at Newmarket was completely different, like chalk and cheese. There it was more like South Africa. At East Ilsley you couldn't go too fast with a horse at the start of a gallop or you'd never finish with him. You had a more difficult job judging the gallops. I'm not the type who likes to see a horse go ten lengths clear on the gallops. If a horse gives me a good feel I'm inclined to stop them straight away. To me, that's enough. I'd rather save it for the race than put in a great gallop. Mastering the tracks wasn't so much of a challenge because I wasn't getting enough quality rides and had to go everywhere: I never saw a particular track very much. The worst thing was finding some of them. I had two rides at Wolverhampton one evening. We got to the town but were held up in traffic, so I asked a man for directions: he said, 'Down there, just round the corner.' Off we went and found it was the dog track he'd sent us to! I missed my first ride and had to go before the stewards. When I told them they all started laughing and chased me out.

However, it was not the whereabouts or topography of Britain's racecourses which caused Roberts the greatest inconvenience but the xenophobia hiding within their weighing-rooms – though he'd be the last man to make a song and dance about it. Hunter and his assistant, a young former City gent by the name of Alec Stewart, hold no such reservations.

* * *

HUNTER: English jockeys weren't very kind to him; there was plenty of squeezing-up on the bends. It's not allowed in South Africa for safety reasons. But he survived: he was young, fit and brave. Some of it was diabolical in the north. They can be like that, it's the northern syndrome I suppose. Football teams get the same reception.

STEWART: I've so much respect for jockeys like Mark Birch, Dean McKeown, George Duffield but there are a handful I will mark down as jockeys who really did Michael no favours when he went up there. Some of them really did behave apallingly, whereas the southern jockeys were more affable and understanding. There's one jockey still riding now who I will never give a ride to if he is the last jockey available because of the lasting memory I have of his treatment towards Michael in a race. And there were these awfully snide remarks all the time. I was an extra travelling head lad and I heard all the chat and I remember thinking how petty and narrow-minded some of the people were – especially when you remember that so many of those northern jockeys go out and ride in Germany or Hong Kong and take the livelihood away from locals without batting an eyelid. It's only a minority: the vast majority would no sooner do that than fly to the moon. There is a small group of very, very silly, short-sighted, small-minded, petty jockeys that treated Michael the same way they treated Julie Krone on her visit to Redcar in 1992. Americans go out of their way to welcome us. I've worked in California, as have many jockeys – and been awfully well-paid for doing so.

So the attitude some of them displayed toward Julie Krone was disgraceful, because all she was doing was helping sell racing to the public; creating a day out that would bring in more of a crowd and therefore help racing and all the jockeys. Michael will always deny it and will always dismiss it as not being that bad. But I was at an impressionable age in 1978, I suppose. I liked Michael and thought it was so awful that someone who had reached such a pinnacle in his own country should be treated so deplorably. It is one of the great pluses of Michael's character that he doesn't let anything like that get to him. To be honest, nobody gets to the top in any walk of life without being like that. Great politicians take enormous insults from the press and people in the street but have the ability to understand it and then totally ignore it. Michael was the same. He understood the resentment but he chose to ignore it. But I could not understand it; I could not understand it at all.

Temperatures were to approach boiling point at Edinburgh and Ayr during high summer. On 5 June Roberts partnered Sovereign Acres to a hard-fought neck victory in the Gallipoli Two-Year-Old Maiden Stakes at Edinburgh. Hunter's filly had made every yard but a furlong and a half into the race she had swerved to her left, carrying Private Sentence (John Lowe) and the eventual second and third, the 11–10 favourite Sovereign Bay (Jimmy Bleasdale) and Manivek (Richard Hutchinson) with her. Despite the incident being so far from the finish the stewards demoted Sovereign Acres to third. On 15 July, the spotlight shifted to Ayr and the Glen Sannox Two-Year-Old Maiden. On this occasion Roberts was adjudged to have pushed Hunter's 5–4 favourite Timonel through a gap at the expense of Border Squaw (Eric Apter), who had, the form book states, 'edged left' towards the rail. Timonel won going away by two lengths, only to be disqualified for 'accidental bumping'. No action was taken against his rider, whom *The Times* referred to as 'Malcolm' Roberts. However, matters were only just warming up. On the Monday Roberts was aboard another Hunter two-year-old, Super Sirocco, in the Tam O'Shanter Maiden. Ahead from the gate they were hampered inside the final furlong by the favourite Inside Quarter (Michael Wigham) and beaten a length. Roberts objected 'for taking my ground': the objection was overruled.

HUNTER: The Edinburgh disqualification, basically, was a jockeys' carve-up: they lied through their teeth. I was not at Ayr but I saw reruns of the camera patrol films and decided to appeal against both decisions. Michael was staying up there and he rang me on the Sunday after Timonel's race and said: 'Jeez, they were tough on me. At worst it was six of one and half a dozen of the other – the horse on my outside came into me just as much.' Then he came to win the race on Monday and was murdered; he objects and doesn't get it. I was livid! You can't have one rule for Saturday and another one for Monday. We took it to Portman Square: Timonel was chucked out and placed last and Michael cautioned for careless riding – probably fairly – but we got Monday's race and the local stewards received a bollocking for not giving it to us in the first place.

* * *

The last of Roberts's 293 mounts that season was Neville
Callaghan's Holernzaye at Bath on 9 October. Half of those
rides had been for Hunter; but the very fact that the other
half of them were spread among sixty-one trainers illustrates
how much effort Roberts had devoted to going anywhere,
at any time, in pursuit of a ride or a fresh contact: he had
one ride for each of no fewer than thirty-two individual
trainers. Only Carlisle, Catterick and Beverley did not
receive a visit. All the endeavour was rewarded with twenty-
five visits to the winner's enclosure, the last after Vedas
Valley's win in a Chepstow seller on 16 September. This
was the eleventh winner provided by Hunter and put Kennet
House's 1978 season in a nutshell: the anticipated
ammunition had not materialised.

Roberts received two genuine opportunities to shine and
he grabbed them with both hands. Henry Cecil was the
benefactor; Water Frolic in the Hermes Handicap at Epsom
on Oaks day and Formulate in the Waterford Candelabra
Stakes at Goodwood on 25 August were the horses and
events concerned. Cecil's jockey could not make the weight
in the former case, and in the latter he understandably opted
for Formulate's stablemate Mixed Applause, the 2–1
favourite. Roberts brought his filly home at odds of 20–1:
'It's Cecil – but the applause is mixed as Formulate zips
in,' joked the *Sporting Life* headline.

ROBERTS: I didn't exactly become resentful in the early
days but there were times when I wondered how long it
would take. Gavin's horses weren't particularly good that

year and there were problems with viruses. Consequently I didn't get the start I needed. It was always just a matter of pushing myself and saying hello again and again until people recognised me and took notice. Some of them used to turn the other way when they saw me coming! I'd sit in the weighing-room sometimes boiling over with frustration, or I'd be at home watching the racing on television knowing I could do things better than the others. It was frustrating to think 'I'd love to ride that horse' or 'I know what he's doing wrong on that horse.' I felt like going up to people and saying, 'Just give me one ride on your horse and I'll show you what I can do.' No matter how well you ride or how many winners you have in a season, you need to ride the top horses to keep on the map. It is very depressing, almost degrading, when you have to sit back and watch, and not have that involvement with a really good horse.

I was still enjoying the challenge of being here, though. It was an honour to be in the company of your heroes – Lester, Joe Mercer, Brian Taylor, Geoff Lewis, Eddie Hide – and a hell of an experience. Everything was new to me and it definitely improved my riding, even though I wasn't riding good horses. I think this is the hardest school in the world to break into; but once you're in it it's the best. You have to get into the right circles before things can happen. I learnt a lot in '78 and was happy with twenty-five winners: I never thought I'd get fifty. If the top riders came out to South Africa they wouldn't ride winners until they'd made an impression.

HUNTER: Michael was a bit disillusioned and lost in 1978.

I was very hopeful that somebody would come along and offer him a lightweight retainer – Cecil nearly did, I believe. Owners are always very fickle and invariably say it's the jockey who lost the race. In the second half of the season they were blaming Michael, not the horses: I'm sure he'd have been back like a shot if he'd had a successful year.

DENNEY: I was disappointed for him. There were occasions when he should have ridden horses but the owners didn't want him; he'd have won on them just as easily. Gavin's horses were only moderate which meant we always had to wait to see where he could find a race for them – that limited our choices for outside rides. Michael stood up like a big man to whatever was thrown at him. He weathered the storm and was determined to come back. He'd been the blue-eyed boy in South Africa but people over here only wanted jockeys they knew. Even with a champion it was hell getting rides.

STEWART: It was an exciting time of expansion in the yard, but Gavin got the second-division Wildenstein horses from Peter Walwyn which he couldn't fit into his own yard. They weren't very good; the second division of the second division. We had high hopes but they didn't live up to expectations. Half Michael's problem was that his style was so different from most of the English jockeys. He's much higher in the saddle in a finish, for example. I think the disloyalty of the owners upset me as much as anything, the business of beaten horses and using Michael as an excuse. Of course jockeys ride bad races – it's only human and it would be boring if they didn't – and Michael rides bad races now and again, but the excuses for why some horses were getting beaten were pathetic. He adapted very quickly, understood our tracks and way of race riding. I think it's a very weak line of defence when you constantly blame jockeys for horses not winning.

The saddest thing that year was the horrible way the press treated Michael. I think there was possibly resentment of a foreign jockey by some of the press who took the side of the smaller jockeys frightened of losing rides. I'm well travelled – Germany, Hong Kong, America – and all I ever see is English jockeys: the English are the worst for taking jobs from others. The press very much rounded on Michael. Whether he was built up into something he was unable to live up to because the horses weren't good enough I don't know. I do know that the press and Gavin's owners became disenchanted with Michael, and I never for a moment thought it was ever Michael's fault.

DENMAN: The great thing about Michael is that he doesn't brood; 1978 hurt, he's a sensitive man and he'll have a couple of beers in the darkness but he didn't let the setback get to him. He was a superstar in South Africa, winning everything, and this was a rude awakening for him, especially once someone – who he greatly respected – told him he should go home. But he knew how good he was; he didn't need people to tell him; he knows inside of him what he's like. And when you're at the top the only thing people can do is try to pull you off the top.

* * *

Roberts flew back to South Africa a chastened man, yet one who was determined to return when the moment was right. Hunter never did manage to crack the big league and relinquished his licence in 1985; but Roberts and Denney kept in touch. Then one day Verna showed her husband a copy of *Pacemaker* magazine that carried a feature on Alec Stewart, now a trainer in his own right.

ROBERTS: Racing in South Africa was becoming very boring: it was the same thing year in, year out. Verna said to me: 'If you don't do it now you'll regret it for the rest of your life.' I had nothing left to prove. I was only thirty but there'd already been the odd article about Father Time catching up on me and I had a lot of support to switch to training; but I knew I'd regret it if I didn't give England another crack. I'd always wanted to have two years.

STEWART: I was asked if I would take him in 1984 but I only had fourteen horses and it would have been unfair on him. I couldn't pay him a retainer. I dissuaded him from coming because I thought the timing was wrong. In my second season I was incredibly lucky, with Opale winning the Irish St Leger and Dubian doing well. When he rang in 1985 I said 'come'.

DENNEY: I approached Alec Stewart at Salisbury in 1984 and he said maybe, if things went well. Then I asked him again in 1985. I think there was some apprehension on Michael's part in the end, but I told him that if he didn't come now he'd never do it. Piggott had retired and the opportunity was there. There was a lot of aggravation getting a work permit and a place to live. The flat in Newmarket was Piggott's until Michael bought it. Trainers like Brittain and Blanshard said they'd support him; Henry Candy suggested a letter to get him known. So I put together this brochure made up of press cuttings and career statistics and circulated it to trainers. It was pretty well received. I wanted to get across Michael's tremendous attributes. Horses do run for him; he has incredible drive and determination; great judgement of pace; and, above all, a brain – he's always in the right place, sizing up how the others are going and putting his horse exactly where he wants it. If we could only beat the twenty-five winners of 1978 I was going to be happy.

Although Roberts had only thirty-one more rides in 1986 than he had in 1978 he comfortably passed the twenty-five mark, ending the season with forty-two successes from 324 mounts. Twenty of them (from 100 rides) were for Stewart and ten (from seventy-four) for a new and increasingly valuable ally: Clive Brittain. Quality kept pace with quantity. Both Stewart and Brittain trained for members of the Maktoum family: Stewart had been an assistant to Hamdan Al-Maktoum's principal trainer Harry Thomson Jones after leaving Hunter. Indeed, Roberts was to open his account at Royal Ascot on his first opportunity for Jones, in the Queen's Vase – 'Roberts roars in on Stavordale,' headlined the *Sporting Life*. He also won four nice races on the two-year-old filly Abuzz, who ran in the name of Mrs Maureen Brittain, and on 27 September he secured his first

Pattern race when driving Brittain's two-year-old colt Bengal Fire through a gap along the fence to snatch victory in the Group II Royal Lodge Stakes at Ascot. Newmarket, Chester and Ascot were now making their presence felt in the column headed 'successful tracks' at the expense of Edinburgh, Ayr and Hamilton; and he made his debut in a Classic, riding Brittain's Sirk in the St Leger.

Opportunities further afield were also starting to materialise. In 1978 he had a few rides in France; now he gained experience of Ireland, Italy and the USA, and with it Group I success. A Phoenix Park excursion in September bore no fruit (the Group II Tattersalls Rogers Gold Cup of 14 May 1988 on Shady Heights was the Irish breakthrough), but on 5 October Stewart's four-year-old filly Dubian journeyed to Rome's Campannelle for the Premio Lydia Tesio over a mile and a quarter. In a pulsating finish Roberts outrode Willie Carson on another English raider, Santiki, to land the spoils by half a length. A month later Dubian contested the Yellow Ribbon Stakes at Santa Anita, though she found the American fillies too good for her.

Things were looking up and seemed set to continue improving. In 1987 Roberts's tally of wins rose to seventy-four (from 554 rides) – but as it did, old prejudices were reawakened in the weighing-room. It was struggle enough to make ends meet without some South African – especially one who could ride as light as seven stone eleven – pinching the rides: and, to cap it all, he was so polite, courteous and eager to please – all traits which, while satisfying the ethos of the South African Jockeys' Academy and Afrikaner codes of propriety, were calculated to grate alongside the informality and lack of grace inherited by the offspring of Britain's cultural revolution that was the 'Swinging Sixties'. Even Steve Cauthen had not been immune: the press welcomed him with open arms in 1979 but gave him a hard time when things were going less than perfectly. Cauthen, like Roberts, played down the issue and rose above it all to become champion in 1984 and 1985 – when he rode winners for Clive Brittain. A second champion, Irishman Pat Eddery, was also among Brittain's jockeys.

An example of the predicament facing young English jockeys was provided by Philip Robinson. Twice champion apprentice, he had won the 1984 1,000 Guineas for Brittain on Pebbles and looked upon Carlburg stables as a major source of rides: now he found himself competing with Cauthen, Eddery and a third champion in Roberts. As the South African's fortunes waxed Robinson's appeared to wane, and before his departure to Hong Kong in 1987 he and Roberts clashed in a tinpot race at Yarmouth on 9 June. Roberts, riding the 2–1 favourite for Stewart, won the race but only after a brush with Robinson's horse at the two-furlong pole. The stewards disqualified both horses, suspended Robinson for five days and reported Roberts to the Jockey Club, since they considered the interference was intentional. Robinson was beside himself with rage and told the press: 'I don't care how much it costs me. I will appeal. I have never known a decision like it because he has come from behind and knocked me over.' Robinson took his case to Portman Square and after a two-and-a-half-hour hearing got his suspension quashed. Roberts was not so lucky: the Disciplinary Committee dismissed the charge of intentional interference but found him guilty of careless riding and stood him down for seven days – his first ban in Britain. In consequence Roberts missed the whole of Royal Ascot. Watching on television proved an ordeal and on Stewart's advice Roberts took his family to the Lake District for a holiday.

ROBERTS: There were a lot of pros in 1978 and no one was worried about who was coming in. But in 1986 there was a vast change; a lot of new faces. The more winners you rode, the more worried people started to get. They tried to upset me, play jokes on me. I just laughed at them and they couldn't get the better of me; they couldn't wind me up. If they cut holes in my socks I'd just laugh. Out on the track I was knocked over a few times – I know on purpose. I just carried on. My attitude was, put me on the ground and then we have a little legal battle; and that I was always prepared to do if I was ever injured. You get it in all walks of life really, and on the whole they were a pretty decent bunch of guys. Philip Robinson would buy itching powder and all sorts of tricks down on the front at Yarmouth. One day he put L plates on Steve's and my back; or he'd tie a pair of tights to your breeches so you went out with a tail. Another day I was in the weighing-room and he comes in and says: 'Ron Boss wants you.' I go outside and there's nobody there. I go back inside and he comes up to me again and says: 'Ron Boss wants you.' I was laying down now so I said: 'What do you mean, I've just been outside and he's not there!' So he sent somebody else to tell me and I'm getting quite cross now and so I shout: 'Tell him to bugger off!' Meantime Ron Boss was in on the joke and the bugger walks up just as I'm telling him to bugger off!

The phone calls I used to get! 'This is Henry Cecil.' So the first day Henry Cecil actually rings me to ride Indian Skimmer I was pretty cool and couldn't believe it was him. One day Sheikh Hamdan rang and Verna didn't believe it was him so she told him I was sleeping and she couldn't wake me up! I know there are a few who are sick about my success but I haven't got time to worry about them. I've got a job to do and I can't afford to go out wondering if I'm going to get knocked over or worrying about what the other guys say about what I do or how I ride. If I did I'd stop riding: you can't go out there with that in the back of your mind.

This kind of behaviour sorts out the professional man from the middle-of-the-road man. I've never seen the real pros behave like that. I like a bit of fun but there's fun and there's fun: cutting up people's clothes isn't fun. I've never been a vindictive person or carried a grudge but some are and do – and one day, bang, you'll be knocked sideways. I soon learnt I had to be careful. I used to say that you must be worried about me or else you wouldn't be talking about me. That really got their goats.

BOSS: What immediately drew me to Michael was his will to win. I had watched him riding and I liked his approach, his forthright attitude; he was hungry. Obviously, he was on a learning curve. His aggressive style was suited to races up to a mile – Mon Tresor was a perfect example in the Middle Park – but he had to learn how to turn off horses out in the country in the longer races, for instance. He was willing to learn – even though he was a champion jockey – and you could talk to him. It usually takes years for a jockey to learn all our different tracks, but Michael grasped things very quickly. He was not afraid to ride the track as he found it; whatever the track or distance, a horse runs its race on one gallon of petrol only and it's the art of jockeyship to use it effectively. The jockey makes things happen, he puts courage into his convictions; Michael was winning on horses that shouldn't have won in those early days. There's no doubt he wanted to get to the top. He was a terrier – but a terrier who also thought about what he was doing. He was not interested in thinking how good he was yesterday. He wanted to know why he had not won races yesterday so he could be better tomorrow. He hated losing! A champion must look after his own interests, physically and mentally. He must be prepared to make decisions that won't please everyone; he mustn't mind offending people. That is inevitable. I mentioned to him the possibility of him becoming champion early on; you could see he wanted it badly. In fact, I bet him fifty pounds at the end of 1987 that he would ride a hundred winners the next season and he didn't believe I was serious about that; I gave him the hundredth and I'm still waiting for my fifty pounds!

Luckily Roberts had also found two more staunch supporters in Stewart and Brittain. Both men stood by him, ignored the adverse publicity and somehow cajoled their patrons into using this unknown South African.

* * *

STEWART: I can't tell you how hard it was to persuade owners to put Michael up. I was only a third-season trainer and it was difficult to dissuade owners who wanted to see Walter Swinburn or Pat Eddery on their horses. I was very happy with Walter and Pat, but having your own stable jockey is a hell of an advantage. I used to ring up Henry Cecil and others pestering them to use Michael so it would be easier for me to persuade my owners he was a good jockey and therefore worth a retainer: he was only waged in the first year. I put my neck on the line.

BRITTAIN: I knew he was South African champion, and a champion in any sport in any country has to be a cut above average, so I had no qualms about using him. But at the same time I had to convince a lot of my owners that he should be used. His style was not automatically recognised as that of a good jockey. People who had seen him ride in South Africa didn't bat an eyelid because they knew how good he was. But it was surprising how few people were prepared to put him up. In the early days I had to talk the owners into using him. I had other trainers come up to me and say: 'What do you see in Roberts? You use him all the time, what makes him a jockey?' I'd tell them he was a champion and a jockey with a brain – what more did they want? They couldn't believe what I saw. I didn't mind because it meant I could have him all the more.

Steve and Pat rode for some owners in the yard, but I'd still have favoured Michael. It would have caused unnecessary friction to have told owners that they didn't know what they were talking about, but they failed to understand Michael's style. He just needed the horses and I was only sorry I didn't have more top-class horses for him in 1986 apart from Bengal Fire and Abuzz. He made some very moderate horses look good and suffered for it, because next time they ran less well – they couldn't produce two performances of a lifetime – and if he was riding the criticism came his way. If it was another jockey the second time nothing was said.

Michael is a very emotional person. There's no way you can call him a softy, but there are soft spots in him. He would have felt the disappointment very badly in 1978. All he did was come here to ride but he got a lot of stick from other jockeys and some of the press who were probably egged on by those jockeys. I heard one or two people pass the remark that 'the South African is no good – they must be monkeys riding out there because he's no jockey.'

South African racegoers – be they owners, trainers, punters or journalists – begged to differ.

6 Muis the Ace

When Michael Roberts flew out of South Africa for his first taste of English race riding on Tuesday, 7 March 1978 he had ninety-five winners on the board towards a sixth consecutive South African title, twenty-eight in hand of Garth Puller. He jetted back in October knowing Puller had relieved him of his title by exactly the same margin through riding 123 winners (from twice as many mounts), while Robbie Sham and Basil Marcus were streaking ahead in the 1978–9 race. Since that historic initial championship of 1972–3 Roberts had exerted a vice-like grip on the title: scores of 129, 148, 127 and 132 secured the next four, during which period no challenger posed any greater danger than had Raymond Rhodes. The closest call was in 1975–6, when Michael Cave got to within sixteen of the champion. Fired by a high-octane fuel concocted from a mix of profound (albeit concealed) disappointment at the nature of the English experience and the wounded pride of a deposed champion, Roberts went after the leaders with a vengeance.

By the end of February he had rattled up sixty-nine winners and slashed Sham's advantage to six, with Marcus dividing them on seventy-one. On 10 March at Milnerton Roberts joined the handful of jockeys to have ridden all four legs of the Jackpot, and in doing so overtook Sham to lead eighty-one to eighty. Although Sham momentarily regained the leadership in June, Roberts eventually landed his sixth crown with a total of 145 – only three short of his best ever and eleven ahead of the runner-up. Some tally, and some effort, after giving his rivals a two-and-a-half-month head start. However, as he would be the first to admit, Roberts needed more than his own skill and determination: he was aided and abetted by an agent, Pat Guilfoyle, and a close friend, Lew Tankel, who invariably acted as his driver. Roberts was the first South African jockey to employ an agent – indication, if any were now necessary, of his pre-eminence and the intense demand for his services. An original application to register Teddy Savage (Herman Brown's assistant) as his agent back in June 1975 had been rejected by the Jockey Club, despite the champion's plea that the pressures of handling his own arrangements once resulted in a fine for accepting two engagements in the same race. When the Jockey Club relented, Pat Guilfoyle was recommended for the job by Jock Sproule, Chairman of the Natal Stipendiary Board. Guilfoyle's stepfather was none other than John Otto, the stipe who had thwarted Roberts's intended debut on Galley Lad in June 1969, while trainers Syd and Russell Laird were cousins of his. In an association which was to last nine years Guilfoyle helped Roberts rewrite South African Turf history.

The heavy artillery in that blitzkrieg campaign of 1978–9 was provided by Bold Tropic. This chestnut colt was bred by the Birch brothers from their imported son of Bold Ruler named Plum Bold, a speedy early juvenile in the USA, out of Tropicana, a South African mare who had achieved some degree of fame by upsetting the renowned Leora Ann in the 1967 Constantia Handicap. Tropicana was trained by Russell Laird, who, not unsurprisingly, turned out to be the underbidder at the Germiston Yearling Sales of 1977 as Bold Tropic fell to a bid of R17,500 from Fred Rickaby, acting on behalf of Cyril Hurwitz. By this stage the esteemed 'Mr Rick' was contemplating retirement and a return to the land of his birth (he recalls Bold Tropic as 'a dark chestnut with a common head but good bone'), which led to Hurwitz's newest star being prepared for his Classic season of 1978–9 by Buller Benton.

ROBERTS: From day one we always knew we had something special because he'd give you a terrific feel. He was very similar to Sledgehammer, but a little smaller and more refined. Sledgehammer was a big, rangy sort of horse and never carried a lot of condition; always looked very fit, had a lovely arched neck and ran with his head up. Bold Tropic ran with his head down; he was a bonny little horse, smaller and more compact, a bit like Warning, the English miler. He trotted up in his first race which was one of my last rides before going to England. I immediately booked myself the ride in the following year's Cape Guineas!

With Roberts still in the UK, Bold Tropic commenced the Classic trail with Robbie Sham in the plate and they got off to a flying start with a runaway success in the Natal Guineas. Thereafter Bold Tropic's fortunes seemed to dip. He was hard pressed to win the South African Invitation Stakes; he could finish only sixth in the Benoni Guineas to the filly Rock Star (in mitigation, he had picked up a bump early in the contest); and then he ran second in the Cape Trial Handicap to the four-year-old Lucky Lad, assisted by the recently returned Roberts. Ante-post favourite for the Richelieu Guineas (the latest manifestation of the Cape Guineas) on 3 February was Horatius, the winner of six races; but Horatius was drawn poorly. By contrast, Bold Tropic received an ideal spot in the centre and – not without significance – Roberts was back on board: Sham had been jocked off. Accordingly, Bold Tropic ended up the 2–1 favourite. Calvados led into the straight with Roberts tracking Horatius in fifth. As the furlong pole beckoned Horatius made his move and Roberts instantly drove Bold Tropic through in his slipstream. The last two hundred yards built into a cliffhanger of a finish in which Bold Tropic prevailed by a neck. This third Cape Guineas for Roberts, after Sentinel and Gatecrasher, equalled the record of the Cape's very own former champion, Johnny Cawcutt.

The pundits believed that the stoutly bred Horatius would turn the tables over the longer trip of the Cape Derby, pointing to the fact that Bold Tropic's sire had not won beyond six furlongs – conveniently forgetting that Plum Bold had never had the opportunity, owing to premature retirement! The Derby proved a cakewalk for Bold Tropic, who won by seven lengths; Horatius was fifth. That afternoon at Kenilworth constituted a benchmark in Roberts's career, for Bold Tropic was one of a four-timer which also included The Skipper, decreed by the South African authorities to be his thousandth winner. The Jockey

Club, in its wisdom, excluded two winners gained in Mauritius, thereby denying Turffontein's claim that Roberts had reached the magic figure at their track on 27 February. Whatever the case, at the age of twenty-four Roberts was the youngest rider to have accomplished the feat.

ROBERTS: In the Cape Guineas you've got to have early speed to keep your place and then when you come into the straight there's usually an exceptionally strong wind – a south easter – and that does blow, I can promise you. It's so strong sometimes you can't hold your stick in a forward position. You've got to hide your horse. I remember sitting there and finally bringing him out . . . and whoosh! They said he wouldn't stay the mile and a quarter of the Cape Derby but I told them they hadn't seen nothing yet. I dropped him right out, crept, crept, and crept – very similar to how I rode Sledgehammer – and when I let the handbrake off the race was over in two strides. It was a walkover!

Rickaby may no longer have held a licence but he still contrived to play an instrumental role in the Cape Derby success of his old patron's latest star.

RICKABY: Benton had gone to New Zealand with Hurwitz to buy horses and my old assistant Rodney Clarkin was in charge of training Bold Tropic. He said: 'Can you help me? I've been told to sprint this horse; what shall I do?' I told him: 'You can't do that. He'll never stay; he's on his toes now. You've got to get him settled; poor old Michael will never hold him in behind if you train him like that. Canter

109

him from the ten furlong start right round every day and let him down one furlong from the winning post, and he'll finish. Just don't tell anybody and hope nobody notices you're not obeying orders.'

Bold Tropic subsequently returned to Natal where he won the Drill Hall Stakes but met defeat at the hands of Anytime Baby in the South African Guineas. After a disappointing run in the July he followed in the hoofprints of Colorado King and Hawaii by carving out a fresh racing career in the USA. Trained by Charlie Whittingham and usually ridden by Bill Shoemaker, he added seven more victories (including four at Grade II level) to the nine (from fifteen starts) he had accumulated in South Africa; he also ran third to the great John Henry in the Grade I Oak Tree Invitational over a mile and a half – all of which tends to endorse Roberts's comments regarding the ability of South Africa's quality performers such as Sledgehammer, Bold Tropic and, later on, Wolf Power, to hold their own upon the world stage.

With Rickaby's repatriation the two trainers who benefited most from the repercussions of Roberts's English experience were Herman Brown and the Kloof-based Brian Cherry, who had developed quite a rapport with Roberts. Furthermore, both men recognised that, for all its shortcomings, the enterprise had made a positive contribution.

BROWN: He definitely came back a more polished rider and, I think, a more mature person. Actually, for his first year, we thought he did remarkably well. Naturally we all watched his progress pretty closely and were trying to get the English papers to follow him. To be honest it was something of a surprise to us when he didn't return in 1979 because once he has made his mind up about anything he is a very determined fellow.

CHERRY: We got together with Gavin Hunter before Michael left in 1978 and he said he'd make a very good jockey out of Michael. I said: 'But he's already a very good jockey: you might make him better but he's already top class!' I certainly didn't want Michael to go back in 1979; I wanted him on my horses! They did improve his riding in the UK: he always sits, looks and picks up all the good things. He knew a lot more about pace, for instance, and going to the front. Most jockeys needed instructions but I never needed to give him any – other than 'I want this one to win and don't give it a hard race!' I think the 1978 trip to the UK did hurt him: inside he would have hurt like hell. But he's a clever boy; he doesn't expose his feelings; he behaves and speaks intelligently when setbacks occur. I always used to tell him: 'Don't pee in the well because you never know when you might need to go back for a drink!'

ROBERTS: To me Cherry was one of the shrewdest trainers I've ever worked with – or even come across. He won a July with a 33–1 shot, Chimboraa, for example, and won a lot of money. He had a very good eye for a horse. I remember he took over a horse from Jo'burg one year especially to run in distance races. He used to train them in short, sharp sessions. I said: 'That horse can't win over two miles!' But it did. I couldn't believe it. He won a fortune! He used to buy sprint types all the time. I rode for him right up until he retired; probably for longer than anyone I rode for. You could talk to the man and he would listen. We had a really happy relationship – closer than those I had with Herman Brown or Fred Rickaby, in fact.

CHERRY: You could see right away that he was streets ahead of the rest; I grabbed him as soon as I could once Rickaby left, and he stayed twelve years. One of the first races he rode for me was at Clairwood, twenty runners, first race of the day. My jockey never pitched up and I had to go looking for a jockey for my filly Mildenhall; I'd got a fortune on her! I went to the weighing-room and this little boy was sat there without a ride – which was unheard of, because he rode in every race. I gave him the colours and he doddled it!

But Michael always did have Lady Luck on his side. When Michaelmas went to Johannesburg for the Benoni Guineas in 1976 I drove the float and Michael asked to come along. Michael begged me to let him drive the float back home after the race. We're driving along and I notice the petrol is getting low, so I told him to stop at the next station. 'No, no, the next one will be all right,' he kept saying as we passed station after station, until I said that if we ran out of petrol he would be the one to do the walking to get some more. We ran out of petrol sure enough – and as soon as Michael got out of the float a car stopped and took him straight to a petrol station. Three minutes is all it took him!

'Tiger' Wright rode for me and so did Johnny McCreedy – and even 'Cocky' Feldman rode for me a little – but this little Dutch boy came along and he was special. It was his brain that made all the difference. A lot of Afrikaners are inclined to be a bit slow, but this little boy could discuss the Stock Exchange with the Chairman of the Stock Exchange! He was highly intelligent. When he was going to ride a horse for you he would tell you everything about that horse, its draw, the track and everything about all the other horses in the race as well. He made my horses look far better than they were. Heracles, for instance, was not a great horse but Michael burgled the South African Guineas on him. When Michaelmas won the Benoni we walked the course on the Friday and Michael showed me where he was going to go coming into the straight because the grass was uncut on the inside; he was going to swerve out. Well, you could have marked his course with a pencil because he took it exactly to win the race on a horse who was more a seven-furlong horse than a miler. But Michael could make them get that bit extra.

Another horse Michael found the key to was Ted's Ambition. I think Michael missed him only once – and he ran poorly. He was a cross type of horse – you wouldn't want to go into his box – but Michael would win these sprints with him out of the pens. I used to tell him: 'The way he races with you people must think you own him.'

Roberts had been the human component in more than one 'flying machine', from Rickaby's durable gelding Abbey Boy, three times a winner of the Concord Stakes, and

Cherry's Computaform National Sprint winner Row To Rio
('He used to get outpaced early on but came in the dying
strides with a hell of a rattle') to a pair of fast females in
Herman Brown's Justine, heroine of the 1973 National
Sprint ('The track was a quagmire after a heavy storm
delayed racing for over an hour') and the ill-fated champion
sprinter of 1980–81, Scarlet Lady. Yet there was only ever
one favourite: Ted's Ambition. A little chestnut by
Caerdeon, a brother to Mrs Gwen Murless's 1968 1,000
Guineas winner Caergwrle, this gelding pulled off a hat-
trick of wins between 1983 and 1985 in the weight-for-age
Concord Stakes over Greyville's five furlongs, in the process
of which he set a track record of 57.4 seconds. The Durban
Merchants Handicap and Steward's Cup were two other
much-vaunted names on his victory roll.

ROBERTS: This was a game horse and one of the best
sprinters in South Africa. I tell you what, he was one of the
few horses who actually used to stick his neck out when he
raced. The crowds loved him. He was a bit different to Road
To Rio: Ted's Ambition would jump out and go like stink
with his old ears pricked. He hated horses pacing him. When
anything got to him he'd respond, stick his neck out with
his ears flat back; he was a great trier.

As the 1980s unwound the plethora of eulogistic newspaper
headlines testified to the almost messianic status Roberts
had attained on the South African Turf. Muis roars on/The
Man they call Mighty Muis/The Natal System: follow
Roberts/ There's no catching Muis/'M' seems to be the

magic letter/Muis the Ace is in a class of his own – these are a random sample, with the last most apt of all. The precociously talented youth had matured into an immensely strong and tactically aware 'elder statesman', even though still barely thirty. For that he could partially thank those six months in England, both character-enhancing and a refresher course in jockeyship at one and the same time. To quote the *Natal Witness*: 'Always the master, Roberts has matured greatly after riding in Britain. He still uses the whip to great effect but much more sparingly than before. He can ride from the front and then ride with equal ease from the back and possesses a devastating finish. He has improved out of all recognition.' Roberts was 'The Main Man': everyone knew it and accepted the fact.

RICKABY: Sledgehammer was something different and so was Michael Roberts. So is Lester Piggott and so was Gordon Richards. They've got star quality and you only get one occasionally. I never thought he'd get a fair chance in 1978. In those days foreigners didn't go down so well in England. He got experience – so it worked in that sense – but he didn't really get away with it because he never had a chance.

BROWN: We always regarded 'Cocky' Feldman and 'Tiger' Wright as the greatest. Everyone used to compare Michael with these two; the older trainers would opt for 'Tiger' and the younger ones would side with Michael. But now it's changing. Even the older ones are saying Michael is the best. He was so much better than any other jockey in the country. He wouldn't just be winning on favourites; he was winning on also-rans. Your horses improved by pounds when he rode them. There wasn't a record we didn't think he could break if he kept riding long enough.

CHERRY: To make it in horse racing from his background was almost an impossibility, but not only did he make it, he made it look easy. This little man has to be put down as Superman! Lester Piggott, Willie Carson, Fernando Toro from the USA have all ridden for me but, honestly, Michael is way ahead of them. We had a great jockey in 'Cocky' Feldman; even 'Tiger' Wright became a little boy when he rode against 'Cocky'. Basil Marcus, Jeff Lloyd and Felix Coetzee are top jockeys, but the moment Roberts gets back from England they become second-rate. It's a toss-up between Cocky, 'Tiger' and Michael who was the best ever in South Africa. And Michael is nearly as good a farmer as he is a jockey! If he spots a hole in a fence when he's driving past he'll stop and mend it; he'll pick up any scrap of paper. His farm is an absolute model of a farm.

DENMAN: He is the idol of every fan in South Africa and one of the greatest sportsmen the country has produced; the best export since Gary Player. The early jockeys did not have his charisma; he is a household name throughout South Africa. Two things stand out as far as his riding is concerned. First of all, every race was a July to him. He is motivated by a childlike enthusiasm which keeps him going and stops him from ever becoming soured. Ego does not enter into it: he gets a simple pleasure out of riding – which is what every rider needs. Secondly, there is that indefinable quality, the X-factor. To be champion you need a whole lot of factors in combination. In my South African experience I'd say that Marty Schoeman had the most raw talent of them all; and Johnny McCreedy was the greatest horseman possessing the most wonderful hands. But in overall ability Roberts is the best. And away from the track you've got to handle the fame and the money: these jockeys are treated like demigods in South Africa. Michael had so much at a young age but he has kept his feet on the ground. His greatest quality as a man is his humility. I have *never* heard him boast. In fact he still gets embarrassed if you tell him he has ridden well. Sometimes I purposely try to rib him that he has ridden badly because he seems to like the other side of the story!

TANKEL: I've been driving the car when, besides Michael, it has contained Robbie Sham, Felix Coetzee, Basil Marcus and Jeff Lloyd – the top jockeys in the country. But if Michael talks they all shut up and listen. Michael has what we call the eye of the eagle: just that little bit extra. The ability to be right at the right time. I remember him riding three winners at Greyville and every one was a desperate short head. Another jockey would have got beat on them. It was a nod of the head at the right spot each time; the timing had to be perfect. I've seen him sick as a dog and ride five winners – and still moan that he didn't have six. He'll analyse the one he lost rather than dwell on the five he won! That's the difference between Michael and the other top jockeys. 'Tiger' Wright was an excellent rider, but in those days he rode for some of the biggest punting owners who were not averse to getting a few horses to run a bit slowly behind; many people have told me that 'Cocky' Feldman was even better but he also rode for the 'money' rather than championships. Michael has been nominated on more than one occasion for Sportsman of the Year but he's never won. The argument against Michael is that he needs a horse. But one year Jody Schekter won it, and he needed a car!

Natal's journalists finally got around to honouring Roberts by voting him – at the third nomination – their Sports Star of the Year for 1988 (he would win again in 1991). Scottsville went one better: it named a race after him on 26 January 1990. Unfortunately Roberts spoilt the script by finishing fifth – on the favourite, too! Never mind: he put matters right by winning in 1991.

Such star status made Roberts a wanted man. Millard, Maingard, Rixon, Payne, Barnard: all joined the queue of trainers clamouring for his services. Being the single-minded professional he was (and is), Roberts consequently travelled anywhere and everywhere in search of the choicest rides. His presence on a horse's back might reduce its odds; but, by the same token, 'maybes' were being transformed into 'good things' which brought the prospect of landing the Jackpot (picking the winners of the last four races on the card) tantalisingly within everybody's reach. All sorts of records hitherto considered inviolable – 'Tiger' Wright's 175 winners in a season and his eleven championships; the possibility of 200 winners in a season; R1 million in earnings – suddenly came under threat as Roberts racked up winner

Michael Roberts and Mtoto together after a training spin on the
Newmarket gallops in 1987. (*George Selwyn*)

'They say staying power comes from the dam': Magdalena Roberts and her first born.

Aged three and already counting his pennies. Fred Rickaby will not be surprised.

Aged fourteen: first year at the Academy – the horse is Anvil Beat. (*Dennis Cleaver*)

At sixteen, Roberts rode the first of 3,300-plus winners – Smyrna. (*Ken Wilkins*)

The first Classic horse: the powerfully built Sentinel is testing those young forearms on the way to the post. (*Ken Wilkins*)

No sign of danger as Sentinel comfortably gains the first of his two consecutive Clairwood Champion Stakes in 1972. (*Ken Wilkins*)

The new champion jockey kisses his trophy.

Herman Brown holds Sun Monarch at the conclusion of morning exercise.

Bull Brand Jockeys International: South Africa's finest ready for battle. (*Ken Wilkins*)

'Roberts whips world's best on super Sledge'. The second horse is Jamaican Music and in third place comes Lester Piggott on Sun Monarch. (*Ken Wilkins*)

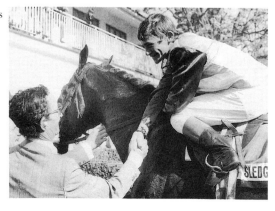

Fred Rickaby greets the returning heroes. (*Ken Wilkins*)

Under the admiring gaze of his jockey and trainer, the 1975 Metropolitan Stakes winner, Sledgehammer, enjoys his own celebratory banquet.

Sledgehammer treats Yataghan like a plater in the 1975 Clairwood Champion Stakes. (*Daily News*)

Majestic Crown spreadeagles his field in the Michaelmas Handicap only fifteen months after suffering a fractured cannon bone. (*Ken Wilkins*)

Gatecrasher – a really imposing individual. (*Ken Wilkins*)

Unsaddling Row To Rio after success in the 1977 National Sprint. The smiling trainer, Brian Cherry, is at the horse's head. (*Ken Wilkins*)

Ted's Ambition roars home at Scottsville.

Bold Tropic gets the better of a cliffhanger finale to the 1979 Richelieu (Cape) Guineas. (*The Argus*)

Peggy and Cyril Hurwitz lead in Bold Tropic after his victory in the Drill Hall Stakes, 1979. (*Ken Wilkins*)

Farmer Roberts with a prize-winning Jersey cow at the Royal Show,
Pietermaritzburg. (*Daily News*)

Wolf Power streaks away to win the 1982 Schweppes Challenge. (*Ken Wilkins*)

'Only Roberts's riding did it!' Northern Princess defeats Senor Santa in South Africa's first match race for twenty years. (*Ken Wilkins*)

'I told you it would be easy, didn't I?' Muis the Ace seems to be saying. (*Anita Akal*)

President F.W. de Klerk presents his country's greatest-ever jockey with the silver South African Sports Merit Award on 24 November 1993.

Michael Leonard Roberts with his father Leonard. (*Anita Akal*)

The Roberts family at Scottsville for the running of the Michael Roberts Handicap: Melanie, Michael (holding the winner's prize of an Mtoto bronze), Verna and Carolyn. (*Anita Akal*)

Ayr, 3 April 1978 – Pakeha gets the British ball rolling, it was Roberts's first win in the UK. (*Kenneth Bright*)

Mtoto powers his way
up Warren Hill,
Newmarket, during an
early morning spin.
(*George Selwyn*)

Debriefing with Alec
Stewart at Newmarket.
(*George Selwyn*)

A grateful pat for Mtoto as he overhauls Reference Point in the 1987
Eclipse Stakes. (*John Crofts Photography*)

In the 1988 Eclipse Stakes, Shady Heights cannot prevent Roberts and
Mtoto from achieving an historic double. (*John Crofts Photography*)

after winner, to the delight of punters throughout the country. To the Milnerton Jackpot of 10 March 1979 he added another at Newmarket on 16 November 1983 – thus becoming the first jockey to assist in fulfilling the punter's dream at a Transvaal racetrack. In point of fact he won on all five of his mounts, the thirty-sixth occasion he had completed a five-timer according to Guilfoyle's records. 'One-man show as Roberts cleans up at Newmarket,' was the press response. Not that this constituted a personal apogee. On 25 September 1982, he had reeled off six winners, a second and a third from eight rides at Scottsville (it could have been seven, as that runner-up was beaten by a stablemate he had rejected); on 22 December 1987 he trumped this display with six out of seven at Clairwood, which included a third Jackpot. Few jockeys ever accomplish one Jackpot: achieving three was extraordinary.

The riding records Roberts coveted most belonged to 'Tiger' Wright. In 1949–50 'Tiger' booted home 175 winners. With only five months of the 1979–80 season completed Roberts had passed seventy and the press were already beginning to sense that the thirty-year-old record could be vulnerable. At fourteen winners a month Roberts was bang on schedule. On 16 July he reached 174; Misty Flight and Me No at Clairwood on the nineteenth gave him the record. 'New Tiger Tamer' declared the *Daily News* beneath a picture of the new record-holder being congratulated by the old. 'It was a bit of an anticlimax,' Roberts told reporters. 'I got off the horses, weighed in and prepared for my next ride.' It was very much business as usual: at the end of racing Roberts flew up to Zimbabwe to honour an agreement with the Mashonaland Turf Club to ride at Bulawayo the following day, a Sunday; needless to say, he rode a winner. His total for the season stopped at 186. In 1980–81 he scored 168. Only Wright had previously topped 150 on two occasions. The following season was to become one relentless quest for the elusive grail that was a double hundred. He passed 100 in February, 150 in May and broke his own record on 10 July at Greyville – by which time he had become the first South African jockey (or trainer) to amass R1 million in prize money for his patrons. He was, some argued, the highest earner in domestic South African sport; his income exceeded that of an MP or Cabinet minister and was not far short of the Prime Minister's.

With four days remaining of the 1981–2 season Roberts's tally had climbed to 198. Racing history was made at Greyville on 28 July, when Lady Anne and Floral Slipper (both trained by Brian Cherry) brought him to the prized milestone that had defeated the country's finest practitioners, from Feldman and Wright to Charlie Barends and Stanley Amos. Roberts's final figure was 203 from 849 rides, a winning percentage of 23.9.

TANKEL: The thing to remember is that although Felix Coetzee subsequently rode 270-odd and Jeff Lloyd over three hundred to take the title in 1991–2 there is much more racing in South Africa nowadays. Jeff Lloyd had something like fourteen hundred rides. When Michael was chasing his titles there were really only two meetings a week, Wednesday and Saturday. Now they're racing five days a week. If a jockey wants to he can ride in Kimberley on a

Monday and Bloemfontein on a Thursday, which were meetings Michael wouldn't consider.

ROBERTS: The nicest championship to win was as an apprentice. The others were pretty straightforward except for 1978–9 when I'd been in England at the start of the season, and 1983–4 when Felix stole quite a march on me. I had to dash everywhere that year! The other great challenge was going for the two hundred, which was just as chaotic.

VERNA ROBERTS: I hardly saw him during the two hundred season. He'd be flying from one meeting to another; it seemed he was always in the air. Sometimes I didn't know where he was! But he was still so relaxed and easy-going. He's always the same until he walks on to a racecourse. The minute he gets home he's relaxed again.

Roberts relaxed whenever the jockey in him gave way to the farmer; or, as *Farmers' Weekly* phrased it in the issue of 20 March 1987: 'Horses mean work to Michael Roberts but rearing cattle is a pleasure.' One particularly gratifying agricultural venture was the herd of pedigree Jerseys he ran at the Umlaas Road farm he owned in partnership with Richard Bruton. His pride and joy was Tetbury Fandancer, who broke the South African milk-yield record in July 1980 – the same week her owner broke 'Tiger' Wright's longstanding record of 175 – and Roberts was a frequent exhibitor at Pietermaritzburg's Royal Show, winning the award for the Supreme Dairy Animal with his Jersey cow Jacqueline. Roberts also dabbled in thoroughbred breeding, and the first horse he bred – Golden Express – won on its debut at Greyville on 3 October 1979. The colt's breeder, naturally, was in the saddle.

Quite possibly the finest monument to Roberts's inexhaustible ambition to be acknowledged the best was his pursuit of an eleventh title in 1983–4. With four months of the season remaining, Felix Coetzee had manufactured a buffer of twenty-three over the defending champion, 112 to 89. Roberts became perpetual motion: he explored every avenue in the hunt for winners. Cometh the hour, cometh the man. It was time for the motoring skills of Lew Tankel to shine.

TANKEL: Nigel Mansell couldn't have beaten me! I performed miracles! In those days winners in Zimbabwe counted and Michael used to go up to Bulawayo every second Sunday. But there was no early morning flight on a Sunday from Durban to Johannesburg to enable you to go on to Bulawayo. So Michael would take the overnight train from Pietermaritzburg – which would never have got him to Johannesburg in time – and get off at Heidelberg, about forty miles away, where I'd meet him and drive like the devil to Jan Smuts to catch the plane. He'd have six hours on the train just to get near Jo'burg! There was no other way of getting to Bulawayo without chartering a plane. By doing things like that he made up the deficit.

When the season closed at Clairwood on 31 July Roberts had scraped together 160 winners for a healthy double-figure advantage over Coetzee and landed his eleventh championship. The next barrier to breach was 2,000 winners. Amos led the South African list with 2,507, followed by Wright on 2,454 and Barends on 2,157: no one else had made it to 2,000. Roberts became the youngest to do so on 21 November 1984 at Clairwood, when Lotus Land became his forty-sixth winner of the 1984–5 season. Nevertheless, the characteristic thirst for winners was beginning to be quenched by the sands of time. This year, for the first time since 1971–2, Roberts lost the South African jockeys' championship in a straight fight.

The Floral Slippers and Lotus Lands of South African racing were fast relegated to the back seat as Roberts increasingly aligned himself with quality at the expense of quantity. Bold Tropic was certainly not the last outstanding South African racer to benefit from an inspirational Roberts ride. Indeed, some would argue that Roberts did not sit on the greatest of them all until the day he rode Wolf Power in the 1982 South African Guineas. This charismatic grey by the American-bred, French-based sprinter Flirting Around (winner of the 1975 King's Stand) was the undisputed favourite of the South African crowds at the beginning of the 1980s. Bred by Birch Bros. and trained by Ricky Maingard, Wolf Power won a host of Graded races between 1981 and 1984 which included the Administrator's Champion Juvenile, Clairwood Champion, Hawaii Stakes (twice), Queen's Plate (twice), Schweppes Challenge (twice) and the Met. – all Grade I. The monarch of all he surveyed at a mile, Wolf Power, though hardly mean, could occasionally be moody but he was invariably magnificent when it mattered most and he became the country's first half-million-rand horse (winding up with R729,037) before a bid of R4 million ensured his stud career would commence in the USA.

ROBERTS: He was Jeff Lloyd's mount really. I only got on him half a dozen times when Jeff got a long suspension in 1982. I won the Clairwood Champion and a Queen's Plate on him and came second in the 1983 Met. He was all right as a two-year-old, not the best, but he came into his own as a three-year-old. He was a brilliant miler with great acceleration – a bit like Mtoto's. I don't think he was quite as good as Bold Tropic or Sledgehammer, though. He became the idol of the racing public; everybody loved him and whenever he ran the track was packed out. He was a lovely, flashy grey and the public really took to him.

Wolf Power's position as South Africa's leading money-spinner proved short-lived. His status was soon challenged by Spanish Pool, a horse he had often encountered and defeated. Spanish Pool followed his sire (the Waterford Crystal Mile winner Gay Fandango) to South Africa after two seasons in Europe where, trained by Jeremy Hindley, he had won five races, notably the 1982 Oettingen Rennen (Group III) over a mile at Baden-Baden to earn a Timeform rating of 116. Whether Spanish Pool actually improved with age is debatable, but his career most definitely prospered once he joined David Payne. Some invaluable assistance from Roberts did not come amiss, either.

ROBERTS: Being an imported horse Spanish Pool attracted

considerable publicity before he even ran. I rode him in a gallop and was tremendously impressed but he was Robbie Sham's ride and I couldn't get on him. Before his first run at Scottsville I rang Joe Mercer to see what he had to say about him and Joe told me he was a short runner. I knew Robbie Sham tended to go early in his races so I sat behind them on Grey Sun, waited, and got up to beat them. Because of that I got the ride afterwards.

Spanish Pool did improve an awful lot once he came out to South Africa. Had he returned to the UK, for instance, he'd only have been a Group II horse. We've seen occasions in South Africa where these kind of horses profit from a longer racing career and they do get better; there's no two ways about it. He was a very versatile little horse at seven furlongs or more. He had a lot of speed and was very effective at a mile. You could sit on him at the back and pick them off. He was a top horse for South Africa but not an outstanding one like Wolf Power – even though he did beat him once – or Sledgehammer.

Spanish Pool won just the once during his initial South African season of 1982–3. However, a third to Wolf Power in the Schweppes Challenge and two second places behind the crack filly Tecla Bluff (winner of the July) hinted at better things to come. Despite coming up against Wolf Power on too many occasions for comfort (he and Roberts seemed to have the 1984 Met. in the bag until the grey pounced), Spanish Pool went from strength to strength and recorded his first major victory in the R300,000 Sun International (formerly the Holiday Inns). Robbie Sham had

been his intended partner, but with Roberts's mount
suddenly scratched Sham was handed a 'present' and
Roberts substituted. As the ten furlongs was stretching
Spanish Pool's stamina, Roberts had to cover him up for as
long as possible before unleashing what was in any case
only a short burst of finishing speed. It turned out to be a
close-run thing. The pacesetters tired unexpectedly, leaving
Spanish Pool exposed in front with over a furlong and a
half still to run. 'They just kept falling back on me, forcing
me to get out of the way and there I was in front and having
to keep him going.' Roberts somehow contrived to nurse
his desperately weary mount to the line before Gondolier
(later to win a July) swept past. Spanish Pool concluded the
1983–4 season on the highest possible note by winning the
Schweppes Challenge from a field which included Wolf
Power making his farewell appearance.

Largely thanks to further successes in the Champion
Stakes and Queen's Plate, Spanish Pool's earnings had
already eclipsed Wolf Power's when the 1985 Schweppes
came round, and after he had defeated Beldale Lustre to
win the Clairwood event for the second time (knocking 0.3
seconds off Wolf Power's track record) they soared to
R883,899. Becoming South Africa's first equine
'millionaire' now assumed priority. Spanish Pool's attempts
to bridge the gap proved fruitless, however (Model Man
would be the eventual history-maker), and he retired the
winner of R913,899 as a result of eleven wins and thirteen
placings from his twenty-seven South African starts.

Spanish Pool's final fling was in the 1985 Champion
Stakes won by Bodrum, formerly a top three-year-old but

without a win in nine months. The man who had rekindled the grey's enthusiasm at the age of five was none other than Roberts. 'Supermuis does it again,' said the *Daily News*, almost shaking its head in incredulity. 'All the while along the rail Roberts had been judging his final dash to perfection. He held up Bodrum through the final 400 metres and allowed him to get closer as they approached the final 50 metres. Then, as the line loomed up Roberts quickly switched his whip from his left hand, pushed Bodrum to full stretch and the big grey threw all he had into it and snatched victory by a short head from Wild West.' On Bodrum's next appearance Roberts helped him to Turffontein's Champion Stakes, but his presence in the irons was never guaranteed. He could now virtually choose his mounts at will and no jockey was safe, however good – as Robbie Sham had discovered. Behind Bodrum at Greyville, for example, was another animal Roberts frequently partnered: Turncoat, a little horse Herman Brown trained for Robert Sangster.

ROBERTS: Bodrum was a cheeky ride because you couldn't rush him early. He belonged to the Oppenheimers: if we had royalty in South Africa it would be them. I have a lot of respect for them and we got on well. They enjoyed their racing and bred their own horses; one year when Mr Oppenheimer bid for a horse at the sales it was so unusual everybody clapped! Turncoat and Bodrum were exact opposites. Turncoat was small and dark whereas Bodrum was big and grey. Turncoat also had a club foot and if you ever saw him going to post you'd automatically scratch him off your list.

* * *

The rivalry between Bodrum and Turncoat was understandably most fierce during their Classic season of 1983–4. The South African authorities had finally succeeded in extracting some semblance of unity and order from the jumble of Classic races held by the individual provinces. A Triple Crown was agreed, comprising the Richelieu Guineas over the traditional one mile (the old Cape Guineas) in February; a new race over nine furlongs in early March at Germiston, to be called the Gosforth Park Classic, which replaced the Benoni Guineas; and finally a new ten-furlong race at Greyville in June, named the South African 2,000. Thus, each of the three major racing centres was responsible for one leg of the Triple Crown; there was a sensible time lapse between each one; and the distances became progressively more taxing.

Having already won the Natal Guineas, Turncoat entered the Richelieu holding an excellent chance of victory – that is, until his high draw was announced. The long sweep into the Milnerton straight is considered the kiss of death to those drawn on the outside who must make that much greater effort. Roberts countered by dropping Turncoat to the tail of the field. With a furlong and a half to run the pair had yet to trouble the binoculars as Bodrum struck the front. Only then was Roberts seen to switch Turncoat to the centre of the track, settle him, balance him, and send him scampering into the lead for a cosy three-quarter-length victory. 'The race truly belonged to the "Mighty Muis" and Turncoat,' raved the press. 'Roberts showed once again that he could hold his own with the best in the world. His fantastic judgement and expert horsemanship was shown to its best; he is likely to become a South African legend in his own lifetime.'

It was generally agreed that Bodrum, who finished one and a quarter lengths behind Turncoat in fourth place, would be favoured by the extra furlong of the Gosforth Park Classic, as he was by the Prix Ganay winner Free Ride, whereas Turncoat's pedigree was that of a sprinter. Consequently, the loss of Roberts owing to a fall from Spring Wonder earlier in the afternoon probably tipped the scales in Bodrum's direction. Turncoat was ridden too near the pace and the grey left him through the final furlong to win by a length and three-quarters. Thereafter Bodrum consistently proved Turncoat's superior, finishing ahead of him again in the South African 2,000, albeit failing to win the race. The pair clashed for the final time during 1983–4 on the very last day of the season. A record crowd of 15,956 packed Clairwood to see them contest the R200,000 Mainstay 1800. It could not be called a two-horse race by any stretch of the imagination. Both Rain Forest and Grey Sun, on whom Roberts had won the previous season's South African Guineas and South African Fillies' Guineas respectively, were among their adversaries. However, on the day Roberts completed his eleventh successful championship to equal 'Tiger' Wright's record there was, as the racing pages subsequently confirmed, 'No stopping the champion jockey. Muis shows why he's champion.' Patiently biding his time, Roberts delayed until the last feasible moment before urging his gutsy little partner to a thrilling victory over Bodrum.

The one race Roberts could not manage to win was the one he – like all South African jockeys – wanted to win most of all: the July.

ROBERTS: On my first visit to Durban for the Academy interview I had to go to the Turf Club and as we passed the track I was told: 'That's the winning-post for the July: one day you'll go past it first.' Well, I haven't yet! I've had thirteen goes and ridden some good horses like Sledge, Majestic Crown, Bold Tropic, Zamit, Gigantic, Turncoat, but the closest I've got was coming second on French Mustard – a last-minute pick-up ride – in 1981, though Sweet Wonder and Bush Telegraph were in a way just as close. I'd earmarked Sweet Wonder as a potential July horse for 1983 after I'd been third on him in the Holiday Inns; I begged his trainer, Bertie Sage, for the ride but I missed a trial on him and he gave the ride to Bartie Leisher. Bartie is a top jockey now but he didn't know Greyville so well in those days. Usually they go flat out all the way in the July; they jump fast so as not to get chopped off at the turn by the outside horses cutting across. But that year was a slow-run race and Sweet Wonder missed the break slightly, got squeezed and was too far out of his ground. I'm sure he could have won. Then, after Mtoto won at Royal Ascot in 1987 while I was suspended, the owners of Bush Telegraph, who was the top three-year-old in South Africa, went up to Sheikh Ahmed and Alec Stewart and asked if they'd release me to ride him in the July. As Mtoto was going for the Eclipse it was never really a possibility, though. Bush Telegraph not only won, he broke the track record!

The top jockeys more or less have their pick of the runners and I've ridden some good horses in the race, like Sledgehammer and Majestic Crown, but they had a lot of weight as older horses. Majestic Crown carried fifty-seven kilos in 1976 and still finished fourth; the lightweights just came past us at the end. Sledgehammer carried fifty-six and a half in 1975. And in my time other good older horses like Elevation and Yataghan were asked to carry fifty-seven or fifty-eight kilos. I think you'll find Sea Cottage won with something like fifty-seven and a half, but that's about all. And the best three-year-olds will have been running in the Cape Classics and be tired out by July. Only eighteen horses can run, as a safety measure, and they are invited by the Durban Turf Club. The race is a handicap but the invitation factor is important, because if you just eliminated from the bottom as normally you'd take out all the best three-year-olds who are down there as a result of running in the Classics and not having a true handicap mark. The handicapper gives them a rating plus a weight-for-age allowance; but the records show that three-year-olds struggle to win with more than fifty-one kilos, which restricts him. Gatecrasher won with forty-nine and a half and In Full Flight won with fifty-two and a half – which is what made his victory so outstanding. The invitation system gives the handicapper and the stewards the discretion to frame an all-aged handicap and not have to eliminate the younger horses. All the same, the system causes a lot of controversy: who's invited and who isn't, kind of thing. The draw comes out with the weights, and that is vital because of the danger of chopping on the bend, even though they use a 'false rail' to fan the horses out coming into the straight which is meant to give everyone a chance. It's still a race I'd like to win. Every year I get calls to ride this or that, but the race is usually the same day as the Eclipse which I always hope to be involved with and the July jockeys have to be declared weeks in advance; getting there and back would be no problem. The race is a lottery, really. The hard luck stories that come out of the July are unbelievable! I will win it one day, though . . .

Most of those present at Clairwood on 28 July 1984, could not conceive of Roberts ever riding a finer race than the one which brought Turncoat victory in the Mainstay. However, the calling card of the truly exceptional jockey is the ability constantly to amaze, the ability constantly to extend the boundaries of excellence, and two further instances of Roberts's genius were still to be set before South African eyes.

The first came in the 1986 Richelieu Guineas on Sea Warrior, a horse Roberts dismisses as 'not much better than a handicapper; he was an outsider and a front runner.' By the sound of it the whole event was no big deal. Others, Lew Tankel among them, recall that day at Milnerton with awe in their voices, eager to dwell on Roberts's performance which they insist was something quite out of the ordinary even by his exalted standards. In utter defiance of a howling south-easter Roberts decided to make every post a winning one. With the wind behind him down the back straight he booted Sea Warrior into a clear lead in the hope that nothing would possess the energy to narrow the gap once the teeth of the gale was encountered in the home straight. The favourite, Ecurie, a filly trained by Terrance Millard, 'the Magician of Milnerton', tried her level best to get on terms but the combination of shrewd stratagem and forceful riding saw Roberts's own brand of wizardry prevail by a length.

Alchemy played no small part in the second and even more eye-catching example, too, because the event in question was the historic match race between the gelding Senor Santa and the filly Northern Princess on 30 December 1989 – the first match race in South Africa for twenty years. The last one, at Gosforth Park on 22 November 1969, had resulted in a victory for Double Eagle over Mr Djanning. The circumstances leading to the match between Senor Santa and Northern Princess arose from the whims of the Transvaal handicappers. They eliminated Senor Santa from the Germiston November Handicap, arguing that his form was not good enough at the one-mile distance. Senor Santa was first and foremost a crack sprinter, but he had run second in the South African Invitation over a mile. A match between him and the eventual winner of the November Handicap over the mile was immediately proposed. Northern Princess was that winner and talk of a match became hot on the lips of every racegoer in South Africa. The ingredients were mouthwatering: a battle of the sexes (well, almost) between two Natal four-year-olds sired by the Natal-based stallion Northern Guest (El Gran Senor's full brother), the gelding trained at Summerveld by Willie Pieters and the filly stabled at Clairwood in the care of Patrick Lunn. The obvious venue was Greyville; the filly would receive just the three-pound sex allowance; the purse was to be R150,000, made up of contributions from the respective owners, the Summerhill

Stud (who stood Northern Guest) and Winning Form. Gavin Howes would partner Senor Santa for Pieters: Patrick Lunn offered the ride on Northern Princess to Michael Roberts. 'Michael will more than likely have to set the pace on the filly as it would make no sense to lope along and allow Senor Santa an opportunity to use his devastating finish. Michael has ridden overseas and in small fields a lot; he has the experience to make the pace.' Match races are invariably decided by superior jockeyship; won by the craftier rider. They tend to be games of cat and mouse. This particular 'Mouse' was about to demonstrate – yet again – that he was too wily a customer for most cats to handle.

CHERRY: I was acting as Michael's agent that year and Patrick Lunn came to me and asked if Michael would take the ride. Well, you couldn't put the two horses together; it was silly to even have a match; Northern Princess was just not in Senor Santa's class. But Michael said 'We can work something out; we can beat this horse.' I thought it was impossible! So, Roberts puts a hole in Gavin Howes's head. He thought that whatever Roberts says before the race, he'd go and do the opposite in the race itself. Michael put it about that he would make Senor Santa go to the front, so Howes thinks this must mean Roberts will go on himself. Then, just before the race, Roberts says he's going to jump and go! Howes doesn't know whether to jump and go himself or whether he should wait. Anyway, this time, for once, Roberts did as he said. He stole six lengths out of the pens and used this advantage by easing in front up the hill and then kicking coming into the straight. Senor Santa got to him but Michael had saved a bit. Reverse the jockeys and the other horse would have won ten lengths.

VERNA ROBERTS: Michael thought through his tactics day after day. We'd be driving into town in the pick-up and all of a sudden he'd say: 'I wonder if I should pop her out and let her go to the front? Or perhaps I should pop her out and then sit at the back?' He was really taking it so seriously and giving it a lot of thought. We'd be going for a walk and he'd bring the race up again. It was a marvellous race and one that sticks in my mind more than most. The crowd was tremendous; the third biggest Greyville had that season after the July and Gold Cup days. The beaches were empty; there were parked cars everywhere.

ROBERTS: Anyone can win on a favourite: it's expected to win. I get a great kick out of winning on a horse when I know there are better ones in the race. I'd ridden both these horses and won on them. Senor Santa was odds-on. He had tons of speed but my filly was a miler. I thought Gavin Howes would go to the front and try to slow things up. I got the number one draw on the fence, which I believed was the best, and thought to myself I must go out in front and try to get Gavin Howes wound up. As it happened, he obviously wanted to drop his horse out. I broke the quicker and let Northern Princess really run for about a furlong and then I eased up on her. I think that may have confused Gavin. I stayed in front, five lengths or so clear, until the slight hill between the four- and three-furlong poles: if you use a horse up there you don't last, you seem to burn them up a bit. I sat and waited for Senor Santa. I'd say he actually went half a length up on me a furlong out, but then I switched my whip, asked my filly for a little more, and off she went.

Greyville went mad. 'I can't believe it! Roberts at his brilliant best! Only Roberts's riding did it!', bawled the racecaller. Mickey Goss, one of the syndicate who stood Northern Guest at Summerhill Stud, spoke for everyone when he was immediately ushered before the television camera. 'It was all a Michael Roberts red herring. Undoubtedly the gamesmanship before the race paid dividends. He put the story all over Durban that he was going to make Senor Santa make the pace. Willie Pieters and Gavin Howes were determined to make Northern Princess go to the front, so Gavin missed the break and gave Roberts a six-length start – and that made all the difference in the end because to make up that gap, which he did, made it very difficult to go on and win the race. It was an unbelievable piece of tactical riding. And how clever of Roberts to slow the pace on the hill! When Senor Santa got to him I thought it was race over. Maybe he didn't stay as well as the filly but Roberts won the race, no doubt about it.'

Press reaction did full justice to the virtuoso performance of a maestro. 'Mighty Muis roars home in showdown of the year,' applauded the *Daily News*. The *Sunday Times* enthused: 'The Muis roars: brilliant was the word to describe Northern Princess after she emerged victorious in the Winning Form Challenge. The 6–10 favourite was certainly not disgraced in defeat but the accolades for the filly are without question well deserved. Racegoers were treated to a spectacle that can well be heralded as one of the races of the decade and they witnessed Muis Roberts at his absolute best as he gave a display which showed why he is rated one of the best jockeys in the world. The two horses came together to do battle at the 200 metre mark and it was at this point that Roberts changed his stick to his right hand and, being the master he is, at no stage did he unbalance the filly. She rose to the occasion like a true champion as she held off a determined challenge from Senor Santa to gain the upper hand, pulling clear to win by half a length in a time that was only 1.4 seconds outside the course record.'

If Roberts never rode again in his native land, this one bravura display was sure to live on in the memory of all who saw it as the work of South Africa's greatest ever jockey.

7 Mtoto Opens the Door

What Michael Roberts desperately needed to lift the English experience out of the humdrum was an outstanding horse to whom he could hitch his star: a reincarnation of Sledgehammer would do. At Salisbury on 8 May 1986 he made the racecourse acquaintance of a three-year-old of Stewart's whose Swahili name translated as 'little boy'. Within a twelvemonth the slow-maturing 'little boy' had grown to manhood and developed into the kind of crowd-pleaser who could not help but haul Roberts into the limelight. Mtoto was the horse Roberts had been waiting for.

ROBERTS: The turning point was Mtoto beating Reference Point in the 1987 Eclipse; after that the phone never stopped ringing. I was amazed by Mtoto's transformation from three to four – I think we all were. When he was younger he used to pull a bit in the early stages and it was harder to get him relaxed. Later on he got more mature and thoughtful and I could switch him off at the back of the field, safe in the knowledge that he had that devastating speed, which we always knew he had. The first time I sat on him was in a seven-furlong gallop and when I pulled him out to go past the lead horse it was like floating on a cloud.

STEWART: I cannot think of a mile-and-a-half horse with acceleration like Mtoto. All the other good horses since Mill Reef that I'd seen never had the absolutely amazing acceleration of Mtoto to go from last to first. From the day we broke him in he was our favourite. I'd paid a lot of money for him – 110,000 guineas, which was a lot to pay for a Busted, but he was the most lovely horse and I was very keen to have him after Opale, who was also by Busted. We sent him to Yarmouth for his first run and he finished third, but in his very next piece of work he chipped a bone in his near hind ankle. We left him in his box right through the winter and although the bone healed he developed a foot problem where his hooves wouldn't grow. It was an impossible situation; we even had a man over from America to put 'hoof bound' on him but that didn't work; he just couldn't keep his shoes on. I felt very frustrated because I knew he was a good horse. In desperation we sent him to spend the winter of 1986–7 in the meadows of the Kildangan Stud in Ireland and the moisture in the ground miraculously cured him. After that he always stood on peat moss at home and his lad, Victor Todd, used to rub ointment round the top of his coronet band to let some moisture back into the foot. My blacksmith, Harry Buckle, also deserved a medal; he always accompanied Mtoto to the races.

I was impressed from day one by his enormous stride, walking, trotting and when we broke him in. It was always hard for him as he was always running into the heels of horses in front of him, because he outstrode everything in the yard; teaching him to settle was very difficult. Generally, horses with a huge stride don't have a finishing kick; you always see them making all and galloping the others into the ground. That's possibly why Mtoto was misunderstood as a three-year-old. At that age he was most aggravating, because we had a horse that worked as well as anything I've ever seen and yet when he got to the track he was only keen on getting out of the stalls and running flat out. In the end I had to run him over a mile, which I knew was too short for him, because in mile-and-a-quarter races he used to pull too much and wouldn't get home.

He was a mirror image of his father, because Busted did exactly the same thing – he ran away with his jockey in the Irish Derby. I knew all about him because Tom Jones had been with Busted's trainer and Tom was my boss and mentor at one time. Mtoto was never highly strung at home but at the races he was like a coiled spring. It was only as a four-year-old when we were able to run in these big races with small fields that we were able to relax him. As a three-year-old in big fields of maidens or in handicaps he was in the middle of them and never learnt to be relaxed. It's amazing how he turned the corner as a four-year-old.

Thus 1987 proved to be the year when Roberts, Stewart and Mtoto each turned his respective corner. Stewart was in his second season as a trainer and still only twenty-nine years old when he made that successful bid for the white-faced bay colt by the Eclipse and King George winner Busted out of the prolific winner-producing French mare Amazer on behalf of Sheikh Ahmed Al-Maktoum. The dashing, blue-eyed young man had enjoyed a privileged upbringing: Perthshire farming family, Gordonstoun public school, working for Lloyd's in the City. However, the prelude to gaining his licence in 1983 had been less routine. Having agreed to leave school a year early ('I was not the best-behaved boy there's ever been'), he departed British shores with ninety-four pounds in his pocket, intending to travel the world for eighteen months. In so doing he unearthed a hitherto dormant passion. Five months on an Alberta stud farm was the period which shaped his future. 'By chance I got a job mucking out just because I had nothing else to do and I just loved the horses. I became fascinated by them. I worked extremely hard and the stud manager made me his liaison man, and so I became involved in pedigrees and breeding. I worked in the City for two years in marine insurance when I returned. I found it quite easy to broke insurance and as soon as I had got it out of the way, it was off to the races in the afternoon.'

Stewart's entrée to the Turf came via Gavin Hunter; two years on, he moved to Tom Jones in Newmarket, where he got to know the Maktoum brothers. In 1983 he opened for business at Moulton Paddocks with a dozen or so horses, one of whom was Opale. A beautiful chestnut and a lovely mover, she became Stewart's first winner – by five lengths at 50–1. Stewart's initial total of six winners increased to thirteen and then twenty-two before he commenced the 1986 season at the historic Clarehaven yard on the Bury Road, which had once housed Classic winners such as Pretty Polly and Spearmint and the Prix de l'Arc de Triomphe winner Comrade. A new yard – and a new jockey.

* * *

STEWART: From the first day we met at East Ilsley I thought Michael a thoroughly likeable fellow. He was charming and made an effort to be extraordinarily friendly towards everyone. His personality has always been in his favour; he's outgoing and easy-going. I knew very little about him other than what I'd heard Gavin enthusing about, and I didn't see much of him then. He lived in Chilton and I lived in Compton and you don't actually see a jockey in the yard very much. What I immediately liked about Michael was the way he quickly assessed situations. He quickly understood why a horse was beaten, what went wrong, how to ride a horse, whether a different track would suit it. It was the understanding of the racehorse that I've always felt is important about Michael. I've never really liked Michael's style but he seems to have the horse in the right place at the right time and he had an understanding of the horse; he didn't have to ride a horse five times to realise where to put it in a race. Style is unimportant. Michael is a good judge of pace and a good judge of where to put a horse in a race at any given time and that is more important. The greatest advantage for any trainer is not having to give orders. There's nothing worse than tying a jockey down with orders. How do we know, legging a jockey up in the parade ring, how fast the pace is going to be? The great thing about having a jockey like Michael is you don't have to give him orders. The only horse we had a definite order about was Mtoto, who had to be absolutely last in all his races.

Michael also used his brain on the gallops. Gallops are just about getting horses fit. I'm loath to let too many jockeys ride work if I think they'll get too overexcited because all I want to do is to get a horse to travel at third gear towards fitness. Michael is very good at that and he knows I get angry if they race too much in the mornings.

ROBERTS: Alec is an exceptionally good stableman and he is a perfectionist. His attention to detail has to be seen to be believed. He likes everything to happen to the book, just like Rickaby – the horses must walk in a straight line or he goes mad – but a completely different style to Clive. When you go out you could ride the gallop blindfold because he will have explained everything to the last blade of grass. I always think that if I could put Alec and Clive together you'd have a helluva trainer.

Being based at Newmarket was a big help. At Gavin's I was a bit isolated and it was more difficult to ride work for other stables. In Newmarket everybody knows each other because you keep seeing the same faces. The only problem I had was learning where the different gallops were and locations like the Boy's Grave and the Red Hut – there is no red hut! I drove around for ages one day looking for it! Back home we've got markers on the gallops; here there are no furlong markers. Every half furlong is a bush and I had to learn to count the bushes.

Mtoto – pronounced Em-toe-toe – broke his maiden at the third attempt (Haydock, 6 June 1986) but this constituted the solitary success of his opening two campaigns. Tried at a mile and a half (King Edward VII Stakes) and a mile (Queen Elizabeth II Stakes) in Pattern race company he finished fifth and fourth, and when burdened with nine stone seven pounds in the Andy Capp Handicap over nine furlongs he was beaten two lengths. The colt's future seemed bleak: at least a stone below top class but guaranteed no mercy from the handicapper. A Pauline conversion was necessary. To win the 1967 Eclipse and King George Busted had undergone just that kind of transformation, a tractable four-year-old with a startling turn of foot emerging from the unlikely chrysalis of a headstrong three-year-old. His son followed precisely the same metamorphosis. Mtoto even made his four-year-old bow in the same Sandown race as his sire, the Group III Brigadier Gerard Stakes (in 1967 the Coronation Stakes) over a mile and a quarter in late May. The second coincidence was the astonishing Busted-like burst of speed Mtoto displayed to streak up the Sandown hill and win, easing down, by two and a half lengths from the odds-on favourite Allez Milord – rated ten pounds his superior in 1986. Mtoto kept improving by leaps and bounds. Three weeks later (minus the suspended Roberts) he added the Group II Prince of Wales's Stakes at Royal Ascot just as easily, which ensured his next target was obligatory: Sandown's Coral-Eclipse (Group I), where he would be confronted by the recent Derby winner Reference Point and the multiple Group I-winning mare from France, Triptych. Nevertheless, in the opinion of the *Sporting Life*: 'Mtoto can stake his claim to stardom.'

STEWART: I had terrible flu at the time of the Brigadier Gerard and didn't go because I felt lousy. I told Michael: 'Whatever you do be last.' It was an evening meeting and I listened on the telephone, in bed. When the commentator said Mtoto had been left in the stalls I'd never been happier. Richard Hills rode him at Ascot and he couldn't believe how fast Mtoto took him past the others: he got to the front too early. He peaked in the Eclipse; he was really at his best that day.

ROBERTS: The race was virtually set up for me because Triptych's pacemaker was chasing Reference Point and it was impossible to maintain that pace. But it meant I was able to switch off Mtoto. He came on the bridle beautifully just before the straight; I looked to see where Triptych was when I made my challenge because she was a funny old thing and used to take her time to pick up. I changed my hands to see how we were going and Mtoto nearly took off, so I had to steady him. When I gave him a couple of inches of rein a furlong later he went past them like a knife through butter. Reference Point hung on for a few strides but I could see we'd got him.

The race had been run to suit Mtoto: Reference Point was a mile-and-a-half horse and in order to capitalise on his mount's stamina Steve Cauthen had set a scorching pace on the good-to-firm ground. The leader was tiring up the hill and a sitting duck for any suitably armed hunter. The rematch, in the King George VI and Queen Elizabeth Diamond Stakes over an extra quarter mile, presented the Derby winner with a wonderful opportunity to exact revenge – particularly if the conditions underfoot were softer. As Diamond Day approached soft ground seemed assured and threw Mtoto's participation into doubt. Forty-eight hours before the race Stewart scratched his star – and was subsequently grateful he had.

STEWART: Mtoto got sick the day of the King George; he was sick for four weeks and got a temperature of 103. We never found out what it was and none of the other horses was affected. By the time he was fit to run we couldn't get a prep race into him and so he went straight to the Arc. He was 96 per cent fit for the Arc and finished fourth but when a horse runs in a race like that at less than peak fitness it takes twice as much out of it. Consequently, he came back a very poorly horse. Nor do I think Mtoto was ever a great traveller. He got himself worked up in the stable complex the day before.

ROBERTS: I wasn't really hopeful of winning. He'd had a few problems after missing the King George and then there was the distance. I went out to ride the same race on him as in the Eclipse. I don't regard Longchamp as a tricky track, you just need the right type of horse. You've got to come down the hill well and a lot don't. From the stands it doesn't look much of a hill but if you walk the track it's quite a sweeping downhill bend. I wish Steve had gone fast and then slowed up, but they went slow out of the stalls and then he really went on with Reference Point. My horse didn't really pick up after hacking into the straight; the winner Trempolino came from behind me. I don't think Mtoto was a hundred per cent in the Arc; he ran badly in the Champion Stakes afterwards.

* * *

In view of his interrupted preparation there was much to like about Mtoto's Arc performance – a strong-finishing fourth, beaten around five lengths in a race completed in record time – and with both Trempolino and Reference Point retired to stud, the major middle-distance prizes could remain very much in his sights for 1988. The season did not commence without mishap. Goodwood's Festival Stakes was selected as Mtoto's warm-up for Royal Ascot; he won all right, but the field had taken a wrong turn out in the country due to some incorrectly placed dolls and the race was declared void. A second Prince of Wales's Stakes proved more of a formality before a similar double was attempted in the Coral-Eclipse. In 102 years only three horses had won the Eclipse twice, the last, Polyphontes, way back in 1924–5. The only danger to Mtoto (6–4 favourite) appeared to lie with the female of the species, the evergreen Triptych (whose Group I tally now stood at nine) and Henry Cecil's imposing grey ten-furlong specialist Indian Skimmer – though both of them would have appreciated softer ground. The remainder had no chance: a scenario which frequently heralds an upset, and the unthinkable very nearly came to pass. After the two mares contrived to delay the start for several minutes the 33–1 shot Shady Heights ambled out of the gate, assumed the lead, steadily increased the tempo round the turn and only just failed to execute one of the shocks of the season. Mtoto, last into the straight, demanded all of Roberts's strength to get up in the shadow of the post and win by a neck. 'Stroppy Mtoto finds encore hard work,' declared the *Life*'s front page.

* * *

ROBERTS: He missed the kick; he started to half-rear in the stalls because one of the mares was next to him. He settled OK but I had to hit him and he resented the stick. Shady Heights had got me beat until I put the stick down and then Mtoto went again. I really had to go for him for the first time. He got to Shady Heights but wasn't going by him to start with.

STEWART: He did get himself in a very stroppy mood that day; even when I saddled him he'd been on edge. Watching the two fillies playing up made him worse and when the stalls opened he was going down which caused him to lose more ground than we had planned. Sandown is a great course for front-runners and Shady Heights was able to dictate his own gallop and quicken to suit himself. For us it was hard to quicken off a slow pace. Michael admitted that Mtoto had to use his speed to close on the leaders and then he had to ask the horse to quicken up again to get to Shady Heights. He knew he had the fancied horses covered and having ridden Shady Heights in the past felt he could pick him off whenever he liked. But in the end it became a bit of a scramble; the leader nearly caught us napping. Something was wrong with Mtoto that day – he had an attitude problem and I remember being very nervous in the paddock that something wasn't quite on song. He was moody and agitated, far more than at any other stage of his four- or five-year-old career. When colts reach that age they do develop stallion tendencies: I have every sympathy with owners who retire their three-year-old colts before this starts to happen.

Eight previous winners of the Eclipse, besides Mtoto's sire Busted, had gone on to win the King George in the same year. The opposition to Mtoto was not strong. Half the field were three-year-olds – though dual Derby winner Kahyasi was not among them – while the Arc runner-up Tony Bin and the St Leger winner Moon Madness represented Mtoto's generation. Not even the rain which began to fall in the days before the big race managed to dampen Roberts's enthusiasm. In an interview headed 'Roberts exudes belief in Mtoto's magic' he informed readers of *The Times*: 'They've tried every way to beat me and they haven't done it so far. You can't go changing your plans just because it's the King George . . . I'm not frightened about having to come from behind . . . I'm sure he'll stay the trip now he settles better . . . he's been working in softish ground at Newmarket so we'll probably get away with it if it's no worse than good to soft.' However, between the appearance of that article on Thursday and race-day on Saturday Roberts began to have second thoughts about how best to ride Mtoto in what was his biggest test to date. Yes, he had contested an Arc and there's no greater test than that, but he had not been burdened with favouritism at Longchamp – he was 7–4 favourite for the King George; nor was the ground any threat on the earlier occasion.

ROBERTS: I was concerned that they'd go no gallop and I'd be at the back and with the short straight I'd get into trouble. Alec said to ride him like always: miss the break, sit last for the first furlong and then do what I wanted. I was happy to do that, but I thought to myself, it's the King George and if I get beat on him doing that people will point the finger at me. I just wanted to clarify things: I really thought they were going to slow us up completely and so I ought to make more use of him. The ground was very sticky and horses with his kind of speed often can't produce it on soft ground.

STEWART: Michael told me that morning he wanted to ride him closer to the pace because he thought in the sticky ground he might not be able to quicken up so effectively. But I could see no pace on that ground and I wanted him to do what we had been doing all season. So I just said: 'You'll ride him from the back.' He was the only horse I insisted on particular tactics for; I was sure we had not seen the best of him as a three-year-old because he never sat at the back. I think he was a horse that had, like all great racehorses, a mental, highly strung element in him.

I also hate that mile-and-a-half track at Ascot because they run downhill for at least two furlongs and it's hard to get them settled. You see horse after horse getting a position and running far too free down that hill, not getting relaxed and then having to go round those tight right-hand bends. I was adamant he had to be last to relax the horse. If we got beat at least I felt we'd got beat for the right reason and not the wrong one of having him up there and not using that turn of foot.

When the stalls opened Mtoto had drifted to 4–1. Lack of a

victory at the distance, coupled with his perceived distaste for the ground and, in stark contrast, Unfuwain's known preference for it, saw the Derby seventh and recent winner of the Princess of Wales's Stakes sent off the 2–1 favourite: the market then went 9–2 Tony Bin, 6–1 Glacial Storm (the Derby runner-up), 7–1 Doyoun (the Derby third and winner of the 2,000 Guineas). Despite these unpropitious omens the race went like clockwork – and Swiss clockwork to boot. 'Magic Mtoto defies the odds: Stewart eyeing the Arc,' announced the *Racing Post*; 'Brilliant Mtoto dominates Ascot opposition,' declared *The Times*.

Stewart's belief that there would be precious little pace early on was vindicated as Glacial Storm led down to Swinley Bottom and completed the initial half mile in 52.23 seconds, nearly four seconds slower than Reference Point had clocked on softer ground twelve months previously. Roberts's yellow helmet could be spotted merrily bobbing along last of the ten. Thereafter the leadership passed first to Moon Madness and then to Unfuwain, but it was abundantly clear to the 30,000 crowd and the millions watching on television which horse was travelling like Pegasus. Once into the short two-furlong straight, Roberts unleashed Mtoto up the centre and he produced a dazzling burst of speed to cut down Unfuwain and win by an expanding two lengths. It was only the third victory by a five-year-old in the 38-year history of the race. Mtoto was immediately promoted to Arc favouritism, as low as 5–2 with Corals.

STEWART: I know I am biased but I can never remember

a horse quickening like he did. I am sure there have been better horses, perhaps Mill Reef, El Gran Senor and Dancing Brave, but I bet Mtoto had the best acceleration. Dancing Brave had a wonderful kick but it took time to happen. Mtoto's was instant. Michael just used to change his hands on him and he went; his killer punch was quite staggering. Especially to be able to accelerate off a slow pace like he did in the King George. That turn of foot demoralises other horses, he came past them so quickly. As Michael said afterwards, on faster ground just how much further would he have won?

ROBERTS: Mtoto just climbed all over them. I knew I was on the best horse beforehand but I thought they'd test me for stamina, which they never did. There was not much more than six lengths between first and last going down to Swinley Bottom and the beauty of it was when I looked up all the horses I had to beat were within striking distance of me. If they had gone like hell I felt I would have to lie a bit closer to the pace in case they slipped me – that can mean trouble in Ascot's short straight. The last thing I wanted was to get beat on him and have everyone saying: 'What the hell's he doing? Does he think he's riding a machine?' Alec said to ride the usual race and don't worry; he would take the blame. The trouble with Mtoto was that as soon as horses were behind him he used to panic; that's why he used to pull and why you had to go in the stalls late. In the early part of a race he'd pull my arms out but once there was nothing behind him he'd drop the bridle.

Receiving my prize from the Queen was like riding

another winner. I have always dreamt about it but never thought it would come true. It was such a great honour. She is such a lovely person and obviously very knowledgeable about racing. Having the involvement of the Royal Family makes English racing; they are part of the scene and lift the sport. The South African press were soon on to me for all the details; the race was shown live on television as an extra race during Gosforth Park races. Wally Segal told me that when I produced Mtoto the crowd went mad; he said the roar was as if it was actually happening there instead of thousands of miles away. It certainly was a great day.

The day was indeed extra special for Roberts and it could not help but wedge his foot even more firmly in the door marked 'jockeys to be reckoned with'. As the 1988 season continued the creaking door veritably flew open. One man's misfortune is all too frequently another's lucky break, and when Steve Cauthen suffered a body-smashing fall at Goodwood on 26 August Henry Cecil suddenly required a top-flight partner for his galaxy of equine stars waiting to plunder the prestigious autumn prizes. The Goodwood race in question was one of three won by Roberts that afternoon. He was hot; he got the call. Messrs Rickaby and Cherry, among others, would recognise this latest manifestation of Roberts's mystical relationship with Lady Luck. Once again he was in the right place at the right time. The Warren Place aristocrats were primed to hit a purple patch. Roberts had thirteen mounts for Cecil and won on nine, seven of them in Pattern races. The six-week period between 4 September and 15 October saw Roberts win the Kiveton Park Stakes

(Group III) and Challenge Stakes (Group II) on Salse; the May Hill Stakes (Group III) on Tessla; the Royal Lodge Stakes (Group II) on High Estate; and the Phoenix Champion Stakes (Group I), Sun Chariot Stakes (Group II) and Champion Stakes (Group I) aboard the current jewel in the Cecil crown, the four-year-old filly Indian Skimmer. After the Champion the *Sporting Life*'s front page screamed: 'Skimmer simply out of this world.'

ROBERTS: I had ridden a couple of winners for Henry in 1978 but it was a surprise really: one morning we were riding work and he came up to me and said he wanted to give me rides. Then he rang up and asked me to ride Indian Skimmer in Ireland. Everything went according to plan. I rode her work on the Wednesday before the race and was impressed: she is certainly the best filly I have sat on. Henry was a bit worried about the ground, but cantering down she gave me the same feeling. There wasn't much pace on early in the race but when Galitzin went on with Shady Heights she dropped the bridle and was completely relaxed. The idea was to kick on early because she took a few strides to get going. I think her only problem was the ground – she always looked after herself when it was fast ground. Once she got the message she shot forward.

The Sun Chariot was just a walkover for her, although in neither of these races was the ground quite right for her. She was a different animal on soft going; in the Sun Chariot, for example, she changed legs an awful lot. On Champion Stakes day it was drizzling all day and the change of ground helped her enormously. I was worried she might think about

155

her race in the Sun Chariot on the firmer ground and she was reluctant to go down to the start. Henry had to coax her; he called her an 'old cowbag' and off she went – she obviously understood what he said! I always get on well with fillies in my opinion and she had this kick. I followed Willie Carson on Shady Heights down the centre and as we passed the Bushes I kicked her in the belly. She quickened up really well, not as instantly as Mtoto, because she used to lengthen and then open up, but she really flew. She was magnificent that day; a marvel. We won by four lengths. A mile and a quarter was her best trip, that's when she could show her brilliance.

Then she went to America for the Breeders' Cup, that year at Churchill Downs. It was her first attempt at a mile and a half but the ground was soft and the track was tight so we were hopeful. It turned out that the ground was bottomless. The American jockeys had told me not to go up the inside if it became bottomless – I shouldn't have listened to them! I thought they would all go crazy but we jumped out and they all pulled up. I couldn't hold this filly. It was the first time she'd pulled in a race. Usually I was niggling her but with this ground she was travelling. I had an opportunity to go up the inside but never took it. Coming round the last turn they all wanted to come out and they pushed me even wider – and the winner, Great Communicator, came up the inner. Saying that, I still had a chance to win but she couldn't do it and we were beaten just over a length into third. Looking back I could have dropped her out the back and tried to creep up late but she probably didn't stay.

* * *

Beside winning Group I races for Cecil, Roberts gained a
third when he and Mon Tresor – a pleasing big winner for a
loyal supporter in Ron Boss – upset the odds-on favourite
Pure Genius in the Middle Park Stakes. In fact he would
have landed a third for Cecil – and thus his sixth of the
season – had not a four-day suspension for careless riding
cost him the mount on Salse in the Prix de la Forêt. This
was his third ban of the season, the previous two being for
'excessive use of the whip'. The more contentious instance
involved Alec Stewart's Waajib in the Queen Anne Stakes
at Royal Ascot. In the course of winning this Group II event
Roberts was adjudged to have slashed his mount down the
offside shoulder fifteen times in the final two furlongs: the
shoulder was a restricted target and Roberts received two
days' suspension.

ROBERTS: If I had not hit Waajib he would not have won.
He was hanging away from the crowd. I knew the horse
well and he would have resented it if I had hit him behind
the saddle. It was too close to the post to put the whip down
and correct him.

The pity of this hoo-haa was that it detracted from a
marvellous piece of race riding. Waajib was talented but as
ornery a horse as could be imagined. In 1987 Roberts had
produced him at the death to win the Prix du Rond-Point
(Group III) on Arc day, a ride many considered to be one of
the jockey's most masterly, and only a fortnight before Ascot
Roberts executed something very similar to secure the

Diomed Stakes (Group III) on Derby day. The Queen Anne, if anything, saw Roberts at his most sublime because on this occasion he took the race by the scruff of the neck and won from the front after the field had taken over half a minute to crawl through the first quarter. 'Scholarly Roberts uses his brains on Waajib,' observed the *Sporting Life*. Stewart still regards this display as unparalleled.

STEWART: That race sticks out in my memory. It was a wonderful exhibition of a jockey using his brains to win a race. Michael outfoxed the other riders. Cash Asmussen was on an unquestionably superior horse – Soviet Star – but Michael dictated the pace and quickened when he wanted to. It's much more difficult to quicken off a slow pace and the others simply could not catch him. Waajib was a terribly difficult ride, too. Michael was dreadfully unlucky to get suspended for use of the whip as the horse had kept shying away from the crowd and all he was doing was keeping him straight and running.

Clarehaven had much to savour in 1988: Stewart won a career-best forty races (thirty of those winners ridden by Roberts) for fifth place in the trainers' table, and Roberts went through the century mark for the first time with 121 (from 777 rides – over 200 up on 1987) to earn third place in the jockeys' list. The single black spot was the Prix de l'Arc de Triomphe, which Mtoto lost by a rapidly diminishing neck to his old foe Tony Bin.

ROBERTS: I must be honest and say I thought it was a

matter of just going round. We went full of confidence. I went through the race and there wasn't one horse to be scared of. Everything went according to plan until we started running downhill, when he was a bit sluggish; but coming into the straight I was really happy because I was looking round and everyone was getting knocked about. I was lucky to have nothing on my inside. I picked Tony Bin to follow because he was travelling nicely at the time. Unfortunately, there was a bit of scrimmaging and I was hemmed in by Village Star for about fifty yards and that may have cost me the race. Mtoto didn't seem to pick up as he usually did when we got out. Perhaps it was because he was getting older and he needed more time. I was flat out and not getting anywhere. He'd always been a horse that travelled on the bridle, pulled out and kicked: this was the first time I'd had to scrub. The Arc was the saddest moment I've ever had in racing.

STEWART: I don't think he was at his best in the Arc. He'd already annihilated most of the field. He'd found it easy to beat Tony Bin at Ascot and had no reason not to win the race, barring accidents. I personally think he sulked because he didn't have his own way out the back. When he had no horses behind him to worry about he loved it: in the Arc he never had things his own way, was caught in a pocket and he sulked. I do believe horses can become sulky at that age – perhaps that was what had happened in the Eclipse. He disliked being bothered by other horses. Deep down I always had the worry there were too many runners in the race. It will appal many people but I think horses who should never be in the race often get in the way of everybody else. I had this awful premonition when I saw how many there were declared at the five-day stage; I kept feeling half of them shouldn't be in the race and are going to get in the way. I shouldn't feel like that; it's an awful elitist view. It was the only race in two years that we couldn't sit out the back and dominate with him. I knew we wouldn't be able to do it and was always pessimistic beforehand. If only he'd been right in 1987 when it was a small field. We knew we'd be taking an enormous risk but we couldn't ride him up with the pace because he'd have run himself out.

'It's misery for Mtoto,' reported the *Sporting Life*; 'Tony Bin pips Mtoto in Paris thriller,' said the *Racing Post*. The majority view insisted that Mtoto was an unlucky loser. Only five of the twenty-four runners were behind the 8–5 favourite at halfway but entering the stretch he was prevented from following in Tony Bin's slipstream by Village Star. Those three or four strides probably made the difference between victory and defeat because Mtoto was a trifle flat-footed when the opening finally came and yet he was gaining hand over fist as the winning-post flashed past.

Whatever the whys and wherefores of Mtoto's Arc defeat, he still departed for Oxfordshire's Aston Upthorpe Stud with an outstanding record. Timeform gave him an annual rating of 134 in both 1987 and 1988, thus pronouncing him to be the best horse Roberts has partnered in his nine European seasons; *Pacemaker* magazine voted him Horse of the Year, Champion Older Horse and Middle-distance Horse of the Year in 1988.

* * *

STEWART: Mtoto was an exceptionally good horse but he was a difficult horse inasmuch as he was only at his best in a very small field when he could sit at the back. I think he peaked in that first Eclipse; in the 1988 Arc it was a big field and he couldn't sit and do what he'd done before, which was to be the last horse into the straight. You take a big chance doing that in the Arc. It worked for Dancing Brave but not for us. But if he had run up in the firing line he'd have run on his nerves and finished nowhere.

ROBERTS: He was a great horse – his acceleration was unbelievable – but he was a bit of a softy. He didn't mind a smack but he disliked being hit too hard or too often. When it was raining, for example, it was an effort to persuade him to leave his box. He hated the rain – he'd try to run under the trees! I can only hope I'll be fortunate enough to get on a horse of his unique calibre again – although I thought the same after Sledgehammer!

Mtoto made 1988 a year Roberts would never forget; arguably, Mtoto *made* Michael Roberts, full stop. 'Watching the tiny South African on Mtoto's back,' observed Christopher Poole, 'never fails to remind me of a working elephant and his mahout. Those powerful little men somehow manage to persuade their partners into galvanised action and so does Roberts despite looking like a pea on a drum. His horsemanship is exceptional and with a mount of Mtoto's class and power the combination is indeed formidable.' *Pacemaker*'s panel of experts awarded him the Jockey of the Year title by eight votes to two over the champion jockey Pat Eddery, 'his patience, sense of timing and his undoubted strength in a finish' being deemed his principal assets. The Horserace Writers and Reporters Association likewise made him the recipient of its Flat Jockey of the Year award. As Paul Hayward had written in *Pacemaker*: 'Many would say that it is not before time, and that it is an indictment of British racing that a man with Roberts's considerable ability had to wait for so long to be given a chance, purely because he came here as an outsider . . . it has become fatuous to talk of him as the ascendant rider in British racing. The waiting game is over. The news is out.'

The long-awaited breakthrough had most definitely been realised. 'The news was out' – yet there was still more to prove, and further prejudice to overcome.

8 Call me Clive

If you had to stake your life on naming one Newmarket trainer with whom Michael Roberts was bound to strike up a profitable relationship the chances are you would nominate Clive Brittain. He and Roberts give every impression of being peas from the same pod: willing to graft all the hours God sends, yet forever sunnily disposed; occasionally mocked for their openness and happy-go-lucky air, yet never vindictive and always approachable; two smiling-eyed, cherubic sides of the same eternally optimistic coin. Bonding was surely inevitable.

To the press Brittain is 'Call me Clive' on account of his habitually genial response to being stuffily addressed as Mr Brittain; the exuberant dancer and snappy dresser; or the eccentric early riser whose string is on the Heath at 5.30; or else a latter-day incarnation of Don Quixote, prone to tilting at windmills by overfacing his horses. 'Brittain positively radiates self-belief. He's like some hyperactive bishop at a confirmation,' Brough Scott once wrote memorably. 'If you didn't know the symptoms you'd swear he was on something more narcotic than fresh air and exercise.' In fact, Brittain's daily intake includes a multi-vitamin pill, primrose oil and royal jelly.

Certainly it is rare indeed for a prestigious race not to feature a representative from Carlburg stables; but the proof of the pudding is in the eating. Julio Mariner, a 28–1 winner of the St Leger, or Radetzky, victor in two Royal Ascot Pattern races at odds of 16–1 and 25–1, are typical examples of Brittain's lance striking a lucrative sail on the windmill. 'There's no reason why I should worry about some people's condescending attitude towards me. If I worried about what other people thought I don't suppose I'd do anything. I'll let the results speak for themselves. I don't believe the form book tells you everything: it's a guide. I do take fliers sometimes but I can't see any point running a horse below his class, they have just as hard a race in winning at Warwick as being placed in a Group race. It's not just blind optimism, and I'm not averse to place money.'

No foreign windmill is safe, either. Brittain was the first English-based trainer to win a race at the Breeders' Cup, with Pebbles in the 1985 Turf; the following spring he even saddled Bold Arrangement to finish a close second in the Kentucky Derby; and later that year he landed the Japan Cup with Jupiter Island. 'My mind's always looking for new ideas and fresh fields to conquer but people have always criticised me because I did things differently. Most of the time I have been trying to make bad horses good. It is the same with Martin Pipe. We didn't come from the "old school", so as soon as we started to do well the knockers stuck the knife in.'

Brittain shared Roberts's green-fingered rapport with horses. Born in Calne, Wiltshire, he was disinclined to follow his father's trade in the local bacon factory: his consuming interest was the horses that grazed in the surrounding fields, and he showed an innate understanding of them. From the age of seven he'd jump out of the bedroom window at 5 a.m. before school – which he frequently skipped – to earn pocket money tending them; and when a horse fair came to town he would disappear altogether for days on end, working for the horse-traders. 'Trap-ponies, dray-horses . . . you name it, I rode them round the pen so the prospective buyers could have a look and when a deal was struck and sealed with a handshake it was the custom for the trader to say: "And luck money for the boy." Then the buyer would give me a coin – half a crown or five bob.'

Besotted by horses and weighing next to nothing, it was only natural that Brittain gravitated towards the famous Beckhampton yard of Fred Darling, close by his home. He spent hours there during the school holidays and it was always clearly understood that once he was old enough Darling would sign him on as an apprentice. The legendary trainer died before this could come about, but his successor, Noel Murless, kept to the bargain. Unfortunately, any hopes of a riding career were dashed by Mother Nature: Brittain (finalist in the five stone seven pounds class at the stable lads' boxing tournament) grew too quickly. Instead he began to concentrate on feeding the yearlings and coping with any awkward customers in the yard. In 1952 Murless moved to Warren Place, Newmarket, and Brittain went along. 'Such was the loyalty of the Murless staff that promotion was hard and although I worked for him for twenty-three years – minus two I spent in the army – I was never more than a lad, officially that is: I never actually got head lad's wages.

But everything I know I learned from Sir Noel. He had the brains and I picked them.'

This acquired knowledge was soon utilised to skin the bookmaking fraternity. 'Backing winners, if you worked at Warren Place in the fifties, sixties and seventies, was like falling off a log, more investing than gambling, and a portion of every pay-out was put away for the future.' In 1971 the victory of Altesse Royale in the Oaks was sufficient for Brittain to take out a licence and a three-year lease on Pegasus Stables in the Snailwell Road. The first winner – Vedvyas – came on April Fool's Day 1972, at a remunerative 33–1. Brittain has long since proved he is no fool. A satisfying total of fifteen in that initial season set the tone; 1975 saw him ensconced at Carlburg on the Bury Road; the first Classic came three years later, to be followed in 1984 by the 1,000 Guineas victory of the marvellous Pebbles, who then preceded her Breeders' Cup success with others in the Eclipse and Champion Stakes. By the time Michael Roberts was introduced into the Carlburg equation Brittain had over a hundred thoroughbreds in a stable which came to boast such innovations as a swimming pool, a solarium and its own spring water from a 90 metre well shaft.

ROBERTS: A lot of people made me feel very welcome when I first came over from South Africa but if I had to single out anyone it would be Clive and Maureen Brittain. They are two great people, nothing is too much for them; but they are the same to everyone. Alec put me on to Clive. As he worked so early it was handy to go there and then on to Alec's. It was hard work to begin with because Steve was there, Pat, Willie and Philip Robinson. But the more work I put in for Clive the more I got back from him. It's the same with everyone in the yard. He listens to any suggestions and everything is discussed openly. There is a lot of mutual confidence. There are certain horses that only the jockey can tell the trainer about – old Sikeston for instance. I might say to Clive: 'He's running in three or four days' time so let's gallop today and the day before I'll give him another blow because he's a stuffy horse.' Clive will say OK and let me work him how I think. There's no competition to see who's cleverer than the other, we just work as a team. There's no undermining; he's very fair and if I suggest something that doesn't work out, well, he just treats it as bad luck.

He can get cross if a gallop is messed up: if he sets a gallop up he wants it done that way. I remember a kid went six lengths too fast in one of User Friendly's gallops and he went absolutely mad, calling him all the names under the sun! He's a great organiser: eighty horses, eight bits of work in forty-five minutes; they all leave the yard on the second turn. He's criticised for aiming high with some of his horses, but he gets results. What's the use of running in a little race with twenty-odd runners if you can pick up big prize money? Owners love it: their horse may earn thousands before winning a maiden.

Out of racing he's very comical – there's never a dull moment – and we usually have dinner together at least once a week to talk things over. Clive did offer me a job in 1991 to ride full-time for him but we're so close the relationship might go if money came into it. The last thing I want is to fall out with him, and bad things do happen when it becomes a business.

BRITTAIN: The first horse he rode for me was Happy Hector at Epsom in August 1978. We had never even met, and I didn't have any idea of what he looked like. I didn't see the race but I was very impressed with the phone call he gave me afterwards: he advised me not to run him again but send him to stud! I thought that was a pretty bold statement for someone with so few winners in this country. Alec asked if he could come and ride work; he came in every second morning and the relationship built up from there. He still calls me Mr Brittain – one of the few that do – which bugs me because we are very good friends and have come through a lot together. Ours is more than a rider–trainer relationship.

I never give him any orders. We discuss what changes he could make in a race if things go wrong. I get them fit and leave the rest to him, which is a great advantage. If you restrict a jockey you often pull against each other. I don't have to think for him. It makes it so much easier when he knows I've got every confidence in him to do the right thing. Once I've legged him up, the horse is his – win, lose or draw. He has ridden some really moderate horses and won on them by giving them such a fantastic ride. They really deserve to have been Group I races because of the effort he puts into it. Every time he goes out he goes out to win, yet he's the first to sit up if the horse has given of its best: he's the first to realise his horse has done its best and you're only going to injure the horse by overtrying on it. On the other hand, it works the other way if he knows a horse has got something else to give: he will not give up until he's got that extra bit out of the animal. It's sheer compassion for the horse but also a sheer determination to get the best possible placing.

He's never been stable jockey here but the lads have a great feeling for him. Lads are notorious for talking through their pockets and blaming the jockey. If there has been anyone to criticise Michael, there have been three to jump on his back and say what are you talking about. If they are behind you they will tell you little bits and pieces about a horse that probably even the trainer doesn't know – and Michael always has an ear open to listen.

Bengal Fire's surprise victory in the 1986 Royal Lodge had already provided the two far from cock-eyed optimists with plenty to crow about if they were of a mind (which they were not) before the Dowager Lady Beaverbrook's Terimon gave the phrase a whole new meaning in 1989. By Her Ladyship's St Leger winner Bustino, this grey had cost 140,000 guineas as a yearling and needed eight attempts to break his maiden; but nine days after so doing in a £1,884 ten-furlong race at Leicester he lined up for the Derby. In a field of twelve his starting price of 500–1 accurately reflected his chance of overturning 5–4 favourite Nashwan.

BRITTAIN: We knew Epsom was the sort of track that would suit him. I could see the race being a four-horse race. Michael said he'd drop him right out the back and pick them off up the straight; and that's exactly what he did. His confidence and judgement of pace got him there.

ROBERTS: I rode the horse to get a place. I dropped him out and took the shortest way home. He kept picking up and rounding Tattenham Corner I was going so well that I was looking for Nashwan and thinking if he doesn't find another gear I'm going to win the Derby. Terimon ran a tremendous race and was only beaten by a great horse. In fact, his best form was probably at Epsom. Two years later he only lost the Coronation Cup by half a length, and the following year he finished a close third.

Nashwan comfortably denied Terimon Derby-winning immortality by five lengths. Nevertheless, Terimon still entered the history books as the longest-priced placed horse in 210 runnings. One Durham client of Ladbrokes pocketed £40,000, having backed him to come second to Nashwan at odds of 2,000–1. Most of Carlburg was also 'on' each way. Just as well they did make hay then, because Terimon proved a very irritating character: third in the Princess of Wales's Stakes; second in the Eclipse; fourth in the Juddmonte International; second in the Coronation Cup; fourth in the King George. His only two victories between that Leicester maiden on 29 May 1989 (when partnered by Brian Procter) and the Juddmonte International of 20 August 1991 came in successive renewals of the Earl of Sefton Stakes (Group III) at Newmarket – in the first of which he was ridden by Ray Cochrane as Roberts was claimed by Alec Stewart for Alphabel.

* * *

ROBERTS: He was such a frustrating horse. The more trouble you could put him into in a race the better; from a jockey's point of view that can make you look an idiot – if you'd got a run you'd have won, sort of thing. You had to be careful. He was a horse you had to put into impossible positions and hope for a run. At home you could put your mortgage on him but he just wouldn't go through with it on a racecourse. One morning Clive said let's try the bugger from the front and he wouldn't go at all. The bugger stopped!

Nobody wanted to go on in the International and he really wanted to go, so instead of having to pull him about I let him go. Sometimes I wished he was human so I could talk to him and find out what was going on inside his brain because he was so cantankerous. No one else was interested in making it, so we were just lobbing and lobbing and I knew that when I picked this horse up he was really going to sprint. These were stayers behind me, so if he went through with his effort we were going to win. And when I eventually asked him he kept on pulling out a bit more all the way to the line.

BRITTAIN: I thought it would be a tactical race so I left it to the master tactician. Michael pulled it out of the bag but we'd had the old horse a few years and knew he was on top song. The situation stood out as being one of no pace. Terimon has two ways of running. If you have to tear at him early in the race he gets bored; and when you eventually ask him to go he won't. We daren't sit back and do that. If by any chance they jumped off and went very fast Michael was going to drop him in stone last and ride him like he did

171

in the Derby. But he was well prepared to get him to the front and switch him off if they were going to fool around. Terimon loved a track with a long straight like Epsom or York. All the way up the straight it looked as if something would come and beat him, but Michael had this confidence to hold a bit back; his elbows were going but he wasn't riding him. When Quest For Fame came at him Michael picked him up, and when Michael picks them up he really does pick them up; they quickened and left Quest For Fame for dead.

Terimon's first Group I success in twenty-five starts was unquestionably due to inspirational jockeyship. At 16–1 old Clive Quixote and his very own Sancho Panza had impaled the target once again.

If Roberts was struggling to win a Group I event on Terimon he was experiencing no difficulty whatsoever in accumulating them on Sikeston. In fact, Roberts collected more Group Is on this bay horse than on any other: five, to be exact. The explanation lies in Sikeston's Italian ownership. In his three seasons at Carlburg just seven of Sikeston's twenty-seven races were in England and he won only one of them (the 1991 Queen Anne Stakes), compared to seven successes in Italy where he relished the heavy ground so often encountered. Italian Group I races, however, are less competitive than those of England or France, for example. Even so, Roberts rode Sikeston to win the Premio Vittoria di Capua at Milan's San Siro as a four-year-old in 1990 and again as a five-year-old; the Premio Roma in 1991 at Rome's Campannelle; and the Premio Presidente della

Repubblica, also in Rome, in both 1991 and 1992.

ROBERTS: I tell you what, I think the travelling used to excite the bugger! He was a fantastic horse over there, and even if you'd taken a genuine English Group I horse to Italy he would have given it a good gallop. The big secret to him was the soft ground; on fast ground he used to tell you he didn't like it. The turf is so much shorter in Italy than over here that you get extremes of going, never a happy medium. In Rome it's either like a road or a bog; Milan is a bit better because as it's surrounded by trees it doesn't get so fast, but when it's heavy . . . ! Sikeston had really big feet and he used to go through it like a duck through water – and he could actually quicken on it, which is very unusual. He also liked to come away from other horses; because they've only the two main tracks in Italy the inside gets very cut up, so when it's soft the runners swing wide round the turn. The further out he was, the better he used to go. You have to walk the tracks in Italy. At home we could never get him to do anything and he always carried this big belly, looking as if he was in foal. We'd give him a blow virtually on the day of a race. But what a character; he was a great favourite of mine, was Sikeston.

Italy had long since constituted a happy hunting ground for Roberts. Every Sunday jockeys flew out of England for destinations throughout Europe: the elite few invariably jetted no further than Paris. Until Roberts undisputedly joined their ranks he tended to be found at the lesser venues in Italy and Germany (and even Spain and Belgium). His initial Italian experience was Dubian's successful visit to Rome in 1986; three years later he took two more Group Is, the Derby Italiano on Prorutori and the Premio Vittoria di Capua on Just A Flutter. Germany welcomed him on 17 May 1987 when he partnered Step Dancer in Munich; Diana Dance on 6 August 1989, at Neuss, was his first winner there. In 1993 he broke further ground by winning in Turkey (Shrewd Idea at Veliefendi, in Istanbul, on 25 July) and Japan (Reward Plunder at Tokyo's Fuchu on 5 December). Of the major racing nations only the USA and Australia remained to be conquered. To make life easier on these travels, Roberts sought dual nationality by taking out British citizenship.

ROBERTS: Basically, it would help everyone concerned. At the moment I need a different visa for each country I visit to ride in. I accept that you are gradually granted longer-lasting visas, but if the visa renewal hasn't arrived in time you have to go to London to collect it and there are so many other niggling inconveniences. At the airports you have to stand in special immigration queues which can take for ever, and you find owners, trainers and other jockeys in your party having to wait for you. Hundreds of South Africans hold two passports – it's not unique.

Although success in Group I races was becoming *de rigueur*, Classic victory proved elusive. Since Sirk set the ball rolling in the 1986 St Leger, Roberts had ridden in fourteen of the twenty-one subsequent Classics which preceded the 1991

2,000 Guineas; yet he had come no nearer to glory than Terimon's Derby.

That same year he did partner the 1,000 Guineas winner Musical Bliss – but only in the Oaks, in which she had scant hope of staying the extra distance. Kaheel's fourth in the 1990 Derby was the only other brightish spot in a dismal catalogue of rides. At the outset of 1991, however, Carlburg sheltered a second grey to carry the Beaverbrook jacket in addition to Terimon. This was Mystiko, a leggy, white-stockinged and flashier grey than Terimon (his best pal in the adjoining box) by the Derby winner Secreto. He broke his duck readily enough, but he was an excitable sort. He badly needed a sympathetic horseman to organise him on the Heath of a morning: he desperately needed Michael Roberts.

ROBERTS: I came back a week before the Flat started and Clive brought out all his top horses the first couple of mornings. I'd never rated Mystiko much as a two-year-old – when he made his debut Basil Marcus rode him as I preferred Revif. Anyway, we jumped away in this gallop and I couldn't hold him. I told Clive we wouldn't be able to train him because he was mad; he didn't like working with other horses. So he gave me a free hand with him. I used to get on him first thing in the morning and ride him like a hack, down the sand track and up the Limekilns all on his own. I got him so relaxed that I used to throw the reins at him and he'd pull up with me. The first time I did it I thought: Clive'll go mad because he wants the horse to work. I said that I was sorry he went up so relaxed but I can't squeeze him or ask him for anything because the horse was happy. Then one morning Clive gave me a little four-year-old filly, rated 85–90, to work with. Little Brett Doyle rode her and I was giving him a stone plus. I told Brett to jump away and go as fast as he could. I also gave him four lengths' start, and after three furlongs I squeezed him and put seven lengths between them in strides. The last horse who had gone up the Limekilns with me like that was Mtoto. I said to Clive that we mustn't work this horse again, we've got him spot on.

BRITTAIN: Michael rode Mystiko in all his work and most of the time on his own, basically working out a system to suit the horse. Sometimes a horse with tremendous speed frightens you and there was a passion about Mystiko; it was our job to control it. You don't win races with wooden horses. The few times we put a lead horse in with him either it wasn't fast enough or Mystiko wouldn't settle in behind. We always worked him first, in darkness mostly: I'd done similar things with others and thought it was worth trying. But I left Michael to pace the work right up to the Free Handicap and the Guineas.

Mystiko was set to carry nine stone two pounds in the seven-furlong Free Handicap; clearly only the skylarks had spotted the impressive gallop, and he was allowed to start at 11–1. Roberts always had him in touch with the leaders and once past the Bushes he let the grey come home in his own time. It was as straightforward as that. This effortless three-and-a-half-length victory thrust Mystiko bang into the 2,000

Guineas picture because although there were plenty of contenders holding the pertinent credentials no one horse stood out head and shoulders above the rest. Marju (winner of the Craven Stakes) was favourite; Mystiko was next best at 13–2; the French pair Ganges and Lycius (first and second in the Prix Djebel) were on sixteens. However, Guineas week had not begun smoothly for Carlburg. On the Monday Mystiko worked poorly: Brittain was unhappy with the horse's stride pattern. He decided to swim the colt on Tuesday and Wednesday. On the Thursday Roberts gave Mystiko a blow up Long Hill and the grey nearly carted him through the woods at the top. End of worries.

As the preliminaries were unwound Mystiko was winding himself up: he was like the proverbial cat on hot bricks during the parade. Roberts's empathy with the thoroughbred was never going to be better illustrated. Today's Classic was a furlong longer than the Free Handicap: Mystiko must conserve all that fire and passion so admired by his trainer. A few tense steps; a hesitant trot; some soothing words in the colt's ear – and Mystiko saunters to post like a contented old moggy.

ROBERTS: It was that very situation we had been practising for. He wasn't stupid and I kept talking to him on the way down; I just sat in the saddle and let him flow gently on his own. When we got to the start he was fine and he almost fell asleep in the stalls. I got a lovely lead from Lester on Bog Trotter for the first three furlongs and Mystiko was travelling so well in himself and saving energy all the time. We led at halfway and he was still doing no work under me. He was bowling along, ears pricked and not using much energy at all until I asked him to gain momentum going into the Dip. I was very conscious of keeping something for the hill when I was expecting the challenges to come, especially from Willie on Marju. But he was brave. He stuck his old neck out and kept digging deeper, though he was probably tying up a bit on the hill. I think we might have had some luck, because Lester took half the field with him up the centre so we had the rail to run on our own and Mystiko loved that. In the finish we were holding Lycius quite comfortably and won a head.

To win for Clive and Lady Beaverbrook made it a great day. We went up to have a drink with her afterwards and she was over the moon; she just kept repeating: 'Marvellous!' We had that horse so right for those two days in the spring it was unbelievable. He made my bones tingle, I can tell you. I'd not enjoyed that sort of feel on a horse since Mtoto.

BRITTAIN: Mystiko was supercharged on Guineas day. Michael knew he could win, but he had to save a little for the last challenger. He let the other horses feel he'd got him beat, but he still had a fraction left and went back for it. Very few jockeys would have had the nerve to sit with a little bit up their sleeve that close to home. They would have gone for it, and had Michael gone for it he would have been beaten. Whenever he gets on a top horse he really makes it sing; he's got that knack of making them look as if they're enjoying it.

* * *

Even as Lady B opened the *Sunday Times* to read about
'Macho Mystiko's Classic win' she had succumbed to the
sales pitch of her trainer and jockey by consenting to run
Mystiko in the Derby. In what was assuming the appearance
of a very open year Mystiko was a 6 or 7–1 favourite,
depending on your bookmaker. Could he handle the
unnerving, boisterous atmosphere of Epsom Downs on
Derby day? Would he stay the mile and a half, given his
ebullient style of racing?

BRITTAIN: Lady Beaverbrook wasn't keen to run him
because she'd seen her Minster Son injured in the race, but
I persuaded her that Mystiko was an athlete and perfectly
built to handle the track. Fortunately she came round to my
idea. He had got more relaxed and I was sure he'd stay the
distance; we already knew he had the class. Sir Noel never
galloped horses over the Derby distance before the race,
and I followed the same path. Then the weekend before the
race Mystiko had to have a corn removed from his near
fore, but he strode out in tremendous style in a five-furlong
gallop on the Limekilns after we removed the poultice. I
certainly would not have run him if I didn't think he was a
hundred and ten per cent.

ROBERTS: Anyone riding a Guineas winner in a Derby
has a right to feel good. It was unfortunate about the corn,
but if it had to happen it was better to know beforehand
than after he'd been beaten. Deep down I'd always thought
he was a Derby horse. It's always difficult to assess how far
a horse will stay, but he was running on strongly enough at

the end of the Guineas and you had to be encouraged by that. You can never be sure, particularly in the Derby which is a law unto itself. I rode him to stay; you can't do anything else. He was a beautifully actioned horse, well balanced, so I didn't think the track would be a problem, and although he was highly strung, wanting to get on with the business, he was getting better all the time, so I was confident he would handle the preliminaries. Whatever happened I wanted to be up in the first four or five, though I was happy to let the race develop and was prepared to go or sit behind, whichever was necessary. Anyway, I couldn't hide him and ended up having to ride him from the front so he could bowl along. My plan was to lob till the top of the hill – I thought they'd leave me alone – and kick from there; but Arokat, the pacemaker for Toulon, just worried around me and it killed me. I was dead before Tattenham Corner.

Mystiko, deposed as favourite after the corn scare but still the medium of the day's biggest on-course bet of £100,000 to £20,000, trailed in tenth of the thirteen. In his seven subsequent races the grey was dropped back in distance, but apart from another resounding success on his home track (all four of his victories were at Newmarket) in the seven-furlong Challenge Stakes in October he never recaptured the sparkling *joie de vivre* of that spring campaign.

ROBERTS: It was a shame he lost his form, but the way he got het up for his races he really couldn't have lasted. But winning the Guineas meant so much to me; much more than the South African Classics. To win an English Classic was my main ambition from day one; to win a Classic was a bigger ambition than winning the jockeys' championship. It's what the racing fraternity always refer to in British racing.

Ah: the jockeys' championship. In 1991 Pat Eddery secured his ninth title with forty-eight winners in hand of Roberts; the previous season he had become only the fourth jockey in British Flat racing history to ride 200 winners or more in a season, with a total of 209. Riding as well as ever and feeding on the adrenalin of winner after winner, his hold on the title seemed secure. The bookies certainly thought so: they made Eddery a 2–1 on favourite to retain his crown in 1992. And Roberts? He was 100–1! One man who believed those odds insulting was Graham Rock. He was taking over from Dick Denney as Roberts's agent in 1992, and he was prepared to back his opinion with hard cash.

King George VI and Queen Elizabeth Diamond Stakes, 1988 – the sparklers are in the bag. (*Gerry Cranham*)

'Receiving my prize from the Queen was like riding another winner.' (*Trevor Jones*)

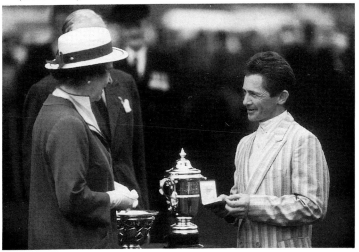

Waajib wins the 1988 Queen Anne Stakes, but that whip action will get Roberts into hot water. (*John Crofts Photography*)

'The best filly I have sat on.' A regal Indian Skimmer wins the 1988 Champion Stakes. (*John Crofts Photography*)

Peas from the same pod, Roberts and Clive Brittain contemplate the next challenge. (*John Crofts Photography*)

At last, Terimon lands the big one – the 1991 Juddmonte International. (*Gerry Cranham*)

Mystiko goes down like an old moggy in the 1991 2,000 Guineas (above)
and runs on like a lion to repel Lycius (below). (*Gerry Cranham*)

'To win an English Classic was my main ambition from day one.' (*Tony Edenden*)

What the public doesn't see:

Going to the gallops on a sharp, sunlit Newmarket morning. Roberts is on the left and Piggott is on the right. (*Laurie Morton*)

Taking to the air in the relentless pursuit of winners. (*Racing Post*)

'Where to next?' Roberts consults agent Graham Rock. (*Gerry Cranham*)

Snatching a quick chat with Walter Swinburn. (*Gerry Cranham*)

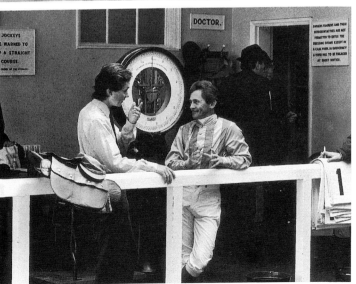

Lyric Fantasy is first, the rest are nowhere in the 1992 Queen Mary Stakes at Royal Ascot. (*Trevor Jones*)

'The Pocket Rocket' becomes the first juvenile filly to win England's sprint championship, the Nunthorpe Stakes. Mr Brooks and Lester Piggott trail. (*George Selwyn*)

Ever a friend to the media, the winning jockey explains how the Nunthorpe Stakes unfolded to Channel 4's Brough Scott, while assorted 'hacks' await the crumbs. (*Trevor Jones*)

Chester, 21 October 1992. The familiar 'Papal Wave' acknowledges the fact that Jasoorah has brought up the two hundred. (*Mercury Press Agency*)

Voted Jockey of the Year for 1992 by the Jockeys' Association. (*Trevor Jones*)

Barathea gets the Sheikh Mohammed retainer off to a Classic-winning start in the Irish 2,000 Guineas. (*Ed Byrne*)

Opera House soon provides a second Group I triumph in the Coronation Cup. (*John Crofts Photography*)

From having been four from the back of the field three furlongs out in the 1993 Oaks, Intrepidity (left) catches Royal Ballerina (centre) and Oakmead (right) at the death. (*Gerry Cranham*)

A tremendous reception for Sheikh Mohammed and his filly prompts a double 'Papal Wave' after the 1993 Oaks. (*Trevor Jones*)

The mature racing machine. Five-year-old Opera House surely looks the part in the process of winning the King George. (*John Crofts Photography*)

The fifth Group I victory of 1993 – Wolfhound takes the Hazlewood Foods Sprint Cup. (*Trevor Jones*)

Roberts and Sabrehill gallop to a facile success at Newbury – only to fall foul of the stewards. (*George Selwyn*)

John Gosden (left) and Anthony Stroud lend an ear? (*Gerry Cranham*)

Clive Brittain mimics all the effort needed for old allies Roberts and Shambo to claim a second successive Ormonde Stakes at Chester, 5 May 1994. (*Trevor Jones*)

'An intoxicating brew of horsemanship and jockeyship': Branston Abby and Michael Roberts triumph at Lingfield Park, 7 May 1994. (*Mel Fordham*)

A farmer at heart.

9 'I didn't think it was all possible'

'Keep your money in your pocket if I were you.' It was Monday, 16 March 1992. Graham Rock had just telephoned bookmakers William Hill to confirm what he had read in the previous day's *Sunday Times* was true. Yes, it was quite correct: the prices quoted on the outcome of the jockeys' championship were indeed 2–1 on Pat Eddery, 2–1 Willie Carson, 10–1 Frankie Dettori, 16–1 Alan Munro and Steve Cauthen . . . and 100–1 Michael Roberts. As a former member of the Timeform organisation and the *Sporting Chronicle* (where as 'Kettledrum' he won the naps table in 1983), stipendiary steward and handicapper in Hong Kong, and founding editor of the *Racing Post*, 46-year-old Rock knew his onions and recognised a sound wager when it presented itself.

ROCK: In John Karter's column William Hill were quoted as offering 100–1 against Michael winning the title. That, for me, was an insult and I immediately rang up and had a hundred-pound bet on my Switch card. I knew nothing about the job of agent – I didn't even know who Michael's agent was – but I'd always been a fan of Michael's ever since he began riding in Europe. I'd always felt he was underrated

183

and wasn't perhaps realising his full potential. He possessed a wonderful judgement of pace: time and time again he seemed to have his horse in the right place at the right time. Being an agent was just an idle thought, but he was the only jockey I'd ever considered taking on.

As luck would have it – and luck had a not inconsiderable role to play – Rock got his man. Roberts had no desire to fall out with Dick Denney, who had been a tower of strength during the leaner years when others had kept their distance, but it was becoming increasingly difficult to field questions from trainers anxious to know why Roberts had not been in touch about this ride or that ride. Perhaps it was time to engage a young 'go-getter'? 'There was no sour grapes on my part,' says Denney. 'I'd got a bit of eye trouble and I was sixty-three.'

ROBERTS: I spoke to Mike Cattermole and John Hanmer – who were agents for Willie Carson and Steve Cauthen – and Clive spoke to J. A. McGrath, who was supposed to send someone to the weighing-room at Newbury one afternoon. I met Graham Rock and asked him if he'd seen J. A. and this chap I was supposed to interview. I thought, this is no bloody good: he's come here to be an agent and he's late – how's he going to be an agent? I knew Graham as a sharp observer. He'd tell me, 'go this side or that side' at evening meetings after watching the early races if ever I was late arriving, for example. So I asked him if he knew anyone. J. A. now says Graham was the man he'd lined up, but I'm sure he wasn't because Graham didn't know a thing about it when I asked him where J. A. and this chap were.

In fact, McGrath was at Ayr not Newbury that afternoon and the identity of his mystery man (most probably Cattermole) has been tactfully consigned to history's unwanted file. Rock had got himself a new job: had he got himself a potential champion jockey?

ROCK: Michael came up to me and asked, could I suggest anyone to act as agent for him next season? I went away and thought about it overnight and the next day went back to him and brazenly suggested myself for the job. At that time the championship was a possibility, no stronger than that, but when we met to discuss the 1992 season during Newmarket's Cambridgeshire meeting I said it was possible if things went his way and Michael agreed. Pat Eddery was retained by Khalid Abdullah, who had transferred many of his horses to France, which meant Pat would have to travel abroad a lot to ride these horses – so that would diminish his prospects at home. Steve Cauthen was similarly committed to Sheikh Mohammed and also struggled with his weight, which effectively ruled him out of contention because he could not take low-weighted mounts. Willie Carson was retained by Sheikh Hamdan. He was also rising fifty and some of his stables were out of form. The only other previous champion was Lester – and he rationed his rides so carefully there was no prospect of his being champion again.

I didn't know anything about the job. I bought a computer to access Weatherbys and Mike Cattermole was very helpful, showing me exactly what was involved in the day-to-day life of an agent. At the beginning I was learning the ropes and made a few mistakes, which cost us three or four winners. We didn't make that fast a start, but things really began to buzz in May and it struck me that Michael might not need that many winners to land the title.

ROBERTS: We spoke after the Craven meeting in April and Graham said: 'I think I can make you champion jockey: are you prepared to work?' I said: 'Crikey, I work every year! It's not a case of being prepared to work.' Graham then went on to say that if he could arrange the rides would I go to every single meeting possible? I couldn't see why not, because that's what I'd been trying to do for the last six years. It was nothing new! 'But Pat and Steve will be away: their trainers will be looking for a third jockey. Who's it going to be?' I had to admit he had a point.

BRITTAIN: I'd told Michael that once he found his feet in this country he had a helluva chance to be champion jockey one day because of his weight compared to others: he was four to six pounds lighter and there isn't a jockey riding who can give him a pound. He had to get there in the end, once he got the support of outside stables. I don't think Dick was getting Michael the outside rides he could have got. I'm not trying to be unkind to Dick because I like the man but, in fairness, his workrate was not the same as Michael's; it's a fact of life that he wasn't doing the job Michael was. Graham Rock is very single-minded which I thought would blend with Michael's single-mindedness. The only doubt I had was that Graham could be a bit abrasive or abrupt and might just put one or two people's backs up. But Graham does have his finger on the pulse and he has a phenomenal workrate, which I felt could make a difference of fifty winners.

Despite his reservations, Rock settled into his new environment as cosily as a cat on a cushion. At the end of August, with fifty-eight racing days remaining till the conclusion of the Turf season at Folkestone on 9 November, William Hill closed their book (Ladbrokes had done so at the beginning of the month) on the destination of the jockeys' championship. As the evening meetings ceased, the current leader – on 163 – was twenty-eight winners ahead of his nearest pursuer. No great shock, bearing in mind those odds of 16 March. But the man a mile in front was not Eddery: it was Roberts, who thanks to Rock's restless energy and encyclopaedic knowledge of the form book had reaped full advantage of 200 more rides than the defending champion.

Eddery had quickly established his customary superiority and it was not until May that Roberts moved up to second place in the table. At the start of Derby week a month later Eddery still led forty-six to forty-two, but Roberts was showing ominous signs of developing a championship-stealing momentum. An Epsom double on 4 June brought him level on forty-nine and he beat Eddery to the half century by five minutes when winning the second race of Goodwood's evening card the following day. Then, on Saturday, he and Brittain's two-year-old colt Anonymous scuppered the Eddery-partnered odds-on favourite Palacegate Episode in Epsom's Acorn Stakes to give him the lead. There was fire in Roberts's belly; his dander was up. After seven seasons consumed by toil, sweat and perseverance he had finally made it to the top and he fully intended to stay there.

The proliferation of feature articles engendered by this ascent of the greasy pole thus made all the sweeter reading: 'The Mouse that roared to the top'; 'Title bid that's built on Rock'; 'Mighty Mouse builds title on Rock of pages'; 'From dairy farm to the cream of the Flat'; 'The making of Mouse'; 'Racing Demon'. In his *Racing Post* column Howard Wright not only underlined the fact but also spelt out a few home truths: 'It's about a 6–4 chance there will be a new name on the Flat jockeys' championship ... and that can only be good for racing. No offence to Messrs Eddery, Carson and Cauthen but it's about time someone else took a turn in the limelight. Racing does need promotion within its own realms and Michael Roberts's emergence will do it a power of good. His salute to the crowd after a win is instantly recognisable and his pleasure in victory is obvious. That he is approachable – and will remain so provided he is treated fairly – is clear from the dozen or so interviews he gave last week, when at least one other might have dodged behind a heavy schedule or at best hidden his deepest feelings in a series of monosyllabic answers (and I don't mean Lester Piggott). Programmed by a new manager determined to make his man champion jockey, Roberts has retained his good manners. A burgeoning book of contacts might not make him the best pal of every jockey in the weighing-room but that's the nature of this game, and Roberts's approach is doing no harm among trainers. After all, he's a trier, and that's what counts among the public too. Good luck to him.' Wright's final point was echoed by Colin Mackenzie in the *Daily Mail* – 'Success has been costly. The weighing-room is the coal face of free enterprise with fierce competition for rides and Roberts has had to suffer more than a degree of envy as he has gathered his rides. His success has some experts puzzled. They complain his riding style lacks the silky smooth skill of Cauthen or the pumping rhythm of Carson or the energetic drive of Eddery' – and, later on, by Julian Wilson on BBC television: 'Some jockeys feel that Roberts, through Graham Rock, has taken their rides. Sometimes he's the odd one out and occasionally parochial resentment comes to a head.'

The winners continued to roll in at a spectacular rate throughout June: trebles at Sandown and Ascot on the twelfth and twentieth followed by a five-timer at Salisbury and Kempton on the twenty-fourth put Roberts twenty ahead of his score at the corresponding stage of 1991. A typical week of bread-and-butter fare read Pontefract (Monday), Salisbury (Tuesday), Beverley and Hamilton (Wednesday), Newbury and Chepstow (Thursday), Sandown and Goodwood (Friday), Sandown and Nottingham (Saturday): around 2,500 miles for forty-two rides resulting in nine winners. Rock was putting Roberts through a punishing schedule.

ROBERTS: I didn't find it a problem. It's probably easier to stay motivated because you're continually on the go and it definitely helps if you're riding winners. Time was often so tight I'd travel to the airport by motor bike to save minutes and I'm terrified of bikes. I was lucky in that I find it easy to switch off. As soon as I get in a car or plane I'll go to sleep, not sit there biting my fingers. It's not easy getting home late from evening meetings and then getting up again at 5.15 the next morning to ride work, but I do it every year. And I do get a lie-in on Mondays and Thursdays!

Graham didn't like to tell me too much too far ahead. He wanted me to concentrate on the day in hand. We don't discuss every race, he's got a good idea of what he's doing and I let him get on with it. We might discuss unraced two-year-olds that I've ridden out or if you've got two or three horses in a race that I've ridden before. I'll pick up the paper and see what I'm riding. He's in the form book all the time and is very sharp. When I get back from work in the morning I might go through the form book myself or watch videos. Whenever possible I like to get on a horse knowing what to do.

ROCK: Michael is absolutely clued-up. He looks through a race beforehand to see how it's likely to develop, although most days he didn't know what his rides were until he opened the morning papers. I began planning his rides immediately the five-day lists came through. I usually found that Sundays and Mondays were the busiest days, fixing up rides for the remainder of the week. Most of the work was done by Wednesday and the following morning I'd begin work on the next week. I started with where the Stewart runners would be. Both Alec and Clive faxed me their entries before they were made so we had a framework to begin with, and then I tried to choose meetings that were most likely to yield winners. I'd usually have a good idea by Tuesday morning where Michael would be going on the Saturday. Then I had to study the form of the races Michael was not required for and try to make an early call to the trainer – catching them as they came off the gallops – asking for the ride. When I contact a trainer to see if Michael can partner a particular horse, he'll say yes, no or maybe. It's the maybes you have to use your judgement on to determine whether the ride is going to materialise into a definite runner or whether it's just a long shot.

You have to be aware of unusual opportunities. A jockey might be suspended, or riding abroad, or retained to ride one horse at some obscure meeting. About half of Michael's rides in 1992 I phoned for, but he was offered many more rides than he could take. We'd talk on the telephone several times a day: when he got home after riding work, later on during the morning and then when he got home in the evening. We'd also meet at the races, of course. His opinion is invaluable, not just for me but also the trainers – which is one of the reasons they were keen to put him up. He can ride a horse and tell them pretty much what is required in the future. The unforeseen lucky break, as it turned out, was Alec Stewart having such a quiet year: his was Michael's only formal retainer and with few runners from Clarehaven to restrict our movements we were able to commit to meetings earlier and therefore get some good rides. I was able to get Michael a few of Richard Hannon's good horses at the beginning of the season when he was short of his regular jockeys, for instance. Both Pat Eddery and John Reid were ahead of Michael in the queue, but we were prepared to wait and it paid dividends. Michael got on some horses that ran well and won; and the Hannon connection took off from there.

Justification for Rock's telephone bill soaring towards £3,000 for the year is amply demonstrated by two bookings, both at first glance seemingly innocuous: the Tom Cribb Maiden Stakes at Leicester on 28 July and Windsor's Lady Caroline Stakes on 27 April. Rock's perusal of the form book for the humble race at Leicester – the last event on the evening card at 8.45 – came up with one horse, the filly Karen Louise from Henrietta Knight's jumps-oriented yard in Wantage. With no obvious claims (unplaced in her last three outings) she was sent off a 16–1 chance in a field of eleven. 'My God, your man must be getting desperate,' another agent had said to Roberts as they flew to the track. Karen Louise made all to win comfortably by three lengths. For both horse and trainer the Tom Cribb Stakes constituted the solitary success of the 1992 Flat season. And Rock spotted it. There were to be countless other Rock-inspired single strikes – twenty-seven of them, in fact – for largely unsung trainers as the season unfolded.

By contrast, that little two-year-old race at Windsor signified considerably richer pickings than its £2,005 face value. Richard Hannon had inherited East Everleigh from his father in 1970 and without the assistance of either Maktoum or Abdullah patronage had developed the Wiltshire yard into something of a winner-producing factory. In the latest five seasons Roberts had seen Hannon's total rise from thirty-three to forty-three, then to fifty-five, seventy-three and finally 126. 'How did it happen? I dunno!' says the affable trainer. 'Nothing changed; we've been training them just the same. I've just got some good horses and owners – you can't train empty stables. Better horses and more of them.' Roberts had ridden his first winner for Hannon back in 1987 (Dancing Diana at Brighton on 28 May), but the lion's share of that huge 1991 tally went to Roger Perham (thirty-three), Bruce Raymond (nineteen), Willie Carson (fifteen), Pat Eddery (ten) and John Reid (nine). Roberts rode seven, from thirty-three rides, in actual fact a better winning percentage than any of the other five. In 1992 he would enjoy almost as many winners (twenty-nine) as he had had rides the previous year. Rock got him 136 mounts for Hannon, only three fewer than Perham, who was attached to the stable.

Roberts had ridden one winner for Hannon by the time Windsor's evening meeting of 27 April came round. That night the trainer planned to give two promising fillies belonging to Lord Carnarvon their debuts. John Reid had first refusal. He agreed to ride the Carnarvon filly in the Blue Charm Maiden but not the second filly, due to contest the Lady Caroline Stakes, since he preferred the chances of Sheila's Secret on whom he had been successful at Kempton. This second mount therefore passed to Roberts. Reid won the Blue Charm Maiden all right aboard Niche, later to win the Norfolk Stakes and Lowther Stakes. The filly Reid rejected was Lyric Fantasy. This tiny 14.3½ hands filly, named after the painting by Augustus John but soon dubbed the 'Pocket Rocket' by the media, was destined to capture public imagination more than any other performer in 1992, thereby presenting Roberts with the appropriate equine icing to adorn a championship-winning cake.

ROBERTS: Niche had won her race and Richard Hannon said to me that Lyric Fantasy would go very close in hers because he didn't think there was much between them. I thought 'Crikey, we're taking on two winners with her.' She was a bit sluggish out of the stalls and I had to give her a couple of smacks; she got up on the line to win by half a length. Her next start was the National Stakes at Sandown and she felt so good; I don't think people appreciated what she did that night. Hannon said to me that it was difficult for two-year-olds to bowl along all the way up the Sandown five furlongs. I didn't know how she had progressed since Windsor but I thought she'd relax. I sat a length off the pace and halfway up I just changed my hands and this little thing went off like a rocket and won by six lengths. I've never known a horse quicken like that up that hill. Then they told me the time, which was under a minute. Then I realised she was special.

Hannon's unerring knack of acquiring and converting inexpensive purchases into money-spinners had become legendary. In an era of petrodollar-dominated yearling sales Hannon had twice cocked a snook at the big spenders by winning the 2,000 Guineas with horses acquired for peanuts, namely Don't Forget Me and Tirol. Lyric Fantasy cost a measly 12,500 guineas at the Doncaster St Leger Sales of

September 1991; she was so small, apparently, that she frequently got stuck under the horsewalker at the stable where she was reared.

HANNON: It's hard to explain what attracts me when buying horses. You either like them or you don't. You go for the individual every time. If it's got a bit of pedigree as well, it helps, but it doesn't worry me so long as there's some speed somewhere along the line. You've got to buy a horse you like. You're looking for good movers and I look for a horse with a good head and a good eye. The thing I liked about Lyric Fantasy was the way she used herself; she wasn't 'tied up' in any way. Had she been a hand bigger she would have been the perfect model. But I don't mind small horses and she had such a great arse end. That's where it all starts; that's where she'd got all the power. She had a backside like a scullery maid and a head like a model. She was no worry to train; a very happy, relaxed filly who enjoyed all her exercise. She had this way about her. Every morning as she cantered past me she'd turn her head and look at me as if to make sure I was there.

Lyric Fantasy did own a 'bit of pedigree' with 'speed somewhere along the line'. She was by the deceased Irish stallion Tate Gallery, a Group I winner as a two-year-old and a full brother to the top-class sire Sadler's Wells, out of a mare called Flying Melody who won a couple of sprints in France. However, Flying Melody's grandam Peggy West was a half-sister to the famed 'pigeon catcher' known as Pappa Fourway, the champion sprinter of 1955. Unbeaten in eight starts which included the King's Stand Stakes, July Cup and Diadem Stakes, this three-year-old colt (as mighty as Lyric Fantasy was minuscule) retired with a Timeform rating of 139, the second highest ever accorded a sprinter by the Halifax organisation.

The obvious next stop for Lyric Fantasy was the Group III Queen Mary Stakes on the second day of Royal Ascot. Once a significant landmark in the career of a future Classic contender, the event had latterly forfeited some of its glitter as a result of seeming to reward precocity rather than potential. However, despite the likes of Book Law, Sun Chariot, Sun Stream, Masaka, Waterloo and Forest Flower going on to win a Classic, the most illustrious name on the winners' scroll was Mumtaz Mahal, the runaway ten-length victress of 1923. This astonishing grey won her first five races by an aggregate of thirty lengths to earn the soubriquet of the 'Flying Filly'. Of her Queen Mary, one witness wrote: 'She literally lost her rivals: she went off with a wonderful burst and before a furlong had been covered she must have been half a dozen lengths clear.' What Mumtaz Mahal and no other juvenile – filly or colt – had managed was to crack sixty seconds for the Ascot five furlongs.

The bookies' shouts of '7–1 bar the favourite' suggested a one-horse race, the presence of ten other winners among the 11–8 favourite's dozen rivals notwithstanding. Lyric Fantasy ran them all ragged. Establishing a clear lead before the gates had even ceased clanging, she kept quickening away to pass the post five lengths to the good. The clock showed 59.72 seconds: Lyric Fantasy had shattered the existing record by 0.43 seconds to become the first sub-minute juvenile at Ascot. Certainly, the sunny, good-to-firm conditions were ripe for record-breaking, but so they were on numerous other occasions during the preceding 200 years when the best juveniles had raced here.

ROBERTS: She was very impressive at Sandown but in the Queen Mary she was even better. She absolutely bolted up: she was brilliant. I've never been so fast in my life. If I'd given her a tap, she would have gone even faster.

The Jockey Club's Senior Handicapper Geoffrey Gibbs promptly gave Lyric Fantasy a rating of 118, the highest ever for a filly at this mid-stage of the season, which furthermore declared her to be the best two-year-old so far seen out. Gibbs had no cause to alter his opinion after Lyric Fantasy subsequently won the Newbury Sales Super Sprint Trophy by six lengths on 18 July – and accordingly raised her rating to 123. How genuinely fast she was would be tested in her fifth outing: York's Nunthorpe Stakes, on 20 August, the country's only Group I five-furlong contest, in which she would be pitted against older horses of both sexes. The event had provided some of the rare occasions when such a generation clash had occurred in Britain: indeed, many sound judges averred the weight-for-age scale favoured a precociously fast two-year-old at this stage of the season. Three juvenile colts won the race in the 1950s (Ennis being the last in 1956), but although the filly Meadow Music won the race in 1904 the Nunthorpe was just a modest seller in those days. Since it had become Britain's acknowledged sprint championship none of the eight

juvenile fillies to participate had come closer than second
– most recently Caterina, and that as long ago as 1965. In
point of fact only one two-year-old filly had competed in
the previous ten years (and only one two-year-old colt, too).
Taking her three-pound sex allowance into account Lyric
Fantasy was set to carry seven stone seven pounds. Therein
lay Roberts's problem: his lowest riding weight was seven
stone twelve pounds, and eight stone was the happy medium
these days. Carnarvon agreed he could put up one pound
overweight. Roberts consoled himself with the thought that
a combination of the warm weather and his hectic schedule
would enable him to pare the excess off his wafer-thin five
feet one inch frame. On Saturday 8 August he rode six
winners from ten rides at two meetings and lost four pounds
in the process, which brought him nicely on target; on the
Monday he rode another four winners to bring up the 150
(the century had come on 11 July) and stretch his lead over
Eddery to twenty-six. 'Plenty of things can happen,' he told
the press. 'I've been very lucky so far this season and things
are going really well.' Cautious thoughts of the championship and even 200 winners were now permissible.

It was inevitable that Lady Luck would choose this
moment to forget her manners. The following morning
Roberts was riding Brittain's two-year-old Shamisen
when she suddenly tried to take off before actually
reaching the gallops: she reared up, twisted to one side
and dislodged her rider, who fell on his neck. Within
an hour Roberts was in acute distress: his book of nine
rides for the day was cancelled. In a blink of the eye the
championship and, more immediately, his ride in the

Nunthorpe – only nine days away – were both in jeopardy.

Like all his colleagues Roberts was no stranger to injury. After that first mishap as a seventeen-year-old – the broken toe at Greyville in June 1971 – his medical history encompassed damage to a knee (June 1975), hand (July 1975) and knee again (January 1988), plus the life-threatening incident in the Clairwood stalls of 17 July 1974 which came just a month after the horrendous crash with Sledgehammer in the South African Guineas. There were similarly perilous falls in February 1976, which resulted in a severe kicking and a spell in an oxygen tent, and March 1984, which thankfully only left him with six stitches over the eye. The following morning he fulfilled a promise to ride a crucial piece of work by appearing with his head swathed in bandages, looking as if he had donned a turban.

ROBERTS: I thought I would be all right at first but when I went out for the next lot with Mystiko I was in agony and I had to bring him back. The filly's head came back and hit me in the chest and she reared up on her hind legs. I only had hold of the buckle end of the reins, lost my balance, fell on my neck and twisted it. I was quite dazed. If she'd come down on top of me it would have been much worse. My chest was very tender and I'd squashed two vertebrae in my lower back. A precautionary X-ray showed there was nothing broken and I was fitted with a neck collar to support the neck muscles. Everyone told me to rest and lie down, but I found it difficult to relax because I'd been on the go so much and on such a high the preceding few weeks. I got bored just sitting around watching race videos. I had hoped to get back inside a couple of days but I'd pulled a muscle at the back of my right shoulderblade and another at the bottom of my back, which was OK when I walked around but gave a lot of pain if I sat on a horse. I could have taken painkillers but it might have done more harm than good by allowing me to run the risk of more serious injury. I was lying and sitting on hot and cold pads to stimulate the muscles and saw my physio, Fiona Morton, every day.

There were a few days when I thought 'this isn't getting better' and I began to get worried. I thought four days would see it come right, so I came back on the Saturday mainly to ride Shambo in the Geoffrey Freer at Newbury. But it didn't. I thought I'd better carry on because I was worried what would happen if it was still the same after three weeks. I was really concerned about losing the lead. I promise you, if it was not for the title race and Lyric Fantasy I'd have taken three weeks off, but those were chances of a lifetime. If they'd tested me I'm sure I'd not have been allowed to drive a car – I was on so many tablets – never mind ride horses. I was in terrible agony. Getting on the horse and setting off was the hardest part. I was wearing a brace holding my shoulders back to protect my spine and it was cutting into my arms. Every race, pulling up, I was leaning back to try and relieve the pain. I eventually left it off. The worst was leaving the stalls; in one race I actually stood up in the irons in the stalls because I thought that might make things easier. While I was riding I was pulling other muscles, compensating, and my shoulders were getting very sore. After I'd won on Shambo the doctor told me I looked terrible and wanted to book me off, but I said I'd get through somehow.

I decided to have injections before the Nunthorpe because I wanted to be sharp at the stalls against those experienced horses. I had eight injections in my back that morning. Fiona put crosses on my back marking all the sore spots. I nearly fainted when the doctor was doing it: the thought of him wiggling those needles about. The room was spinning – I'd no food in my system because of trying to make the weight. The injections did help me a lot. I had the same two days later and I began to improve. Perhaps I should have had them done earlier.

Until the injury my weight had been dropping fine. I'd been sticking to fish and salad as my diet so as to avoid having to sweat it off in the sauna because that doesn't suit me – it drains my strength. The last few days before the Nunthorpe became a struggle. Toast and Bovril for breakfast, a little melon or a few prawns and three or four cups of tea to combat dehydration at the races, and a little fish at night. The warm weather was a great help – I actually lost a pound and a half when I rode at York on the first day – but the back injury meant I was not a hundred per cent, and you do feel miserable at home when you are starving yourself. But if Lyric Fantasy was a hundred per cent I could not see anything beating her.

Roberts displayed quite incredible willpower to weigh seven stone six pounds stripped on 20 August and thus be able to ride Lyric Fantasy at the agreed weight of seven stone eight pounds. As if the neck and back pain were not enough, he flew to York fighting the nagging effects of flu and a sore throat after feasting on a hearty breakfast comprised of sixteen assorted vitamin and antibiotic tablets. Although he had ridden in nine races the previous day he took the precaution of opting out of the first two today – one of which should have reunited him with that little madam Shamisen. However, overcoming an old man's gait, he still walked the course and noted the longer, potentially speed-sapping growth of grass ahead of his stands-side draw. His partner was dwarfed by her ten rivals, several of whom looked twice her size, as she walked calmly round the paddock: Hannon had had her vanned rather than walked across the Knavesmire from the stables to prevent her from getting as stirred up as she had been at Newbury. With the notable exception of the 1991 Nunthorpe and Breeders' Cup Sprint winner Sheikh Albadou, all the contenders for the title of champion sprinter were in attendance, plus a challenger from Canada in Diamonds Galore. By the off, more than £100,000 had been wagered on the 11–8 on favourite.

Her opponents set out to make victory as difficult as possible. Freddie Lloyd blazed from the stalls chased by the Canadian visitor, with the diminutive filly's distinctive orange rubber split noseband just visible at their flanks. Devised to prevent the tongue from going over the bit and restricting the airways, these Australian nosebands are standard equipment on Hannon's runners: breathing room equals power. With two furlongs to run it seemed momentarily as if Roberts might be slightly concerned, but any such impression demanded instant revision as the power was suddenly switched on. Lyric Fantasy barely needed to exert herself, quickly taking the measure of Diamonds Galore and comfortably resisting the late thrust of the July Cup winner (and another Hannon representative) Mr Brooks. Nevertheless, she still clocked a time of 57.39 seconds, a juvenile track record. Two of England's oldest racecourses, first Ascot and now York, had seen history rewritten.

The headline writers for the trade papers could not contain themselves: 'Lyric proves pure poetry' (*Racing Post*); 'Fantasy win is stuff of dreams' (*Sporting Life*). Even Geoffrey Gibbs could not suppress his excitement: 'It was an incredible performance and I rate her the best juvenile filly since the International Classification was begun in 1978. It was an immense credit to her abilities. It always looks an immense amount of weight for a two-year-old to get – twenty-six pounds – but these older sprinters are very grown-up horses. They know their job, jump from the gate and go. What often beats two-year-olds is their sheer inexperience and not being able to cope with the sheer professionalism of the older horses. The weight isn't the final factor.'

ROBERTS: This was definitely her best performance. Down at the start I was pulling her ears, talking to her and she was so calm. I knew she probably wouldn't be able to lead all the way against these experienced older horses, but this didn't worry me because she never was a tearaway or a filly that had to go and win her races out of the stalls or kill them off in the first three furlongs. From halfway she was really motoring and that's when her speed showed; I knew then she would make it, but I didn't want to use her too soon. When I finally asked her, she did it sweetly. She had matured so much and it was hard to believe she was only a two-year-old. She could have run fifty-six seconds if I'd wanted. Fabulous; different class to anything I had ever sat on. It made all the dieting worthwhile. Verna had done a fantastic job varying my evening meals with all sorts of dressings on my salads to go with my bit of fish but my body was crying out for some good meat and I couldn't wait for a nice steak that evening.

Lord Carnarvon had toyed with the idea of sending Lyric Fantasy to Longchamp for the Prix de l'Abbaye, Europe's all-aged sprint championship, run on the same afternoon as the Arc: changing his mind, he rerouted her to Newmarket's Group I Cheveley Park Stakes, which invariably determines the identity of not only the season's leading two-year-old filly but also the winter favourite for the following year's 1,000 Guineas. At six furlongs it was further than the Pocket Rocket had run before. Getting the trip was not Roberts's only problem. Just three fillies entered the lists against Lyric Fantasy, but one of them was Clive Brittain's Sayyedati, on whom he had won the six-furlong Cherry Hinton Stakes (Group II) and the Moyglare Stud Stakes, a Group I race in Ireland over seven furlongs; she would have no difficulty with the distance.

ROBERTS: Actually, I made up my mind pretty quickly that I would ride Lyric Fantasy although I could have ridden Sayyedati if I'd wanted to. Over five or six furlongs I didn't think there was another filly to beat her. She had so much speed; she hadn't done anything wrong and she'd beaten some of the best sprinters in Europe. I was banking on Sayyedati going to Ascot for the Group I Fillies' Mile and didn't expect her to go for the Cheveley Park at all. I thought she'd be better over seven furlongs or a mile as she was more the Guineas filly. Obviously they were two great fillies. Deep down I believed Lyric Fantasy would get the six furlongs and although Sayyedati had it in her to beat me she still hadn't shown on the track the mind-boggling work she'd done at home. I didn't think anything could beat Lyric Fantasy over the shorter distance. As it happened she ran way below form in the Cheveley Park and gave me a bad ride. When I got on her back she was nervy and fidgety; she'd never behaved like that before. She relaxed all right in the race itself but we were beaten before the Bushes. And, of course, Sayyedati did go on to win the Guineas and prove herself one of the best milers in Europe.

Sayyedati was never headed and downed the 2–1 on favourite with something to spare by two lengths. Coincidence freaks were quick to spot that Mumtaz Mahal had also lost her unbeaten record in race number six. Although Lyric Fantasy was still the top-rated filly in the International Classification on 122, seven pounds above Sayyedati (and three pounds below Zafonic), her reputation was a touch dented: Timeform, for one, declared she had been overrated by the press and decided Sayyedati was her superior by one pound.

* * *

HANNON: I was very disappointed with what Timeform had to say about her in their *Racehorses* annual, as they said 'she can't be rated the outstanding youngster that her public relations machine, official and unofficial, constantly made out.' How they can crab a filly with her record I just don't know. She was one out of the ordinary. I've never seen anything as fast: amazing at the gate. She would just sit there like a little terrier with her nose pressed hard up against the inside of the stalls – when they opened she was gone like a rocket. She had gone in her coat by the Cheveley Park but she had been working well enough. You could say that she ran well because Sayyedati was a good filly. But that wasn't her true form; she must have gone over the top.

Roberts could ill afford to dwell on Lyric Fantasy's reputation. For sure, the filly had illuminated his season with brilliance, but there was still the championship to secure: and the prospect of reaching the 200. He had sought a cushion of twenty winners over Pat Eddery by the time 'night-racing' ceased on 29 August. That afternoon he passed the £1 million mark in win prize money with a treble at Newmarket before travelling down to Windsor for another winner courtesy of Alec Stewart's Shuailaan: this widened the gap to twenty-eight, 163 to 135. Eddery was powerless: totally, in fact, since he was serving a five-day ban for careless riding. It seemed only an act of God could come between Roberts and the coveted title. One such 'act', in the guise of Shamisen, had nearly proved costly – though not remotely as damaging as a midsummer incident almost proved. On Friday, 10 July Roberts followed an afternoon stint at York with four rides at Chester's evening fixture, the last of them at 9 p.m. Along with fellow jockey Jimmy Quinn and trainer/gambler Barney Curley he then embarked on the flight back to Newmarket. Their light aircraft never left the ground: instead it wound up in a drainage ditch, its pilot, Neil Forman, and three passengers lucky to be alive. Their delayed, and hastily rearranged, return ended more happily, incorporating as it did comical scenes reminiscent of a Whitehall farce or a 'Carry On' film.

ROBERTS: The air strip we went in on – Hawarden – closed at six or something and Pat's pilot said he used a farmer's grass strip down the road. We followed them in and it was the worst landing. It wasn't the pilot's fault. The grass was so long and so rough, they were cutting it for silage, and you couldn't see the bumps. We were bouncing around, nearly going through the roof! We rushed back after racing so we could land back in Newmarket before it got dark. I'm always very nervous taking off, it's my biggest fear. I've learnt a lot about flying, being in the front so often, and I reckon if something happened to the pilot I could bring the plane down: Neil's shown me the ropes and it's much like a car. But once you're halfway up after take-off there's no point of return. You could be over a housing estate or a town – anywhere. I hate take-offs.

Usually you get to around 70 or 75 m.p.h. and off you go, but we hit this bump, it threw us into the air, we came back down and now we're running out of runway. I think one of the wheels must have gone when we came back down because when Neil tried to pull us up we didn't have enough

207

power and had to abort. There was a big hedge and some trees in front of us and we went straight through the hedge like a bulldozer. How we missed the trees, I don't know! Then we spun around in the next field. The red light on the wing was flashing in the grass and I thought a fire had started and I told myself to jump as soon as we stopped, before the plane went up in flames. Anyway, we spun nose down into this ditch and all the while the engine is droning and racing, and smoke was coming out of the propeller. As we landed I kicked the door open and jumped. I thought the water would only be knee deep but it was green, slimy stuff that went right over my head. I was only dressed in my riding clothes! The farmer took us to his house and cleaned us up a bit: we were quite shaken and Neil was cut and Barney Curley had hurt his back.

We spent two hours in the hospital before being discharged and by now we were starving. We hired a taxi to take us back to Newmarket but we were so cold and hungry; we were dressed only in these striped hospital overall things and slippers on our feet. We stopped in Leicester for some food at a kebab house and they thought we'd escaped from a loony bin! 'Don't you like hospital food?', one bloke said to me. Then all of a sudden, the shock set in and we began shaking; and then we all burst out laughing. We were very lucky. The Lord was with us.

VERNA ROBERTS: I do sometimes worry about the travelling: the flying is a constant worry. There was a crash one time where two light aircraft came down over Reading. I rang Michael's agent to ask him whether he would be flying over Reading and he said they were. They flew over the same spot half an hour after the crash. I don't know why they can't have proper landing strips – in this day and age something should be done. Terry Ellis, Pat's agent, rang up immediately after the Chester crash. They were watching the plane trying to take off. Michael didn't get home until four in the morning, by which time the press had already got hold of the story.

Roberts was undeterred. Having snatched a few hours' sleep he took to the air again on Saturday and was rewarded with a treble. The championship gradually began to assume the appearance of being cut and dried, but the race to achieve the elusive double century added an extra dimension to the '100–1 outsider deposes nine-times champion' story and helped maintain media interest. Consequently, the pressure on the Roberts household was unrelenting. As the BBC unit departed, Anglia's crew would arrive; the members of the press corps came and went in a haze of anonymity. Somehow Michael and Verna Roberts coped: no one was turned away if at all possible. Under circumstances in which tempers could quite easily – and understandably – become frayed, they were invariably contained.

VERNA ROBERTS: He was just the same old Michael. It will happen, was his view of getting the two hundred; it was just a matter of when. There are more newspapers over here so there's far more pressure. Now and again they'd do an interview with Michael back home, but most of them were conducted on the racetrack. And we'd only just got television in South Africa when Michael was champion and then only for one hour a night. But it wasn't until September that home began to resemble a madhouse. Michael does not find it easy to switch off once he comes in after racing. The whole evening won't be racing, but we'll talk about some of the races; sometimes I have to bring it up. If he comes in at midnight after evening racing he can't go to bed. He'll sit and read *Farmers' Weekly* for hours: he can't relax in front of the television watching a film or anything like that. So many times back home he'll say: 'I'd love a cup of tea' and then walk out the back door and not come back. Our maid will say: 'I'm not making any more tea until he sits down!'

He's always been a workaholic and he's never changed. He's very self-critical; he likes everything to run smoothly; he's a very organised person. When he does something he does it properly, and he expects everyone else to be the same; totally and utterly a perfectionist. When he employs a farm man he tells him to do something properly or not at all. One had spent two days setting up some gates and when they were completed one gate was hanging half an inch lower than the other. Michael told him to take the whole lot down. I said: 'Does it really matter? This is a farm.' And Michael said: 'Yes, I know. But one is lower than the other and I wanted them level.' In his workshop on the farm everything has its very own box; everything is washed down, cleaned and oiled on Saturdays. It's absolutely immaculate! So is his car – no eating or smoking in it. It's the discipline instilled by the Academy; smartness and good manners at all times. He hates bad table manners. You can read it on his face. He'll be removed from the company; he can't handle bad manners. Afrikaners have a very strong upbringing: they're very strict with their children and it's very much a case of respecting their elders. On the other hand, Michael will chat with anyone, it doesn't matter who they are or what they do. He'll stand and talk for ten minutes to the petrol pump attendant whether I've got shopping in the car and am desperate to get home with it or not.

BRITTAIN: I call Verna the Empress State Building! They are a very close family and Michael would not be able to see the season through at the rate he works without Verna there to put the blocks on him sometimes. If anyone rings up who is likely to give him hassle she is quick enough and sharp enough to head them off. If someone rings up to be rude at any time she's well capable of dealing with them. She's a pretty strong lady. They're a team, a perfect match in my opinion.

STEWART: Verna is a lovely girl, a very able horsewoman herself and extremely level-headed. I think if there's a happy marriage and things have gone wrong during the day at the races but you've got someone to come home to as level-headed and sympathetic as Verna, then life is made tolerable. She realises that, however good Michael is, if the horses are not good enough there's no way he's going to win on them.

ROBERTS: Graham kept saying to me: 'Stay out of the Stewards' Room: don't take unnecessary risks.' He kept telling me what I'd be missing if I got suspended. I had one or two lucky escapes where I was waiting in the weighing-room for them to come and call me. But I tried to be careful with my race riding. If a gap was a bit tight I'd think twice and move away. The hardest thing was the whip. When you're going forward and the post is getting closer and you know you're going to get up with one or two more smacks it's pretty much impossible to remember how many smacks you have left to use.

To have got that far and not got there because of a suspension or an injury would have been very disappointing. But I was not counting my chickens. Twice earlier in the summer I'd gone ten up on Pat and both times he pegged me right back. He came back from one suspension and rode seven winners in a day! I thought to myself, it's impossible to beat this man: to come back and on the first bloody day ride seven winners! What chance have I got? It would take me a week to do that! But I watched him a bit, though, after the York suspension in August and I could see he was a little bit unhappy. I'd have been prepared to stay on to ride on the all-weather in November and December if it was necessary, but in fairness the all-weather racing gives the lads who don't ride many winners the chance to get a few rides. It's different during the course of the Turf season but I didn't want to ride purely on the all-weather if I could help it.

Winners naturally became harder to find with only the one meeting per day. As September slipped into October Roberts suffered his longest losing streak of the season – twenty-

eight rides without a win. But the drought presaged a deluge.
Ten winners in six days raised his score to 197, an immense
effort from Rock (nine different trainers were involved)
when any number of runners in the huge autumnal fields
are intent upon earning their winter corn. The last three
winners really had to be squeezed from the form book. The
Queen's Ingenuity at Redcar on 14 October was followed
by twenty-nine consecutive losers before Iota brought
Roberts to the brink of history by winning at Chester on the
twentieth. Some history, however, had already been made.
In Folkestone's Hurstmonceux Handicap the previous day
Tender Moment became Roberts's 1,000th domestic ride
of the season, equalling Gordon Richards's total of 1936;
Alau's company in the Burwash Maiden an hour later gave
him exclusive possession of the record. 'Mouse runs up the
clock,' was the typically tabloid flourish from the *Sun*.

ROBERTS: I thought it was possible to get the two hundred
the day Iota won. When I missed it that day I knew the next
day was the day because Jasoorah was a bit of a good thing.
Getting stuck on a hundred and ninety-eight or ninety-nine
was always in the back of my mind. You hear so many bad
luck stories, an accident or something. It would have been
disastrous if I'd been off for three weeks with a broken leg
and been left wondering through the winter what might have
been. I was close to tears after passing the post on Jasoorah
and I had a huge lump in my throat trotting back. Everyone
was so happy for me; the crowd, the other jockeys, the
officials – everybody. I was glad to have got it out of the
way – it was such a relief – and to do it on one of Alec's

horses made it extra special. I rode two hundred winners back in South Africa but to do it here is something else.

Despite the recent memory of Eddery's double century in 1990 (attained two days later than Roberts's but from 163 fewer rides), newspaper reaction was reasonably euphoric, ranging from 'He's done it!' (*Racing Post*) and 'Roberts joins elite 200 club' (*Sporting Life*) in the trade papers through 'Hard-working Roberts joins exclusive 200 club' in the *Daily Telegraph* to 'Double Top' and 'Two Ton Mouse' in the *Sun* and *Daily Sport* respectively.

Only four other men had shared Roberts's feeling of supreme satisfaction. Fred Archer achieved eight double centuries in ten years (1876–85), featuring a total of 246 from 667 rides in 1885 for a winning percentage of 36.9; Tommy Loates scored 222 from 863 mounts in 1893 (25.7 per cent); Richards broke 200 on twelve occasions between 1933 and 1952, beating Archer's record in the first such season with 259 from 975 mounts (26.6 per cent), which he improved to 269 in 1947 from 835 rides (32.2 per cent). Thirty-eight years were to elapse after Richards's twelfth double century before Pat Eddery reached this milestone with 209 from 891 mounts (23.5 per cent). Roberts's total would eventually stop at 206 from 1,068 rides, a winning percentage of 19.3 per cent (Archer's 1884 figure of 241 came at a phenomenal 41.8 per cent).

Tributes continued to flow from all sides, near and far, as the 1992 Turf season limped towards its conclusion on 9 November.

* * *

STEVE CAUTHEN: Michael is a great rider and a great tactician; always using his brain in a race and always using his brain to get on the right horse – which is half the battle. His determination to become champion was unswerving. He's worked night and day, day and night to do it, which is very tiring. You must have tunnel vision to become champion jockey: almost block everything else out, and he did that perfectly.

WILLIE CARSON: I've probably ridden more horses in recent seasons than most jockeys since Gordon Richards and I know it gets very tiring, especially when the 'night' meetings are on. Michael hardly missed a meeting. I could see he was getting tired. His workload was very, very tough indeed and he worked very, very hard indeed. Riding in a thousand races shows that.

ALEC STEWART: His success highlighted his lack of success in 1978: it's horses that make champion jockeys. Graham Rock was an important factor, but I would mention two other points. Michael did get a lot of the top rides that other jockeys couldn't manage because of weight or travelling – and for that he must thank Graham Rock, who got him on the right horses. The loyalty of Richard Hannon was also important. Michael did him some favours early on and he stuck with him. Secondly, there is Michael's wonderful temperament. You need a character like his to achieve what he has. He is fantastically dedicated; very placid, he never raises his voice, nothing ever seems to bother him. I know it would aggravate me, but not Michael.

I was quite angry at him one day for how he'd ridden a race and later I felt quite ashamed for having been angry with him – yet it hadn't bothered him at all. It meant a lot to me to provide him with the two hundredth winner because we were very conscious of the fact that we'd provided him with so few beforehand. So much hard work had gone into his year and there had been so many near-disasters and calamities, like the plane crash and his injury.

CLIVE BRITTAIN: Michael had built up over the preceding three years something like ten different stables. It's fair to say he would have been champion anyway, but it's also fair to say not with two hundred winners. He was all ready for it: Graham was the extra fifty winners. I rate Michael up with the best. In any year a champion will always look good, but he fits in neatly with Pat, Lester and Steve and if he wants to keep going in the way he has been then he can be champion again. Two things stood out, for me, in 1992: firstly, his determination to take off the weight in order to ride Lyric Fantasy at York; and secondly, the way he overcame the pain after that fall on the gallops to get himself back to work as quickly as possible.

GAVIN HUNTER: I always thought his success was a certainty after his first couple of seasons with Alec. I went so far as to say he was one of the top six and would be in the first three for winners – although, I must admit, I stopped short of saying he would be champion! But it didn't surprise me the way racing is run today. Eddery and Cauthen were going to be in France so much, and Carson may not have the drive for it any more. And Graham Rock was a walking form book. His contribution had to be massive. It's impossible to get it right every time in handicaps, but to get it right in nearly every race was the mark of someone who was going to prove invaluable. As for Michael, he's almost got an American clock in his head in terms of timing and judging pace. He knows exactly how fast a horse should be going at a particular stage of a race; although he often looks as if he isn't going to get there, he always does. It doesn't matter whether he's making all or coming from way back out of the clouds. He's a little seven-stone gnome, just like Willie Shoemaker! He talks so much sense, too.

HERMAN BROWN: Whenever any of us got together Michael's progress was all we would talk about. 'Has he ridden any winners lately?' We get little coverage here, you see. And then the next thing we knew he'd ridden another five or something. Deep down we knew they would have to shoot Michael to stop him! You knew that whenever he got his nose in front he would get everything from his horse, and it would be the same in the championship race.

BRIAN CHERRY: I was just amazed it took so many years to win the championship because he's so determined; ruthless. Verna used to send me cuttings through the season because there was very little coverage out here. But there is no doubt about it, this little man has to be put down as Superman!

FRED RICKABY: When I returned to England I lost interest

in racing but as Michael started to climb the jockeys' list my interest returned. I read every line written about him and watched him on television as if he was an adopted son. It was his obvious fitness and ability to keep a tired horse balanced which thrilled me most. He has an affinity with horses and can urge them to keep finding a bit more. Sometimes during this season it looked to be hopeless but Michael has always been a super-optimist and never gives up. Right on the post he has squeezed that crucial dying gasp which has made the difference between winning and losing a race. I think it's the fear of losing his winning percentage which kept him going! I still get enormous pleasure from watching a great jockey win races that most others would have lost. I am naturally biased, but nothing is impossible when Michael is involved.

LEW TANKEL: Because of the political situation we are a little bit fanatical about our sportsmen who go overseas and do well. We take more of a personal interest than other countries because we've been isolated. The sports boycott hurt us more than anything: not buying our gold or our fruit or whatever wasn't serious, but isolating us in sport was a disaster! There was no *real* champion in South Africa apart from Michael once he won his first championship back in 1973, and we knew he'd do it over in the UK before he called it a day.

ROBBYN RAMSAY (Durban's *Daily News*): Michael is a remarkable person who has worked so hard for everything that he has achieved during his career. He never changes –

a quality which endears him to us all. Year after year he returns 'home' just the same as when he left – totally unaffected by his successes. I find it highly amusing to watch him receiving detailed instructions from some of our young trainers who have been in the game for about two and a half minutes! Far from being offended, Michael graciously takes it all in his stride, but if you happen to catch his eye . . . !

DOUGLAS ALEXANDER (South Africa's *Sunday Tribune*): It would have been an ostrich feather in their cap had Oudtshoorn heeded my suggestion and made Muis Roberts a freeman of the town. I'm no racing fan, but I felt so proud when Roberts won the British championship that I wrote to Oudtshoorn proposing that they bestow their freedom on him. It would not only honour the likeable, unassuming Roberts but would be a wonderful publicity move for Oudtshoorn tourism as Muis is now a household name to millions of racegoers worldwide. To my dismay the proposal got the thumbs down. A letter from the municipality told me that the freedom of Oudtshoorn has been bestowed on only one person – a former mayor – in the town's 145-year history. It was traditional, the letter added, to grant this honour for services to the community, not in recognition of outstanding achievements in sports or other fields. Not that Oudtshoorners are not proud of Muis. Not long ago the municipality presented him with a beautiful saddle and special riding boots made by hand from ostrich leather for his contribution to sport and horse racing in South Africa.

* * *

Oudtshoorn may have been unable to grant Alexander his wish, but Roberts's exploits were certainly not ignored by the mother country. The Association of Racing Clubs of South Africa made a presentation to him at Greyville in November 1992 and a year later it was announced that he was to receive the silver South African Sports Merit Award in recognition of his international achievements. When one considers that Roberts's co-recipients included Olympic medallist Elana Meyer and the respective captains of the national rugby and cricket teams, Naas Botha and Kepler Wessels (previous recipients had been of the calibre of Graeme Pollock and Gary Player), it becomes easier to appreciate the magnitude of the honour bestowed upon him; he was the first jockey to be so recognised. 'I've received many awards over the years but I would rate this particular acknowledgement as one of the highlights of my career. I was absolutely thrilled.'

VERNA ROBERTS: We both wanted this British championship more than any of those that had gone before, because Michael had had to work his way in. A lot of the boys don't work nearly as hard. I've seen him during the summer getting up at 5.15 having only got to bed the previous night at 11.30 – and that goes on seven days a week. There was jealousy and some of the things, like the phone calls pretending to be trainers asking him to ride this horse or that horse, we would never have been subjected to in South Africa. In the beginning you think it's just you but you find out eventually that it's done to everybody.

* * *

GRAHAM ROCK: Michael is very tough. He put himself through the mill and it paid off. There was a feeling in the middle of the season that he might have been getting too many rides, but people in racing are conservative; they are used to an established order. In fact, he just rode more for people he'd ridden for in the past. The championship gave me the greatest satisfaction; it's the glamorous thing. Getting a thousand rides was more a test of endurance than anything else. I'd have liked him to have reached two hundred and ten really; the two hundredth winner itself I watched on SIS in my local bookmakers in West Byfleet. Michael is a good man to work with because he is ambitious and very determined. Also, he knows an enormous amount about racing – not just race riding. He would make a first-class trainer.

Rock's acumen and quick wits had yielded winners for fifty-six different trainers. Clive Brittain topped the list of contributors with forty-four winners from 279 opportunities (Roberts missed only nineteen of Carlburg's scorers), while Richard Hannon provided twenty-nine winners from 136 rides; Alec Stewart's virus-plagued yard gave nineteeen; twenty-six individuals provided a single winner; and if any further proof was needed of Rock's contribution, it could be gleaned from that winning percentage of 19.3 which was a 4 per cent improvement on the previous two seasons. Roberts had rattled up nine four-timers; two five-timers; and, on 8 August, that six-timer at Lingfield and Newmarket that would have tied the British record for the most winners in a day had Eddery not won seven on 26 June. He had earned £1,314,994 in win prize money (plus another £528,729 in place money) for his patrons, and any punter who had staked £1 on every one of his 1,068 conveyances (worth £54,000 in riding fees!) wound up £34.18 in credit.

Little fish had tended to predominate. Although eleven victories abroad included the Group I Premio Presidente della Repubblica (Sikeston) in Italy and the Moyglare Stud Stakes (Sayyedati) in Ireland, his domestic Group I successes were confined to Lyric Fantasy's Nunthorpe and Ivanka's victory in Ascot's Fillies' Mile. Altogether, Roberts won eleven of Britain's 106 Pattern races: back in the 1988 season of Mtoto, Indian Skimmer et al. he had won no fewer than nineteen. Not that he was complaining as his great rival and the deposed champion presented him with the Wilfred Sherman Trophy, which accompanied the championship, in front of the Channel 4 cameras at Doncaster on 7 November. He was, of course, the first of his nationality to lift the title, and only the sixth 'foreigner' – if one excludes English-nurtured Irishmen like Eddery and Steve Donoghue – to do so in the wake of Americans Lester Reiff (1900), Danny Maher (1908, 1913) and Steve Cauthen (1984, 1985 and 1987), and the Australians Frank Wootton (1909–12) and Scobie Breasley (1957, 1961–3). Few men had been champion jockey in two countries – and fewer still in two hemispheres – let alone ridden a double century in two different countries. Roberts's worldwide total of winners now exceeded 3,000, easily surpassing Stanley Amos's South African record of 2,507. Britain's two premier racecallers each had a particular memory of Roberts 1992 vintage.

PETER O'SULLEVAN: There were quite a few because he has this gift of really galvanising them without ever being hard on them. Given his injury and the weight situation Lyric Fantasy at York was pretty special, but the ride he gave Host in a televised race at Newbury in October took some topping. They looked beat all the way up the straight but Michael kept getting more out of the horse to repel every challenger. He does strike up a very swift empathy with his partners and another enormous plus is the way he observes everything during a race. That and his dedicated study of the form book stands him in good stead; he's always got something constructive to say and he is quick to assess a horse's potential. Any owner he rides for has a lot of extra pluses going for him.

GRAHAM GOODE: Perseverance is the hallmark of a Michael Roberts ride and I remember one perfect example I called on Channel 4 at Newmarket in August. Inherent Magic was one of a treble he rode that afternoon and was typical of a jockey riding with supreme confidence. At the two-furlong pole you'd have torn up your ticket if you'd backed the horse but Michael never gave up, kept on nagging away relentlessly and got up on the line to win by a short head.

So, after bidding Europe farewell with a victory in a Listed race at Saint-Cloud on Stewart's Revif, Roberts set off for

Durban (via an international jockeys' race in Zimbabwe) and the haven of Barrington Farm, Karkloof, where 1,000 acres and 500 head of cattle ('506 and more to come' was the last message during calving) were awaiting the boss's inspection. The journey home was marked by conspicuously greater joy than that of 1978.

ROBERTS: I could not have seen all this happen without Graham. He does all the work. I do the riding: he gets the rides. I was the first in South Africa to get an agent and I've seen others suddenly start riding winners left, right and centre once they've got one. You've got to keep ahead of the play. It's the guy who rings up for the ride first that the trainer says 'Yes' to. He doesn't know whether Pat, Steve or Willie are going to ring up for it. He'll think, 'If I can get Roberts I'll take him.' If you're smart like Graham you get an advantage. You've got to know the form and know which horse to go for. I don't think I suddenly started riding any better; I just rode better horses. I had more quality rides in 1992 and Graham obviously made a big difference. All credit to him, as virtually every aim he set for us was achieved. The odd comment was made about his aggressive approach to booking my rides but all agents tread on toes. That's their job, and that's what they get paid for.

It was the most I've ever ridden for Clive. I always thought I had a bit of a chance if both my stables came good. I'd got over 200 horses there, which is like riding for one of the big yards. Winning the Nunthorpe on Lyric Fantasy was the highlight of the season. She was something special; a little machine. If there were any disappointments in such a year it was missing the Classic-winning rides on User Friendly for Clive. When she made her debut Alec had a filly called Anghaam in the race so I had to ride that. I was riding work for Henry Cecil at this time and his filly Midnight Air was going very well at home. She was due to run in the Cheshire Oaks, so when Clive mentioned he was considering that race for User Friendly I said not to bother because she couldn't possibly beat Midnight Air. If User Friendly had gone to Chester I could have ridden her because George Duffield was riding somewhere else for Sir Mark Prescott. Unfortunately, Clive listened to me and sent User Friendly to Lingfield for the Oaks Trial instead – and I was at Beverley!

And I was offered the ride on Dr Devious in the Derby by an agent acting for the owner! I was supposed to be riding Aljadeer for Henry Cecil until he went lame. Anyway, Graham received this fax and a phone call but we then found out that Peter Chapple-Hyam had already given the mount to John Reid two days earlier. We had not seen anything in the papers about John Reid being on the horse but we didn't think it was right to make a fuss about it. If Rodrigo de Triano had dropped out of the race Lester would have switched to Dr Devious, so all in all it was a bit confusing. I ended up riding Thourios for Guy Harwood and finished tenth.

I do think back often when something important is achieved. And then I think to myself, what's next? I've had my share of knock-backs but usually something is always happening. Even 1978 was an experience. Once you've ridden in the UK you can call yourself a proper jockey because the tracks are so different. So to be champion jockey here is everybody's dream. It was unbelievable to have got both the two hundred and the championship in the same season and I was thrilled to have beaten Gordon Richards's record of a thousand rides. I didn't think it was all possible. Incredible, really! I never thought I could do it this year, but it happened and they can't take it away from me. It definitely felt as good as I thought it would.

10 Dignity in the Face of Difficulty

Barrington Farm, an hour's drive from Durban at Karkloof, is the latest successor to the 'smallholding' Roberts fashioned out of a corner of Herman Brown's yard at Summerveld to shelter the likes of Barney and Matilda. A 'proper' smallholding at Summerveld preceded the Umlaas Road dairy (and fresh produce) venture that nurtured Tetbury Fandancer and Jacqueline, after which Farmer Roberts turned his attention to beef cattle at Buffels Bosch, Lidgetton. With the aid of his self-bred Red Angus stud sires, Mr Red Eagle (a Gold Medal Performance animal) and Mr Red Barry, plus thirty-nine breeding females, he soon began collecting more awards at the Royal Show. Nowadays it is Barrington Farm where Roberts annually seeks sanctuary from the mayhem of the racetrack and the prying eye of the media.

ROBERTS: I can relax here and perhaps I should have bought the place earlier. I've got twenty acres short of 1,000. I rear cross-bred Hereford/Simentals to use the Red Angus bulls on, and I grow 600 acres of maize. Because of my grandfather I've always had a soft spot for Jersey cows and after going over to Jersey I bought a couple of females.

227

One of them, Fairfield Dainty Jill, was reserve super cow on Jersey in 1992. We've recently transplanted an embryo from her and exported it to South Africa. I did have a few mares and was quite successful, breeding two decent horses in Kumluckie and Golden Express. I tried to get my mares to the top stallions but the fees were so high and if you can't breed to the top sires you're wasting your time. But being round the cattle is a welcome switch-off from racing: no phones or people troubling you. Every October I'm like a schoolkid, crossing off the days on the calendar until I get back to the farm. When I get back I think: how can I go back to the UK? It's cold, it gets dark at four o'clock! But come February it's the other way round and I get itchy feet to go back and see how all the horses have developed over the winter. We enjoy life in the UK very much, not just racing, but all our family is in South Africa and it's hard to leave everything behind. And I enjoy my farming, even though it's only for four months.

However, this particular sabbatical was destined to become far more eventful. Once before, back in August 1988, Steve Cauthen had inadvertently presented Roberts with a heaven-sent opportunity; now, at 6.07 p.m. on Monday, 18 January 1993, a three-paragraph fax from Sheikh Mohammed's Darley Stud to the Press Association set in motion a train of events that led to a second. Cauthen and the Sheikh's advisers were unable to agree terms for a new contract. The American, it was reported, refused to accept a penny less than the £750,000 he had received previously; to widespread regret, Cauthen vacated the English Turf. The hunt had already begun for a jockey to wear the maroon-and-white jacket on Sheikh Mohammed's regiment of aristocratically bred equines: in excess of 500 – every estimate varied – dispersed among a dozen or so trainers, notably the Newmarket quartet of Cumani, Stoute, Cecil and – most notable of all – John Gosden, the Sheikh's principal trainer, whose Stanley House stable was home to over 130 of them. Irish champion Mick Kinane was favourite for the job. He had donned the Sheikh's colours to win the 1989 Irish Oaks and 1990 King George VI and Queen Elizabeth Diamond Stakes on Alydaress and Belmez respectively and was much admired by the Darley Stud Management. Overtures were made to Kinane five days before Cauthen's decision was finally made known and a definite offer put to him on the eighteenth itself. To universal surprise Kinane rejected the approach, citing as reasons his contentment with existing ties in Ireland and Hong Kong.

With most of the top jockeys – Eddery, Swinburn, Carson, Munro, Asmussen – already under contract, the champion jockey naturally became the prime candidate. Alec Stewart paid him a retainer but he operated without a contract, and his arrangement with Clive Brittain was purely of the verbal, gentleman's variety. Roberts had ridden only twenty-six horses for Sheikh Mohammed in 1992 (seven more than Kinane, in fact), but back in 1988, of course, he partnered Indian Skimmer and Salse to victory in Pattern races. Over a New Year drink at the Carlton Towers, Graham Rock had inquired of Anthony Stroud, racing manager to Sheikh Mohammed, whether Roberts might be in line for any spare rides; as it happened, Stroud was now in South

Africa on holiday. Roberts flew down to Cape Town and the details of a one-year contract were ironed out.

STROUD: Steve's departure was unexpected really in so far as once he'd given his decision he was pretty adamant. We tried to keep him and offered to go over to the United States to discuss the new contract, but he had made up his mind. The contract was decreased in overall monetary terms but it was still very lucrative, especially with winning percentages from so many good horses. Of course, Steve had been at the top for a long time and he had recently married – and he'd always had to control his weight. We asked our four top trainers for their ideas: John Gosden and Henry Cecil wanted Mick Kinane; Michael Stoute and André Fabre, who trains most of the French animals, went for Michael Roberts. Frankie Dettori looked to be committed to Hong Kong. I also favoured Mick Kinane, so in the first instance we approached him.

With Stroud out of the country Robert Acton, a director of Darley Stud, spoke to the press: 'We have a wealth of untapped talent, especially among the three-year-olds. Our breeding enterprise is aimed at producing Classic horses and Michael will no doubt come in for some star rides. We feel that it is Sheikh Mohammed's turn to win some colts' Classics and it could be that Michael, who has a habit of being in the right place at the right time, will be as lucky for us as he has been for others in the past.' Roberts was not about to disagree, and on 9 February duly accepted terms. Little could he have realised just how ironic Acton's final sentence would turn out to be.

ROBERTS: I had no inkling Steve was going to pack up, none whatsoever. I was surprised when I got the call out in South Africa early in the New Year asking if I would be interested in the job. I was shocked to hear Steve was giving up; there had been no rumours or anything like that circulating in the weighing-room. They were looking for jockeys who were interested. Mick Kinane was their number one, as I understood it, and they were negotiating with him. They were fair about that from the very beginning, but if there were any hiccups, they said, then we must talk. Only a week before I'd received a letter from Alec confirming my retainer for 1993. In fact, I could have had Sheikh Hamdan's in 1988 but I didn't want to lose Mtoto; and I could not ride Tom Jones's or Major Hern's – who had the best horses. I did lose Salsabil, but I'd have missed Mystiko had I taken the job.

I met Anthony in Cape Town to discuss everything and signed the contracts when I got back to England in March. The job did not include the Fabre horses but covered all the English horses, including Cumani's. From the beginning I was riding everything in the UK: it was in the contract. I'd ridden for all the trainers and there wasn't one of them that I could say I didn't know much about the man or his methods. So that never worried me at all.

I couldn't believe Kinane turned the job down because it was only a matter of time before the Sheikh had one or two champions with that class of horse. I'd not been looking at the horses as possible rides the previous year so there was nothing I could say was a future champion, but there were a lot of fabulously bred horses who had not run at all. It was mind-boggling – there were over 300 three-year-olds alone! Taos had won three out of three for John Gosden and Barathea two out of two for Luca Cumani, so I was looking forward to getting to know them – and Majority at Barry Hills. Of the older horses, Wolfhound in the sprints and Opera House over middle distances took the eye.

I couldn't see the job hindering my chances of retaining the championship. I thought it would make it easier. I wasn't really required to go abroad as much as Steve had done and I felt I had a big weight advantage over him so I would probably ride many more of the horses here in England. It had to be a big advantage to have so many horses at our disposal: no champion gives up his crown that easily.

Opinions on that score were divided. Rock's freedom to pirate choice mounts in large fields of three-year-old maidens or juvenile contests, which had yielded so much profit in 1992, would be heavily curtailed – and even choosing between the numerous Darley Stud representatives in them seemed to constitute a potential minefield. Ladbrokes eased Roberts slightly from 4–6 to 4–5 for the title; William Hill, in contrast, tightened him to 4–7 from 8–11. Whatever the fates held regarding the championship Roberts could expect quality rides in abundance and the right to be treated with the respect accorded all champions. This deference, however, seldom lasts long in any sporting sphere. During this honeymoon period Roberts joined a select band of jockeys from round the world invited to contest the International Jockeys Challenge at Dubai's Nad Al Sheba circuit. He also had time to philosophise on the attributes and attitudes that had served him so well: his rapport with the thoroughbred; riding styles; race riding.

ROBERTS: I don't think about my strengths. They're gifts, really. I've always felt comfortable around animals; felt I was able to communicate with them. I talk to my mounts a lot, to get their trust and make them concentrate. I've heard one or two trainers say you've got to be strict with them, but I think that is wrong. You've got to get some feeling between the animal and yourself so it will have confidence in you. I believe you can make average horses run good races by helping them relax, drawing out the maximum of their ability.

When I started we were taught to ride with our backs straight, which you can do if you drop your legs. The shorter you ride, the higher you're going to come. But if you're sitting long, you are pushing just with your arms; if you come up, you are using your body more, you drive. I used to get shouted at by Cyril Buckham to drop my irons but I wouldn't. To me it's useless sitting long because there's no power when you push. You've got to come in with your weight behind it, like throwing a punch. You must use your shoulders. You may not look pretty but you'll be more effective. If you've got free-running horses as in America you don't need the power, but here you do. You have to pick the horse up and throw it forward, especially when the ground is soft. I've never been concerned with looking pretty; this toe in the irons business is a load of baloney.

You've got no power from the irons; all you've got is a pretty boy. Anyway, my leg bones are too short to sit long! Sometimes I look at a race and think if only that jockey had been a bit more aggressive he could have won that race. As long as you don't jump around and unbalance the horse it's OK. Some people might say that Lester or Pat are not so stylish in some close finishes, but they get every last ounce out of their mounts. Anyone can look stylish on a 5–1 on shot. It's when the jockeys are going ding-dong in a finish that you want to look at them; they won't look stylists then! I believe you should throw everything in bar the kitchen sink at the finish; then you can say: that guy gave the horse every chance of winning.

Good timing is the product of confidence. I now have the confidence to wait as long as necessary in a race. When you are struggling there is that added pressure at the two-furlong mark. You feel the eyes of the world are on you and you make mistakes. You may go too soon and find the horse dies under you. I have the confidence not to do that now. I never go into a race with a set plan unless I've actually been given instructions. Front-running is the easiest race to ride – if they leave you alone; using the horse's stride and there's no chance of meeting trouble. It is an advantage on the demanding tracks over here. The horses are fitter; you couldn't do it so easily in South Africa. In England the horses are trained to run a mile and a half or two miles and sometimes I'll come back and wish I'd made more use of an animal.

In the UK trainers send their horses out fully fit; it is very seldom that a horse will need the outing, and trainers go straight to the distance dictated by the horse's pedigree. They also tend to exercise the horses over a lot further distances for longer periods of time than South African trainers, which makes them much fitter as a result. In South Africa, though, it's impossible to do the same because of the hotter climate. Generally speaking, English horses are better-behaved than South African horses because they are so well handled on a day-to-day basis – the lads make all the difference. You seldom get a fractious horse causing chaos and being well-nigh impossible to control, and when you do they are not persevered with at the expense of others for so long as they are in South Africa. We have the horses out far too long before races in South Africa, which allows fractious or nervous types to get upset.

Every horse you ride is an individual, and I like to let a horse run his own race. I like to settle them inside the first hundred yards or so and then play it from there. I don't agree that it's a bad thing to miss the break; it often has its advantages. You can more easily dictate to a relaxed horse. In South Africa there is almost an obsession to break fast and rush over to the fence, even though the usual tactics are to come from behind, whereas in the UK they generally start kicking from the three furlongs – which might still be too early in South Africa.

The shortest way home is the best way in my book. I'd rather lose a place or two in the race than race too wide – you lose too much ground. If the going changes, that's different. Ground on the fence can become terrible – like in Italy – and it does not pay to be on the fence in those circumstances. Sometimes there might be a good narrow strip near the rail; you can run with your knee on top of these plastic rails to make use of even the narrowest of strips. You can get shut in, but I'd rather come the shortest way. I always walk the course before racing. Watering systems are not perfect. The wind tends to carry too much across the track and it can be like day and night on opposite sides of the course; and you may get racecourse traffic such as the stalls going down one side of the track only. We have to irrigate a lot in South Africa, and as a farmer I've learnt from experience what effect the wind can have. The result is that you'll often find strips of poached ground down the centre where the water hasn't reached.

South African racing is as clean as anywhere in the world nowadays. You'll hear stories that in the old days there were bands of jockeys fixing races, but in my career everything has been very well monitored, particularly as most of my experience has been in Natal which is one of the strictest authorities. I've been approached once or twice to 'stop' horses for money, but I told them I wasn't interested; I wanted to win races. There's no point trying to cheat in South Africa because you can't get weight off a horse's back anyway. The handicapper works to set rules. If you run in the first four your race figure won't move; if you win you go up five to seven pounds, no more; if you run second you might go up one pound; if you are out of the first four you'll drop one pound. Do anything wrong in a race and you are done. The stipes pay as much attention to the first furlong as they do the last. We do race very tight in South Africa. Jockeys are inclined to be tied to orders, especially the younger ones who, if the boss says 'sit third or fourth' will sit third or fourth even if it means walking. Often this leads to races being messed up because they are all trying to be third or fourth and a lot of jostling results. It's only those of us who've ridden abroad, like Felix, Basil, Jeff Lloyd and myself, who tend to possess the confidence to kick on in front whenever that happens.

South Africa is spoilt by having some fabulous courses. The way I see it, you can't call yourself a proper jockey until you're familiar with every track in the UK. There's so much variation and foreign jockeys do find it difficult. I've ridden every one [in fact, Carlisle is the only one at which Roberts has not yet been successful] and, to me, it's more a case of which tracks you don't like. Graham reckons I'm one of the best round Beverley but it's far from being one of my favourites! I love riding Epsom, on the other hand, and lots of jockeys don't. I've had lots of success there: once you've got a horse running you take a lot of catching.

I get a lot of fan mail from all sorts of people and that's something I really appreciate. They write to thank me, wish me luck before a big race or commiserate with me if I get beaten. Some are really touching, like the letter I received from some pensioners who won money backing me and could afford to go out for a decent meal. The public don't come racing to see sour faces. If they show their appreciation I think it's right to reciprocate. Sure, I get despondent when things go wrong, but I don't believe it's worth dwelling on it for long. If we had plans to go out for dinner then we go – although there might be less noise than if I'd had a winning day! Life is too short to walk around with a long face. A smile costs nothing.

237

* * *

The custom of waving beatifically to the crowd after a notable victory had earned Roberts the affectionate soubriquet of 'the Pope' from English racegoers, but during the first two months of the 1993 season his experiences warranted anything but a smile or a wave. Although Intrepidity's Oaks victory was the jockey's third Group I success for his new patron, following that of Barathea in the Irish 2,000 Guineas and Opera House in the Coronation Cup, those with ears attuned to the sound of drums in the day-to-day jungle of tittle-tattle that is racing's communication system were already picking up a note of discord from some sections of the Darley Stud camp. Roberts's judgement, for example, was being called into question. In the Thresher Classic Trial at Sandown, faced with the choice between Majority (trained by Barry Hills) and True Hero (trained by John Gosden), he sided with the former: True Hero won. In the Craven Stakes, acknowledged as the most valuable trial for the 2,000 Guineas in recent years, he opted for Luca Cumani's Barathea instead of Emperor Jones from Gosden's: Emperor Jones won. In the Musidora Stakes, York's trial for the Oaks, he partnered Michael Stoute's Iviza instead of Gosden's Marillette, and again he found himself on the wrong horse. It was being bandied about that Roberts was even being 'put away' during the discussions which preceded the finalisation of riding arrangements. The job was too big for him, he was trying too hard, ran the second accusation; he had twice fallen foul of the stewards, resulting in seven days on the sidelines; and Pat Eddery held a lead of twenty in the jockeys' championship. The whispers grew louder; the knives were not slow to glint. 'Roberts roasted' (*Daily Mail*, 12 May); 'Mouse cheesed off' (*Sun*, also 12 May). On television, Derek Thompson (Channel 4, 3 May) and Julian Wilson (BBC, 18 May) ended post-race interviews by raising both issues. The media sensed a story, all right. The buzzards were abroad.

Indeed, a hint of the measures some were prepared to take was revealed before the season even started. Back in March Roberts had been voted Jockey of the Year for 1992 by his fellows (he had already won his second such award from the Horserace Writers' Association). Apparently, he won by a single vote. No one can tell the jockeys how to vote. However, to the majority of neutrals, only the fifth man in 200 years to ride more than 200 winners on the Flat was a worthy choice. Nevertheless, some of the jockeys demanded a recount and one was moved to say: 'It spoiled what should have been a very good night. It should have gone to George Duffield – nearly everyone I've spoken to says they voted for him.' It seemed some jockeys still found Roberts's rise difficult – to the point of impossible – to stomach. In the poll for National Hunt Jockey of the Year Richard Dunwoody defeated Peter Scudamore by one vote: no recount was demanded in that instance.

ROBERTS: When you are in a top job there are bound to be some people who want to see you fall. It's human nature; it happens all over the world. There's no getting away from it. Some sections of the press were trying to stir things up, which was a bit annoying because I've always tried to be fair to the media – yet here they were trying to knock me. It was getting on top of me a bit. They were always speaking after the result. If they were so smart, why didn't they say: horse A should beat horse B and Roberts has picked the wrong one? We can all be clever after the event. They were talking absolute rubbish: they were writing a story that happened yesterday and calling it tomorrow. Most of the races concerned were 'trials'. For example, the Sandown race when I chose Majority instead of True Hero: we were never going to beat Tenby so it didn't matter where we finished. I was impressed by how Majority had won at Doncaster. Then it poured with rain and Tenby and others were taken out overnight; I said to Graham this True Hero could win now and he did. We were third; had True Hero been second to Tenby and we'd been fourth nobody would have been bothered. But the press made a big story out of it. It was the same thing in the Craven. If I'd ridden Emperor Jones, who was 16–1, instead of Barathea, the 11–10 on favourite, and Barathea had won, what would have been made of that? If Emperor Jones was a better horse, why did he start 16–1? All that was upsetting, stirring things up with no foundation.

With the amount of horses running under the Darley Stud banner I thought we would be firing in winners straight away. But after a few weeks I could see that it was going to take a little time. There were not going to be any precocious two-year-olds and many of the older horses were geared towards races later in the season.

Ironically, I got suspended for whip infringements at Redcar in May and Ascot in June before the new regulations enforcing a maximum of five strokes instead of ten was introduced. I thought it was crazy! The old rule was working well enough. Personally, I'd sooner see a horse receive twelve flicks of the whip if they're delivered correctly but, if you're only allowed five, horses are going to be struck with more force because jockeys will be conscious of making every one count; and one jockey will stick to the rules and another won't – and he'll probably win the race. Compared to South Africa, say, horses here are trained to relax and they need a lot more driving in a race. The Jockey Club Disciplinary Committee did contact me at the start of the season and warned me to be careful about hitting horses down the shoulder. My problems had never involved hitting behind the saddle.

STROUD: An organisation like ours is always expected to be successful – it's rather like Liverpool Football Club. We did start slowly, but when the press get their teeth into something they don't let go and on this occasion they were adding two and two and making five. The explanations for Michael's choice of mounts was perfectly straightforward. Ray Cochrane had always ridden Emperor Jones; Pat Eddery was the only jockey who got on with Marillette – although I did want Michael to ride True Hero at Sandown.

The champion's fortunes showed no sign of long-term revival as the season accelerated into midsummer. His decision to stick with Barathea in the Eclipse rather than partner Opera House backfired when the older horse (assisted by that man Kinane) landed the spoils, with the

Irish 2,000 Guineas winner only fifth; and it was not until 5 July, a month later than in 1992, that he reached fifty winners. His cup of woe also ran over with three further suspensions, which amounted to another nineteen days out of the saddle.

Incurring the wrath of the stewards was as much an occupational hazard as the risk of injury. Roberts first incurred their displeasure (a ban of three meetings for dangerous riding) in August 1972 but thereafter, as his single-mindedness and high profile increased so did the regularity of his *tête-à-têtes* with the stewards. 'They still do me every year in South Africa: it's part of the season! I think it makes their day.' In Britain the incidents at Ayr in 1978, Yarmouth in 1987 and Ascot in 1988 are the instances that spring to mind. However, the third of 1993's suspensions quickly developed into something of a *cause célèbre*. On 17 July Roberts won the five-runner Arlington International Racecourse Stakes at Newbury on a three-year-old colt, owned by Sheikh Mohammed and trained by Henry Cecil, called Sabrehill. The 'incident' occurred fully three furlongs from home in the mile-and-a-quarter event when the 13–8 on favourite appeared to brush Bobzao in coming off the rails to make his challenge. Sabrehill drew away to win by an exceedingly comfortable four lengths. Bobzao's trainer Terry Mills (not jockey Richard Quinn) lodged an objection and the stewards, having called upon the advice of the 'stipe', William Nunneley, relegated Sabrehill to last; furthermore, finding Roberts guilty of intentional interference, they imposed on him a ban of ten days – the minimum punishment for such a crime.

242

Almost to a man the racing press was as astonished as it was outraged. The *Racing Post*'s senior race reporter George Ennor expressed his disgust in a piece captioned: 'A miscarriage of justice: a damning verdict on the Sabrehill affair'. Most observers were anxious to highlight the inconsistency of this decision with that taken in the instance of the St James's Palace Stakes at Royal Ascot, when Kingmambo not only barged his way to victory but kept the race. Roberts immediately set in motion an appeal, in which study of the head-on and side-on videos of the race (showing Quinn shifting the weight of his body to the left side of Bobzao to keep Sabrehill shut in) raised Roberts's expectations of success. However, after a two-hour hearing on 22 July the Jockey Club Disciplinary Committee (Anthony Mildmay-White, Sir John Cotterell and David Brotherton) failed to share his optimism.

ROBERTS: I was shocked at the outcome. I just couldn't sit back and take ten days. People commit murder on the track and still don't get ten days. I was surprised the stewards even called an inquiry in the first place. There was no barging or bumping; we brushed, that's all. Nobody goes out to interfere intentionally – you would have to be out of your head. What happened wasn't even an 'incident'. It was just slight contact. After we had gone a furlong there was no gallop, but there was no point panicking. I didn't want to pull back because people would have accused me of lacking confidence, so I moved in behind Pat on Port Lucaya. I was absolutely hacking and Bobzao was a neck or half a length down. I went for the gap and there was slight brushing for two strides, that's all. If it had happened on the turn nothing would have been said. The other horse was not affected and we won easily. It wasn't as if there was a barging match. Bobzao tried to keep me in, but wasn't going well enough to do so. How could they say that was worse than what Kingmambo did to Wharf at Ascot, where Wharf bounced off Kingmambo, and the stewards took no action? I won't deny we made contact but it's the sort of thing that happens all the time on the racetrack and was definitely not intentional interference. I knew exactly what I was doing and wouldn't choose to do anything differently; not one person in the weighing-room thought I'd lose the race.

I went to Portman Square confident that, at worst, the suspension would be reduced to four days for careless riding. Richard Quinn was very supportive and said that he never had the horse to win the race. We looked through the films – including some that weren't available at Newbury on the day – but the stewards felt I was boxed in on the fence and that, on purpose – those are the words they used – I forced my way out. I could not believe it. At the time I thought I got a fair hearing at Portman Square, sitting there and seeing everyone taking it all in, listening to our pleas and our case. But it must have gone in one side and come out the other side. To still call it intentional interference – call it careless if you like – was wrong. I'd like to be able to take it anywhere else in the world to see what they'd make of it. I'll have on my record something I don't think I deserve. It was very harsh; it will stick in the back of my mind for a very long time.

* * *

The ban meant Roberts missed all of the 'Glorious' Goodwood festival, in which Sheikh Mohammed had, as one would expect, several fancied runners (he won the Goodwood Cup and the Stewards' Cup). At least Roberts was able to commence his fifth 'holiday' of the season on a happy note: he won the King George VI and Queen Elizabeth Diamond Stakes for his employer on Opera House, and twenty-four hours later won a Group II race at Veliefendi, Istanbul, on Saeed Manana's Irish-trained Shrewd Idea. Roberts seized the opportunity to convert the Turkish trip into a much-needed restorative holiday far from the madding crowd.

The championship was beyond recall: Eddery was some forty to the good. So, too, was any hope of his contract being renewed for 1994 as his rollercoaster existence continued. In August he received a two-day suspension in consequence of Sheikh Mohammed's George Augustus being demoted from first to second in the Group I Aral Pokal at Gelsenkirchen; the luckless Sabrehill was beaten in the Group I Juddmonte International at York after looking an assured winner – Roberts, some said, hit the front too early (he had, however, been riding to orders); and he lost the ride to Barathea in the Prix du Moulin at the insistence of part-owner Gerald Leigh because 'he couldn't settle the horse'. In fact, by the time Wolfhound provided Roberts with a fifth Group I success of the season (and Gosden's first ever in Britain) in Haydock's Hazlewood Foods Sprint Cup on 4 September the 'secret' was secret no longer. Once Anthony Stroud had given him an apparent vote of confidence ('We are happy with him and he is doing an excellent job. We have backed him one hundred per cent and will continue to support him until the end of the year – Michael did only sign a one-year contract. Who knows what might happen after that') the cynics and hard-bitten pros knew they had been reading the smoke signals correctly. In the *Daily Mail* Colin Mackenzie surmised: 'I interpret this as a strong indication that Roberts will have to rediscover the delights of freelancing next year,' in a piece headed 'Roberts losing grip on Sheikh's job: renewed speculation linking Michael Kinane with lucrative Arab retainer increases pressure on the beleaguered champion jockey.' The *Telegraph*'s version – 'Speculation increases on rift between Roberts and Sheikh' – saw J. A. McGrath write: 'The knives are out for Michael Roberts who now seems certain to lose his job . . . informed insiders say he will not be reappointed at the end of the year. I am told by insiders that Roberts has generally underestimated the power of the trainers involved as a lobby in the Sheikh Mohammed organisation.'

As its fangs sank ever more firmly into the story the media refused point-blank to let go. Another jockey in contention for Roberts's job besides Kinane was a rejuvenated Frankie Dettori (once more the 'golden boy' now that the winners were flowing and a run-in with the police forgotten), and after the pair had run a dead heat in Doncaster's televised Scarbrough Stakes on 8 September the post-race interview inevitably turned to the Darley Stud riding arrangements for 1994. A visibly flustered Roberts could only prevaricate embarrassingly. If his lips were diplomatically sealed, those of various columnists in the *Sporting Life* were most certainly not. 'As Roberts has discovered to his cost he is dependent on rival trainers' opinions – and they are not always as helpful or as accurate as they should be' (Monty Court); 'Michael Roberts is, as far as I know, the same Michael Roberts that rode 206 winners last year . . . yet one could have been fooled into thinking otherwise. One of the Sheikh's trainers is reputedly less than keen, goodness knows why, to put him up. He was nominated Jockey of the Year by his fellow professionals, then there was a scandalous claim that the voting was rigged. He came here from South Africa, he's bright and talented and he's a great ambassador for the sport. So what is the problem?' (David Ashforth); 'Dignity in the face of difficulty . . . try telling a random bunch of betting shop punters that Roberts may not be up to it where a top job is concerned and hear them laugh. When Steve Cauthen beat Pat Eddery 197 to 195 a few years ago the papers were full of the battle every day. Both men admitted to near exhaustion. Last season Roberts surged past the 200 mark, scarcely turned a hair and received compliments best described as polite. If he wins the Arc for Sheikh Mohammed it will be his sixth Group I of the season. Will he quietly be asked to stay in a pivotal role? I don't know. Either way, he will have played a difficult hand with style and grace. Perhaps it's time we started thinking of him as a true champion' (Ian Carnaby).

Official confirmation of what everyone in racing unofficially knew already eventually surfaced at 5.30 p.m. on 21 September (just as Roberts was about to start his seventh ban of the season). He was out; Frankie Dettori was in – but only to ride the Gosden-trained horses. To Stroud fell the unenviable task of facing the press; the explanation went as follows: 'His contract will not be renewed for 1994 as part of a policy decision not to retain one specific jockey for all the Darley Stud Management's horses and trainers. Under the new arrangement where riding plans will be agreed by consultation between the individual trainers concerned and the company management it is hoped that our association with Michael will continue for many seasons to come. The decision is no reflection on Michael. We have had a retained jockey for the past three years and we now feel this is the best way forward. Sheikh Mohammed has given it a great deal of thought. The change has been made because of the size and geographical difficulties involved. Michael is an excellent man and has had a very successful time with us, winning five Group Is. He has been desperately unlucky to have had thirty days of suspension which is a big chunk out of the season. When Steve left quite suddenly Michael was very good to step into the breach. Obviously, whoever you are, everyone has views on riding plans. Jockeys are very emotive subjects but at the end of the day everyone is united in agreement.'

The 'explanation' had a distinctly hollow ring to it; and, needless to say, anyone with anything to say on the matter now accepted the opportunity.

STEVE CAUTHEN: The Sheikh's operation has got too many horses for one jockey to do the job properly. You are trying to ride the best out of 600 horses and at the same time keep all the trainers happy. Very often there would be four or five to choose from and each trainer thought they had the best horse for that particular race. Inevitably, that situation can lead to some conflict. It wouldn't matter who was in the job – Michael Roberts, Pat Eddery or Mick Kinane – it would still be very difficult. My job was to get on the best horses and give the right advice. But it's not easy keeping tabs on so many horses from so many different yards. Pat's job with Khalid Abdullah seems to work out much better because he has a smaller number of quality horses to choose from – it's the best job in the world and if I were offered a similar one to it I would come out of retirement and ride until I was sixty! The Sheikh's team have been trying to sort out what suits them best for some time, and this is probably the most workable solution. I feel sorry for Michael but I'm sure he'll land on his feet. After all, he didn't do too badly as a freelance, did he?

MICHAEL STOUTE: I have to agree with what Steve says. It's beyond any one jockey to keep tabs on so many horses. When you are dealing with a lot of backward horses, many of whom have not run as two-year-olds, how can a jockey be expected to get it right?.

LUCA CUMANI: It is just too many horses and too many trainers. And when the jockey gets on the wrong horse the press love it and give him a hard time. It is much better for each trainer to have his own jockey. It enables the jockey to get to know the horses better.

* * *

CLIVE BRITTAIN: I recognised Michael's talents earlier than most. He is a top-flight jockey. If anything, this is a bonus because I have a chance of claiming his services again. I just hope I have some good horses. This won't worry Michael. He is not sour about it, but he would have liked to have kept the job another year. He was just getting used to the different training styles of the Sheikh's trainers.

ALEC STEWART: Being retained jockey to Sheikh Mohammed is not an easy job because there are so many horses to choose from. I don't think that Michael ever really knew which horses to get on. He's a first-class rider and is a little down at the moment, but he'll come back. And he still did very well. It was a big disadvantage for Michael not being able to ride work on a large number of horses he was riding in public. At least when he was with me he was able to get to know the horses at home, and therefore had a much better idea about them.

GRAHAM ROCK: I still don't know why he lost the job. There was never any bad feeling to my knowledge, but the whispering started very early. I don't think you can blame the press; they flushed out a story, which is their job. A lot was made of Michael's choice of mounts in the Sandown trial. After Tenby came out we could have switched to True Hero, but we didn't want to mess people around. John Gosden had booked another jockey and it was early in the relationship. At the time it seemed best to leave things as they were rather than risk offence by changing horses.

There was no way Michael could ride work on even half

the horses and we often ended up choosing the ride which would cause least embarrassment and least offence to trainers. That is a lousy way to pick winners.

Press treatment of the news was almost wholly sympathetic towards Roberts – somewhat ironically in view of previous contributions from certain quarters that were hardly calculated to aid Roberts's cause.

COLIN MACKENZIE (*Daily Mail*): Only a week ago Sheikh Mohammed's racing manager Anthony Stroud denied that any agreement with Dettori had been made. Clearly this was not the case and it does their cause little good to be economical with the truth. It was patently unfair to Michael Roberts, whose confidence has become dented by ongoing rumours that his job was at risk, to keep him in the dark. It also misleads the betting public who are not able to determine which jockey bookings are significant and which are not.

DAVID ASHFORTH (*Sporting Life*): The Dettori–Roberts saga is an example of how not to deal with the press. For weeks there has been speculation that Roberts's contract would not be renewed and that Dettori would ride for John Gosden next season. But Gosden and Anthony Stroud reacted to what must have been a stream of enquiries by refusing to comment on the truth of the rumour and bemoaning the tedious speculation on the subject. When a rumour is true, you cannot make it go away by sidestepping it. If you want to encourage even more tedious enquiries, that is the way to go about it. How could this stonewalling be in anyone's interest? Why could Darley Stud Management not have answered enquiries by at least acknowledging that discussions were taking place and indicating when they expected to make a statement? Darley Stud Management seems to regard information as something dangerous, not safe to be let out. There is an element of fear in its relationship with the press.

JOHN OAKSEY (*Daily Telegraph*): Surely the volley of half-truths and contradictory denials from which Michael Roberts emerged with such dignity ought to sound the death knell of the single-owner contract. History does not relate whose brainwave it was in the first place to engage one jockey for all Sheikh Mohammed's 600-plus horses. But as Roberts's predecessor Steve Cauthen said generously: 'The job is far too big for one man to do properly.'

IAN CARNABY (*Sporting Life*): People have commented on the Michael Roberts affair in restrained fashion but he was actually treated in the shabbiest of ways and there is no escaping that fact. For a number of weeks Sheikh Mohammed's spokesmen played a dead bat to every question concerning the non-renewal of his contract, even when the racecourse was alive with rumour. Then, when Frankie Dettori was recruited, the hope was expressed that Roberts would 'still ride for us when possible'. Some hope. Personally, I'd love the South African to answer in fairly direct and succinct terms if approached to ride anything in maroon and white in 1994.

* * *

JOHN SEXTON (*Sporting Life*): Whether he likes it or not,
John Gosden is irrevocably cast in the role of the man who
scuppered Michael Roberts's retainer with Sheikh
Mohammed. Despite all his protestations of innocence, the
fact that he will be employing Frankie Dettori as stable
jockey next year automatically points the accusing finger.
The decision effectively took close to 100 of Sheikh
Mohammed's horses out of the equation for Roberts and if
that didn't cost him his contract I don't know what did.

John Gosden found himself perceived as the real villain of
the piece as far as the press were concerned. There had to
be a villain: John Harry Martin Gosden seemed to fit the
bill. Son of the noted Lewes trainer John 'Towser' Gosden,
his first racing memory was as a nine-year-old watching
his father's Aggressor toppling the public idol Petite Etoile
in the 1960 King George VI and Queen Elizabeth Stakes.
Gosden was still only sixteen when his father died, so there
was no question of him taking over the licence: indeed,
paternal advice had always concluded with: 'The one thing
you do not want to do is be a racehorse trainer.' Young
Gosden did try. He was bright. He took a degree in land
economy at Emmanuel College, Cambridge, and went out
to Venezuela to put it to good use. But he soon came under
the spell of the early morning workouts at the local racetrack.
In 1974 he returned to England and became an assistant to
Sir Noel Murless until the latter's retirement in 1976. Then
followed a year in Ireland with Vincent O'Brien, the glorious
season of The Minstrel, Alleged, Artaius, Try My Best –

Group I winners all. Quite an education already; and after spending 1978 in California with Tommy Doyle he felt sufficiently confident to stay there and strike out on his own.

Gosden was twenty-eight years old and his Santa Anita barn housed three horses: two with leg problems and one with 'the worst problem of all, no ability'. But his legacy, his brain and his network of superb contacts were going to prove a powerful combination. He soon tasted success in stakes races with ex-English animals such as Devon Ditty, Millingdale Lillie and Star Pastures, and in 1983 he collected his first Grade I races with Bates Motel, notably the Big 'Cap itself, the Santa Anita Handicap worth over half a million dollars. In November 1984 even these achievements were surpassed when Royal Heroine won the first running of the Breeders' Cup Mile at Hollywood Park. Gosden was now more than holding his own with such giants of the California scene as D. Wayne Lukas and Charlie 'Bald Eagle' Whittingham. Some even dared to suggest that he was the new Whittingham – a parallel not unhindered by his own thinning locks. Big money races continued to be plundered through other English émigrés like Alphabatim and Zoffany; in 1986 alone Gosden netted $4.7 million in stakes.

Here was someone begging to be head-hunted by the mushrooming, seemingly all-consuming, European racing empire of the Maktoum brothers presided over by Sheikh Mohammed. Horses, jockeys, studs, yards, trainers; all had a price and the Maktoums were willing to pay. In March 1988 the news broke that Sheikh Mohammed had purchased

Stanley House stables in Newmarket's Bury Road and that John Gosden was to be installed there to run the operation. The one-time home of Hyperion and countless other Classic winners in the colours of Lord Derby was a far cry from the Santa Anita backstretch; the lush turf of a windy heath vastly at odds with a dirt track on a hot, sticky Los Angeles morning. The necessary adjustment did not take long. The first Gosden winner arrived on the second day of the 1989 season: Intimidate, in Kempton's Quail Stakes. The rider was Michael Roberts.

The towering six feet four inches Gosden and the diminutive five feet one inch Roberts struck the eye as unlikely bedfellows, and as rumours of unrest grew the hyperactive and inquisitive collective mind of the media focused ever more sharply and concluded that this physical disparity must extend to a clash of personalities. There was unrest; the racing press were correct on that score; but it was not a case of Roberts and Gosden literally being at loggerheads. At fault was the very nature of the job Roberts was being asked to do. It was too tall an order from the very outset. Cauthen had begun to realise this and undoubtedly so had some members of Darley Stud Management. Riding arrangements were crying out for some kind of revision. Cauthen's unexpected departure, however, provoked a knee-jerk reaction. The retained jockey has gone; a new one must be appointed straight away. For once in his life Roberts, though the right man, was in the wrong place at the wrong time.

GOSDEN: It was not the way one would have liked to have

seen things done; the statement which announced the change in riding arrangements was certainly a belated one. It was unpleasant for everyone involved and some of the comments in the press did not amuse me. I seemed to be getting the gun pointed at me and I was fed up with people suggesting I was behind Michael's departure. I'm a big boy and I'll carry the can but I'm not malicious. Ideally, it would have been nice to wait until the end of the year but there had been an approach to Dettori from Daniel Wildenstein and we couldn't afford to sit and wait. It was logical that I would want a young jockey on the way up and with whom I could build a relationship. Frankie is a great, up-and-coming rider, whom I've known for a long time since he came out to California. He has got that star quality which we need in the game. I've always admired him and I think he has a great attitude to life. As stable jockey he can get to know the horses, the yard and the staff.

This is no reflection on Michael. I never had a cross word with Michael and am never likely to. There was no animosity between Michael and me. I thought what Steve had to say made so much sense and it put the finger on the whole problem. How can one jockey be expected to sort his way through 600 horses with twenty-odd trainers? Logistically, it's impossible. As Steve said, you often find yourself at the wrong course, let alone on the wrong horse. You can't have one rider for so many horses. That will never occur again. Steve found it frustrating and was often on the wrong one – and he was the greatest international jockey we had seen in twenty years. In the end even he found it impractical and unworkable.

I never regarded Michael as having lost his job. He signed to ride for one season and that's precisely what happened. The prospect of two years was never definite. The contract was honoured on both sides; some people have tended to forget that. The truth is, Michael's job doesn't exist any more. If anything, the job went, not Michael; it was the job that didn't fit, not Michael's face. Steve was finding it that way and I'm sure that contributed to his decision. He got on the wrong horse more than once; so did Pat Eddery in the Derby! Unfortunately, if the press see an opportunity they will take it. The nasty stuff sells newspapers.

Those three races in the spring won by horses from this yard which Michael chose not to ride started some rumblings and in the end created some tension. But Michael made the right decision on each occasion. I did want him to ride True Hero at Sandown, but Barry Hills said Majority was working exceptionally well. I was a little disappointed because the race Majority had won at Doncaster was a modest maiden, as they often are at that early stage of the season. Barathea was definitely the correct choice for the Craven. He was a far better horse than Emperor Jones and the press were not totally fair to Michael over that. As for Marillette in the Musidora: she was a difficult filly and only Pat Eddery ever won on her. Iviza looked to have more potential and there was nothing wrong in Michael choosing that big strapping filly with a possible future over one who had, after all, run nine times as a two-year-old. Again, the press made a great song and dance about it, which was unfair.

Things were not going to be easy for Michael and me if we did try to develop a trainer–jockey relationship under the revised conditions in 1994 after the events of 1993. I wanted a young rider like Dettori and once he became available that became the issue – and the situation gradually became more difficult as the year went on. I don't think Michael had any chance of retaining his championship from the beginning. A jockey will not ride a lot of winners in this job. There are so many races that Darley Stud horses can't run in: claimers; sellers; 0–70 handicaps. They are all ruled out, virtually. And a jockey loses the two-year-olds: ours have mouthwatering pedigrees but they will be late developers and only lightly raced as juveniles.

Since he has been over here Michael has proved just how good a jockey he is. He is the best tactician around; he really thinks a race out and reads a race before he even comes into the paddock. I tend to walk the course before racing and he's the only jockey I find out there looking for the best ground. Some jockeys ride totally by instinct; Michael's got instinct but he thinks into the bargain – and that can't be said for everyone.

I work pretty well every horse at once, quickly, and they're gone, done. This was not conducive to making more use of Michael on the gallops; he might only ride a couple of horses a week. This made it difficult to build a relationship. He could have been a little more involved. I remain surprised that he never ever came to the yard and Graham Rock only visited the office once; that always seemed a little bit strange. Steve would come to breakfast after work: certainly, he had a different pace of life, but I was surprised not to see more of Michael in the yard. But Michael was always chasing rides. He was always busy.

He'd hop off one horse after working, jump into a car ready to hop on another somewhere else. He and Graham Rock were dealing with too many trainers, perhaps. They were doing their utmost to please everyone and that's impossible. But, and I stress this, there was never any tension between Michael and me.

STROUD: I spoke to Michael a month before the announcement, i.e. August, and said we'd not be retaining him in 1994. We could have dropped him after Ascot, which might have been cleaner, but Sheikh Mohammed is a very loyal man and the contract was for a year. Yes, you could say it might have been better to have announced something earlier in order to quell the rumours; on the other hand, we'd been pestered so much during the negotiations with Michael Kinane at the start of the year that it seemed preferable to get it all sorted out before saying anything.

We had talked about the size of the job and the problems it might cause. Until you try, though, you don't know the logistics. We always encouraged Steve not to ride on Mondays and to take a day off. The majority of our horses are in Newmarket, so the jockey can get round, and by reducing the job to just England we did feel it was possible. Michael was champion jockey, a top-class athlete and a top-class person, so there was no reason to believe he would not fit the bill.

I felt incredibly sorry for Michael. The press have got a job to do: sell newspapers. Often in racing the press gets tangled up in issues and this was one of them – the whip rule is another example. They just would not let go. Here was a man whose confidence was low and they didn't help the situation. A lot of people forget that Michael was hired on a one-year contract and wasn't necessarily going to carry on. It's not as if this was a longstanding association that had broken up, such as that of Dick Hern and Joe Mercer back in 1976, for example. We wanted to finish the year before making any announcement, but when Wildenstein became keen on Dettori we had to move.

I couldn't be more full of praise for Michael's conduct through all this. He'd also had to endure the Sabrehill business, which was totally out of order. Certainly, to be suspended for a month out of a seven-month season was not helpful, but, if anything, these suspensions had the reverse effect on renewing his contract. Eventually it became obvious the nature of the job had to be altered – and a talent like Dettori had become available. There also seemed a lack of chemistry between Michael and John Gosden. Michael acted like a true gentleman throughout the year; and no one else could have won the Oaks on Intrepidity.

ROBERTS: My big reservation about the job is exactly what came to happen: my biggest fear and worry was that I'd built up such a good relationship with a lot of trainers, I'd take this job, and it would end after a year with me having to go back to square one and build up all those relationships over again. But it was the best offer I've ever had in my life – and the easiest decision to make. There wasn't a better job anywhere; the calibre of the Sheikh's horses. It was a great honour. As it turned out it was right for me to accept the job because my main trainers didn't do very well in

1993. Clive only had thirty-four winners and Alec only had eleven. I had the same kind of season that Steve had been having, except I probably won more Group Is. I had a great year and rode some fantastic horses. That's why us jockeys are in this game. In the end it's quality that counts.

I have to agree with Steve about the job being a tough one. It is a very big job and there are so many horses to choose from that it's sometimes like being a newspaper tipster trying to pick the right one. I didn't find it easy even to get to each stable to ride all the horses work. Competition among the trainers was very high. You're often trying to please one person while not upsetting another. I'd have to ride one for John Gosden and then rush over to Luca Cumani's to sit on one of his. Most people were very helpful but you need at least a hundred and ten per cent assistance from everyone involved to get it right all the time.

To be honest, I found it very strange that I couldn't ride more work for some trainers. Some were marvellous and others weren't that marvellous, especially on riding work. It's very important, I feel, when you've got a stable jockey to use him as much as possible – which I believe was lacking from the whole operation a bit. Some trainers were more helpful and passed on information. Otherwise Graham and I were left to work from the form book and try to weigh things up, and with lots of runners you're trying not to upset people. I believe I could have put more work into the job: they could have made more use of me, which some of the trainers didn't. Why, I can't answer. Messrs Cecil, Cumani and Stoute would put me on the important horses in the morning whereas with the Gosden set-up I rarely had the opportunity of riding work on the horses I'd be riding in the near future: I wouldn't be riding the horses in races I'd be riding in work. I could have ridden two or three lots as well. To me it's absolutely useless to ride a horse in work that is two months off racing, or is going to run in three weeks' time and might need the outing. I feel you must ride the horses you're going to ride in races in the near future; get to know them and find out how fit they are. This is more important to me because you can then ride a race according to your judgement of morning exercise. I asked John if I was needed for more work and I also mentioned it to Anthony Stroud once or twice – and I assume he had a word with John. Perhaps he thought I was too light to put in with a group of lads to work, but I just don't know. I'm not saying John was doing anything wrong; I'm just talking about my relationships with other trainers. I feel I could have put more into it if I'd been asked. And it would have made my life easier concerning choice of mounts.

I would have loved a closer relationship with John because it would have given me a base to work from. But, as I was retained by Darley Stud Management, I was trying to please everyone. I was never asked in for a cup of coffee after work, for instance, which the other trainers frequently offered, so their horses could be discussed. I was brought up to wait to be asked. I never even visited the yard. I'd love to have gone there but I was never asked. There was never much communication. Whatever I was reading in the paper came as a shock to me because I heard nothing about it beforehand. I didn't – and don't – listen to gossip. I'm an up-front person, I think. As I said to Anthony before I took the job, if anything goes wrong, if there are any complaints, talk to me.

John was always very nice to me. The only occasion we discussed a horse that was beaten was True Hero, at Ripon, at the beginning of the season. I went too soon and Beneficial beat me. I told John I should have won and initially he said nothing. Then, when we flew back together, he said yes, perhaps if I'd waited longer I might have won. That's the only time we really actually talked about horses. I'm afraid to say that is where everything stemmed from: a lack of communication. I've had some good jobs here and back home and communication is the great factor in getting things going, developing a good working relationship. We didn't have any bad words because we didn't have any words. The only time we spoke about the job was over a cup of coffee at my place after I'd lost the job. I said obviously I must have been doing something wrong, something you didn't like about the way I rode. John replied that he would have preferred to see me give a horse a bit more rein because he believed horses were a bit too keen with me. And so I said: 'Maybe. It's a shame we couldn't have spoken earlier; we could have done something about it.'

A month before the announcement Anthony said that they didn't know what was going to happen for 1994; so deep down I was still very hopeful something could be sorted out. Maybe John Gosden would have his jockey and I'd ride the other horses. That's why I could never say anything to the press because I didn't know. I'd have been happy with that kind of modified arrangement. Then a week before the press release came I was asked to go up to the office at

Dalham Hall and that was that. I knew something was wrong, of course, from all the press coverage, but nothing was being said to me directly: communications again.

I don't regret the year and I'm proud of it. I don't think anyone can point the finger at me. My only regret is that I wish they'd given me another year: it's a matter of time before they have three or four champions. And I'd have loved to have had the chance to work from a base. I'm sure they weren't very happy with me having so many suspensions. It could have been one of the reasons I lost the job, I don't know. The suspensions did affect my morale. I'd come back, everything would be running smoothly, the winners would start flowing and, bang, I'd get suspended.

I did think it would be relatively easy to remain champion jockey. I had a six-pound advantage over Steve and I was not required to go to France. But it proved that you can't be a champion jockey if you don't have two-year-olds to ride, especially the early ones. If you analyse it you'll see my problems with trying to be champion again came right at the start – before all the suspensions really had an effect. The two hundred and the championship the season before was a challenge, but on the whole I'd rather have quality than quantity – and 1993 was a quality year.

Basically, I'd like to draw a line through 1993 and just remember the good things. But, I have to say, given the same opportunity again, I would jump at it because of my respect for the bloodstock. I certainly hope that John Gosden gives me the opportunity to ride further winners for him.

CUMANI: In a high-profile organisation like Sheikh

Mohammed's there will always be pressure on the jockey – from outside and from within the organisation itself. The job was unmanageable inasmuch as it does a jockey no good when Sheikh Mohammed has two or three horses in a race and the jockey happens to wind up on the wrong one. Often it won't have been his fault; he may have been on the right one to begin with but horses are horses and they don't always perform on the day. Picking the wrong one is no reflection on the jockey. However, the media and the racing public tend to leap on these instances. If this factor was eliminated from the job – by some miracle – it would be quite manageable.

The press have their job to do. They have to make headlines and we have to live with that. Steve Cauthen was a guy, outwardly at least, who seemed to handle pressure well, yet he cracked in the end. It is a job that can crack anybody. The only advice if you work for Sheikh Mohammed is: Don't read the papers: it is harmful!

Michael's great strength as a jockey is his desire to win, which is reflected in the fact that horses do run for him. He transmits his will to win to the horse. He was an extremely valuable man to have on the gallops, although work in the morning was not always plain sailing because there were so many horses he had to try and ride; but he fitted in as many as was humanly possible. His value on the gallops derived not only from his jockeyship but also from the fact that he is a man who thinks about what he says and therefore makes intelligent comments, not just off-the-cuff ones. I only put him on the best horses, the ones he needed to know; there was no point putting him on the run-of-the-mill animals.

Barathea, of course, was the best he rode for me. Nine years out of ten he'd have won the 2,000 Guineas but unfortunately he came up against an exceptional horse in Zafonic. After that Barathea was derailed slightly as he had to fly the flag in the Derby: if Sheikh Mohammed had had a genuine mile-and-a-half horse I doubt if Barathea would have contested the race – there were always grave reservations about his stamina. Mr Leigh took the flak for Michael losing the ride in the Prix du Moulin, but it was not entirely down to him; it was a management decision – although it was nothing to do with me.

I do think it will be better for everyone if trainers have their own jockeys instead of owners having their own jockeys. The jockey feels more involved with the whole stable and the relationship is far better. It's much easier for a trainer–jockey combination to work successfully; just look at how successful Steve Cauthen was when he just rode for Henry Cecil; or Walter Swinburn and Michael Stoute; myself and Ray Cochrane or Frankie Dettori. There are more top-class freelances at present, Michael included, and he'll quite possibly come in for some rides from me – though not necessarily on Sheikh Mohammed horses. I shall be trying to fit the horse to the jockey.

STOUTE: I was happy with Michael's appointment because I'd always been an admirer of his. He is an exceptionally skilful rider with a keen tactical brain. I can remember, for example, many races at the smaller tracks when we'd have particular tactics worked out for a race and he'd be the one to mess it up for us. He's a great one for always varying his tactics; and it's the sign of a top-class jockey to win races at the smaller tracks that you're not supposed to win. He thinks about the race beforehand and always gives the horse a ride. Full commitment is always there.

He didn't ride a lot of work here. There would often be time-clashes but I'd call him in for the important horses. He was always an excellent contributor; he would work a horse and get off and be totally confident in what he wanted to tell you.

On reflection, it's possible the retainer as it stood was too tall an order. But, to be fair, no one was saying anything about it when the approach was originally made. Steve himself never really uttered it until later on when Michael was in difficulty. It was a job any jockey would tend to grab with both hands. If Michael had gone and won the Guineas or the Derby it would have changed the issue, and the entire complexion of the season – and it could so easily have happened.

It's very easy to pick the wrong horses to ride in the spring: the jockey comes back and he doesn't know them. How fit is horse A as against horse B? The press were only stating a fact when it turned out he had chosen the wrong horse, so you can't blame them for that. It was the same with Walter Swinburn here: it's easily done, even within one stable. This sort of thing does get to jockeys, though. Michael missed Opera House in the Eclipse, but if I'd had to choose I know I'd have chosen Barathea. We were very frightened of him and were hoping he'd go to Paris for the Grand Prix instead of the Eclipse.

I have nothing but the highest respect for Michael and

I'll certainly be prepared to offer him rides in the future.

HENRY CECIL: Michael had ridden for me before when Steve Cauthen was sidelined after a very bad fall, and struck up a very good association with Indian Skimmer, Salse and High Estate. He is motivated, in my opinion, by a burning ambition and yet off the track he is a real gentleman and very good company. He was a very good work rider in the mornings when his judgement was of considerable value. I will always regard Michael as a friend.

So, Roberts and Gosden, apparently such kindred spirits, were in reality divided by some intangible albeit yawning chasm which ultimately proved unbridgeable. All manner of tangled webs have a habit of emerging from outwardly the most straightforward of relationships. When all is done and dusted, success and failure, triumph and disaster are not strangers but near neighbours, an uneasy juxtaposition with which fate tends to make much sport. The trick, as Kipling observed, is to treat these twin impostors just the same. In that Roberts succeeded admirably. Had Dettori been available in February, it is safe to assert he and not Roberts would have received the call; but Dettori was not an option and the chalice – golden to the touch yet poisonous of content – passed to another. Gosden had to wait eight months to get his man: Roberts had to endure eight months living with the aching suspicion that he – the reigning champion jockey, who had won his title through becoming only the fifth rider to achieve a double hundred – was merely a stop-gap. For any champion jockey to be placed in this insulting predicament is at best bizarre and at worst unforgivable. Roberts could hardly have achieved more in the name of Darley Stud Management: for a quality-oriented organisation, success in five Group I races should have spoken volumes. But they made not a scrap of difference. Roberts was surplus to requirements by mid-April or mid-June – depending upon which source you prefer to accept – when the season was barely at the halfway point. However adroitly the members of Darley Stud Management may attempt to convey the opposite, they, and only they, have reason to reproach themselves. Michael Roberts is far from being Mother Teresa but he came closer to being a saint than anybody else in this sorry affair: more sinned against than sinning.

The 'good things' of 1993 referred to by Roberts came in several forms. He may have finished only seventh in the list (his lowest placing since 1987), having ridden 114 winners from 715 domestic rides (respectively down ninety-two and 353 on his championship season), but they still earned slightly more prize money (£1,326,907) than 1992's 206 winners. John Gosden provided him with twenty-eight winners from 117 mounts – while saddling sixty-nine winners for Sheikh Mohammed altogether. In 1992 Gosden had given Cauthen thirty-seven winners from 152 domestic rides – virtually an identical percentage of wins to rides as his successor. As far as Darley Stud's three other Newmarket trainers were concerned, Roberts won nine (from fifty) for Michael Stoute, seven (from thirty-six) for Henry Cecil and five (from twenty-five) for Luca Cumani. All told, Roberts won fifty-seven domestic races for Darley Stud; Sheikh

Mohammed, as a matter of interest, won 143 in his own right. Roberts also won six abroad: the Prix Dollar (Group II) at Longchamp on the Gosden-trained Knifebox; the Irish 2,000 Guineas (Group I) at the Curragh on Barathea, and the Premio Sirmione at San Siro on Inner City, both for Cumani; the Tattersalls Gold Cup (Group II) on George Augustus and the Trusted Partner Matron Stakes (Group III), both at the Curragh, for John Oxx; and the Bosphorus Trophy (Group II) on Shrewd Idea for Michael Kauntze at Istanbul's Veliefendi. The number of Roberts's juvenile winners had been halved, from forty-four to just twenty. In 1992 no jockey partnered more two-year-old winners than he; in 1993 fifteen jockeys rode a greater number. Such was one of the ramifications of the Darley Stud retainer. Another was the number of trainers for whom he had ridden a winner, which dropped dramatically from fifty-six to thirty-eight. Brittain yielded seven victories from ninety-one opportunities and Stewart – in what was a disastrous season for him – none whatsoever. One piece of history, however, did come Roberts's way. On 11 June he became the third jockey to ride a winner at three different British meetings on the same day: Alinova (2.10 at York); Learmont (5.30 at Sandown); and Contract Court (7.35 at Goodwood).

The more obvious bright spots of 1993 were the quality horses Roberts rode to win quality races throughout Europe. He collected seventeen Pattern races from England, Ireland, France and Turkey, all bar Shambo's Ormonde Stakes on behalf of Darley Stud. Steve Cauthen had won five Group Is for Darley Stud in 1992, a total his successor equalled via Barathea (Irish 2,000 Guineas), Opera House

(Coronation Cup and King George VI and Queen Elizabeth Diamond Stakes), Intrepidity (Oaks) and Wolfhound (Hazlewood Foods Sprint Cup).

ROBERTS: Barathea was still a big baby at the start of the year but I thought he was going to be something really nice. I rated him very highly. He was a little disappointing in the Craven but he needed the race; he was a big, burly horse. He came on a lot for that race but unfortunately he came up against Zafonic in the Guineas. Suddenly I saw this big head cruising up to my girths; I was going pretty well and I thought I'd give him a race but Zafonic had so much speed. Take him out of the race and I'd have been a good three-length winner. Zafonic must have been a freak: it was a decent field and his time beat the track record that had stood since 1948. I was over the moon at winning the Irish Guineas on him, but I don't think it was his true running. The ground was quite holding and when he hit the front he wasn't sure of himself; he edged left until Lester came at us on Fatherland and you could feel him then begin to exert himself, stick his head out and go and win. I was surprised to be punished for careless riding as Fatherland had moved in to the right. I did come off a straight line in the last twenty-odd metres of the race, but it was all over and you can't fiddle around changing whip hands at that point – it might unbalance the horse. His best Classic form was with Zafonic at Newmarket. After he finished his preparations for the Derby I was getting excited. He had begun to relax and really seemed to have come to himself. I was sure he'd get a mile and a quarter all right but the full mile and a half

271

was another matter. In the race we were upsides the winner – Commander In Chief – the whole way to the straight but then just didn't get home. So I thought a mile and a quarter at Sandown in the Eclipse would be perfect for him: give him a breather on the bend and he'll outsprint the older horses on the fast ground. If there had been even a shower of rain I'd have switched to Opera House, but on the ground I just thought Barathea's speed would be too much for Opera House over a mile and a quarter. They took me off Barathea for the Prix du Moulin, they said, because I hadn't settled him at Epsom and Sandown. He was a big, sixteen-one, keen type of horse and maybe I didn't settle him as well as I should in the Eclipse. I rode him again to be second in the Queen Elizabeth II Stakes but he didn't progress the way I thought he would.

Intrepidity gave me one of the hardest races of my life in the Oaks but she must have had so much class to win without really coming round the track. I love Epsom, because if you get a horse that acts it scoots round; but if you don't it's a nightmare – and it so nearly was in the Oaks. The word was spread around that they wanted Lester to ride Marillette, which upset me a little bit because that only left Iviza and she was the third string: everyone assumed Thierry Jarnet would ride the French filly. So I told Anthony that if Lester rode Marillette I wanted to ride Intrepidity; Sheikh Mohammed himself rang me to say he wanted me to ride her in the end. The first time I sat on her was in the paddock and her lad said to me: 'She likes sleeping.' Come late, were my instructions. Crossing the road after one and a half furlongs or so she was squeezed –

by Iviza of all horses – got tightened up and touched the heels of the horse in front, and nearly threw me out of the saddle and over her head. At the top of the hill she wouldn't go and when I looked up I realised they were all on the bridle except me. I had been pushing all the time and I gave her two cracks before we reached Tattenham Corner. She started to come good down the hill and I became confident once we crossed the road at the head of the straight. I knew we'd pick them up because I thought they'd gone too fast. If you'd asked me any time bar the last two furlongs if I'd like to get off and ride something else I'd have said yes. But it was only her fourth race and she was trained in France on flat, perfect ground: this was an experience for her. I'd seen the tapes of her French races and Thierry Jarnet had exactly the same problems with her. In the Irish Oaks she felt fresh beforehand but she never travelled in the race itself. I heard rumours that André Fabre wasn't happy taking her there; he wanted to save her for the autumn and the Arc.

When I first rode work on Opera House he worked lovely, but I never thought he would end up the best older colt in Europe. When he got beat in the Ganay I was delighted with his run because the ground was terrible and he lost by only a short neck. I was always very confident in the Coronation Cup. Had we been beat we'd have been very unlucky, because we were taken so wide by User Friendly in the straight. But he loved a fight and I knew we'd get there. One drop of rain and I'd have chosen him in the Eclipse; but he lacked instant acceleration. He was a battler; a tough, genuine horse. In the King George, I looked across at the six-furlong marker and everything was virtually off the bridle and yet I was travelling really good. When I released him up the straight no one was going to beat me because he was so tough. I knew I had Commander In Chief beaten as early as Swinley Bottom, and it was just a question of hanging on to Opera House until the two-furlong pole. I was always very optimistic after he'd done a marvellous piece of work ten days before the race.

We wanted a bit more give in the ground for the Irish Champion Stakes, and there was some criticism from Ted Walsh, the Irish television commentator, who said that I'd only made a half-hearted effort to win because I was thinking about the Arc three weeks later. We thought he'd win the race, but he'd done very little work since the King George and he preferred some cut in the ground; there was no point in being hard on him. We just cantered for the first five furlongs and when I kicked him in the belly on the turn he quickened nicely. Willie loomed up on my outside on Muhtarram, so I showed Opera House the whip, but he would not have won however many smacks I'd given him. Why give him an extra smack and risk souring him for the next race? Everyone wants to win these Group I races: you don't just sit there and go round for fun. I think people also underestimated the winner, who was a speed horse; Opera House was a mile-and-a-half horse and this was a mile and a quarter. Then in the Arc itself the ground went the other way and came up too heavy. I was going exceptionally easy into the straight and thought the race was in the bag. But on that ground he only lengthened, whereas on a better surface he could actually quicken; he would usually find two lengths inside the final furlong. The ground definitely beat me. But he gave me a great ride and we were only beaten a neck and half a length by Urban Sea and White Muzzle. Opera House was definitely the best of his sex that I rode for the Sheikh.

Wolfhound was one of the horses I was really looking forward to riding. He had a great first run at Sandown to only lose the Temple Stakes by a head when he obviously needed a race. I thought he'd win the King's Stand at Royal Ascot, but the five furlongs was proving too short for him and he was second again. Then he ran another fine race to be second to Inchinor over seven furlongs at Newbury in August before giving me a fantastic ride in the Group I race at Haydock over six furlongs; he picked up really smartly to go and collect Lochsong, who could motor.

Sabrehill was the biggest disappointment of the year – getting beat on him at York in the International. At the beginning of the year Henry put me up on Sabrehill one morning and told me he could be Sheikh Mohammed's best horse; one who should have been in the Derby but for injuries. He was still big, but as he got fitter and fitter he once or twice put in some brilliant pieces of work. Then, just before he ran at Newmarket, he did a sluggish bit of work, so I rode Lacotte, the favourite. This was a mistake because I knew both horses well. Sabrehill improved a stone after that first run and came on again after the infamous race at Newbury. At York, Henry said in the paddock to start making my way home from the three pole. This was unusual for him, to give such precise instructions, but if I'm given orders I try to carry them out. I tracked White

Muzzle when he kicked after the slow start because he was a mile-and-a-half horse. Unfortunately he didn't give me the lead as long as I wanted or expected. Sabrehill's acceleration was breathtaking, and to be caught after that really gutted me because if I'd left him at the back for another half furlong or so I think he'd have won on the bridle. I went too soon on him, that's the long and the short of it. When a horse lengthens he will keep going, but when a horse quickens like that it doesn't last so long. With my experience, had he not been one of the Sheikh's horses, I'd have ditched the orders and hung on to him much longer. But he was lame soon afterwards and never ran again. He had just the three races – two of them pretty eventful ones for me. It's always easy to talk after the event, but I feel Sabrehill could have been one of the very best horses I rode for the Sheikh.

Epilogue 1994

In spite of what all the 'knockers' may have said to the contrary in the course of a traumatic 1993, Roberts had nothing left to prove, as a jockey or a man, when the 1994 Turf season got underway at Doncaster in March. The resumption of freelancing did not precipitate an instant shower of spring winners: instead, they came at a trickle as his patrons, particularly Clive Brittain (with whom, in fact, Roberts does now have a formal arrangement), were slow to strike form. But, adhering to that trusty dictum 'an ounce of loyalty is worth a pound of cleverness', Roberts got on with the job and provided irrefutable evidence that if the horse was good enough so was he.

Our story turns full circle and ends almost where it began: an assignation with Shambo and an appointment at Chester. Mrs Maureen Brittain's seven-year-old bay horse had been ridden by a veritable who's who of top jockeys – Messrs Piggott, Eddery, Carson, Swinburn, Dettori, Reid, and, on one occasion, even Felix Coetzee – but not one of them could win a race on him. Each one of his seven victories had been gained with the assistance of Michael Roberts. The first, in July 1990, was at Chester, and on 5 May 1994 Shambo was attempting to win the Group III Ormonde

Stakes for the second consecutive year. The 'selection boxes' in the trade papers stated that not one of the country's nineteen leading tipsters thought Shambo stood an earthly. From the outset, Roberts had to push and shove his four-legged friend around the Roodee for all he was worth, but straightening up for the last time they ranged alongside Shrewd Idea and League Leader in a three-pronged drive for the line. Roberts put Shambo's nose in front for the very first time right on the button.

Two days later, southern racegoers witnessed an action replay. Down at Lingfield Park, Roberts demonstrated precisely the same green-fingered touch with Mr David Abell's Branston Abby. The five-year-old mare is another seasoned campaigner of considerable ability; twelve victories in thirty-six races say as much. But she possesses a mind of her own and can become a flighty madam, prone to an excess of nervous energy when a race is in prospect; on one occasion she carted a prominent rider to the start. And yet, when Roberts is aboard she excels herself. Working his silver-tongued magic, he only has to whisper a few sweet nothings in her ear and she becomes putty in his hands. Six wins and two seconds is the outcome of their eleven pairings. However, none of those successes was achieved over the seven furlongs distance of the Maxims Club Chartwell Fillies Stakes (Listed). Adding a further complication is the fact that Branston Abby needs to be dropped out and covered up for a very late challenge, not a simple task from an outside draw in a field of just eight runners. The consummate ease with which Roberts accomplishes the exercise belies its difficulty. Branston Abby gets up to win by a head. By any standard, it is as intoxicating a brew of horsemanship and jockeyship as one is likely to imbibe anywhere during 1994.

How much longer will 'Muis the Ace' continue to hide trump cards up his sleeve and play them at will? 'I don't think I'll be around as long as Lester. I want to finish before my nerve and judgement go. I'd like to have a shot at training when I pack up, but I shall probably end up as a farmer – that's where my heart is.' In the meantime? A second jockeys' title would be welcome: 'Just to prove the first wasn't a flash in the pan.' Winning the July and the Arc also appeals: 'But the big one is to win the Derby. It's the race everybody talks about and remembers twenty years later.'

Whether or not these ambitions are realised and however long he continues to race ride, one suspects the singular race riding pleasure Roberts will carry to the grave will be the same exhilaration he was smitten with as he used to ride bareback on his grandfather's farm during the school holidays. 'Just to get on a horse and go flat out: the faster I went the more I enjoyed it and I always get the same thrill; feeling the horse accelerate away and the wind blowing in my face.'

APPENDIX I: Number of Winners

South Africa

1968–69:	0		
1969–70:	17		
1970–71:	59		
1971–72:	74		
1972–73:	121*		
1973–74:	129*		
1974–75:	148*		
1975–76:	127*		
1976–77:	132*		
1977–78:	95	*UK*	
1978–79:	145*		
1979–80:	186*	1978:	25
1980–81:	168*		
1981–82:	203*		
1982–83:	162*	*Rest of World*	
1983–84:	160*		
1984–85:	141		
1985–86:	79		MAURITIUS: 6
1986–87:	25	1986: 42	JAPAN: 1
1987–88:	33	1987: 74	TURKEY: 1

1988–89:	46	1988:	121	EUROPE:	49
1989–90:	31	1989:	107		
1990–91:	20	1990:	128		
1991–92:	32	1991:	118		
1992–93:	24	1992:	206*		
1993–94:	18	1993:	114		
		1994;	81		
TOTAL:	2,375	TOTAL:	1,016	TOTAL:	57

GRAND TOTAL (up to 15 November 1994): 3,448
* = Champion

APPENDIX II: Principal Races Won in Southern Africa

1. South Africa

Cape Guineas: 1972 Sentinel; 1975 Gatecrasher; 1979 Bold
   Tropic; 1984 Turncoat; 1986 Sea Warrior; 1991 Star
   Effort
Cape Fillies Guineas: 1977 Festive Season; 1991 Star Effort
Cape Derby: 1979 Bold Tropic; 1985 Impressive Style; 1994
   Comareen
Natal Guineas: 1972 Cast Away; 1976 Michaelmas; 1982
   Lucky Abbot; 1983 Turncoat
Natal Derby: 1974 Majestic Crown; 1975 Prince Desire;
   1979 Dunmore
Natal Oaks: 1977 Gun Mettle; 1982 Liberty Silk; 1983
   Spring Wonder
Benoni Guineas: 1976 Michaelmas
South African Guineas: 1972 Sentinel; 1973 Sabre; 1981
   Heracles; 1983 Rain Forest
South African Fillies Guineas: 1983 Grey Sun
South African Derby: 1980 Smuggler's Den
South African Oaks: 1984 Novenna
South African St Leger: 1979 Dunmore
Eastern Province Derby: 1976 Gay Pretender

283

Mainstay 1800: 1984 Turncoat

Metropolitan Stakes: 1975 Sledgehammer

Holiday Inns/Sun International: 1975 Majestic Crown; 1984
   Spanish Pool

Hawaii Stakes: 1984 Bodrum

Queen's Plate: 1975 Sledgehammer; 1983 Wolf Power;
   1984 Spanish Pool

Somerset Plate: 1976 Sledgehammer; 1977 Macheath

Gold Cup: 1971 Rainstorm; 1977 Don The Stripe

Gold Vase: 1980 French Mustard; 1982 Hawkins

Clairwood Champion/Schweppes Challenge: 1972 and 1973
   Sentinel; 1975 Sledgehammer; 1982 Wolf Power; 1984
   Spanish Pool

Greyville Champion Stakes: 1984 Spanish Pool; 1985
   Bodrum

National/Computaform Sprint: 1973 Justine; 1977 Row To
   Rio; 1986 Honey Bear

Cape of Good Hope Nursery Stakes: 1981 Craftsman

Allan Robertson Fillies Championship: 1975 Rebellious;
   1976 Shelter; 1981 Breyani

Woolavington Cup: 1973 Sentinel; 1976 Sledgehammer

Administrators Champion Juvenile Stakes: 1984 Be Noble

Tibouchina Stakes: 1981 and 1982 Just McKenna; 1984
   Flying Rosie

Clairwood Winter Handicap: 1979 Sunshine Man

South African Invitation Stakes: 1979 L'Attaque; 1987
   Priceless Asset

Drill Hall Stakes: 1973 Sentinel; 1975 Sledgehammer; 1979
   Bold Tropic

Gilbey Stakes: 1979 Row To Rio; 1981 Scarlet Lady

Concord Stakes: 1973 Sentinel; 1983, 1984 and 1985 Ted's
   Ambition
Frank Lambert Stakes: 1980 Row To Rio; 1981 Just
   McKenna
Transvaal Champion Stakes: 1973 Sentinel; 1974
   Sledgehammer; 1983 Spanish Pool; 1985 Bodrum
Bull Brand Jockeys International: 1973 Sledgehammer
Smirnoff Plate: 1972 Glenever
Cape Merchants: 1977 Free Enterprise; 1978 Macheath
Durban Merchants: 1979 Calvados; 1983 and 1984 Ted's
   Ambition
Rupert Ellis Brown: 1974 Sledgehammer; 1980 Destroyer;
   1983 Swift Call; 1985 King Kaul
Chairman's Stakes: 1984 Ted's Ambition
South African Fillies Sprint: 1973 and 1974 Justine
Natalia Stakes: 1976 Twing; 1979 Veraland; 1980 Gay
   Mam'selle
Keith Hepburn Champion Stakes: 1973 Sentinel; 1976
   Tudor Blue
Dick King Stakes: 1973 Sabre; 1977 Noble Kingdom
John Skeaping Trophy: 1981 Zamit
Breeders Challenge Stakes: 1977 The Drum; 1981 Ted's
   Ambition; 1982 Rule by the Sword
Flamboyant Stakes: 1972 Dream World; 1975 Party Line;
   1986 Melly Maloy; 1988 Right Back; 1989 Northern
   Princess; 1990 Canzonet
Natal Breeders Stakes: 1972 Glenever; 1973 Magic Square;
   1981 Ted's Ambition; 1982 Sugar Cane
Port Natal Handicap: 1976 Lightning Shot; 1979 Costain;
   1980 Ever Faithful

Josef Dorfman Memorial: 1978 Kings Rhapsody; 1984
  Opera Hat
Stewards Cup: 1973 Sentinel; 1977 Row To Rio; 1980
  Young Captain; 1983 Ted's Ambition
Michaelmas Handicap: 1973 Kings Palace; 1975 Majestic
  Crown
Strelitzia Plate: 1974 Just Jane; 1976 Shelter; 1977 Wedding
  Guest; 1981 Breyani
Gordon Kirkpatrick Memorial: 1979 Row To Rio; 1981 War
  Ribbon; 1985 Harry Flasher
Germiston November Handicap: 1974 Foreign Agent
Cape Flying Championship: 1975 Sentinel
Johannesburg Spring Handicap: 1978 The Maltster
Johannesburg Merchants: 1980 Bizet; 1981 Rotterdam
Clairwood Merchants: 1975 King Of Tonga
Durban Nursery: 1979 Kellerbar; 1982 Hero Worship; 1986
  Kirklevington
Easter Handicap: 1979 Faithful Hussar; 1980 Sunpath; 1981
  Swan Prince; 1984 High Fling
Java Handicap: 1980 Lawn; 1983 Peace Talk
Debutante Stakes: 1981 Magic Vision; 1985 Do A Dance
The Dingaans: 1980 Swan Prince; 1989 Topa Inca
Lonsdale Stirrup Cup: 1981 English Statesman; 1983 Royal
  Play
Natal Free Handicap: 1981 Peace Talk; 1985 Harrington
Transvaal Summer Champion Stakes: 1987 Parisian
  Affair
Kruger Day Handicap: 1984 North Star
Centenary Sprint: 1982 Ted's Ambition
Johannesburg Goldfields Handicap: 1980 Dunmore

Christmas Handicap: 1971 Sentinel; 1989 Chief Of Men
The Sarie Marais: 1974 Justine
In Full Flight Stakes: 1973 Glenever; 1974 Sledgehammer
Festival Juvenile Handicap: 1973 Sledgehammer
Easter Bonnet Nursery Stakes: 1973 Sun Monarch
Champion Nursery Stakes: 1973 Sun Monarch
Summerveld Free Handicap: 1973 Majestic Crown
The Presidents Trophy: 1974 Sentinel
New Year Nursery Plate: 1975 Bold Monarch
J. G. Hollis Memorial: 1975 Jamaican Chief; 1983 Lotus
   Land
Lady's Bracelet: 1976 Free Enterprise
Summerveld Stakes: 1978 Bold Tropic
General Tyres Handicap: 1975 Peri Peri
Merchants Handicap: 1973 Glenever
Kings Cup: 1974 Glenever
Jack Stubbs Memorial: 1975 Sentinel
Duco Dulux Cup: 1975 Sentinel
Allen Snijman Stakes: 1988 Castleton
Province of Natal Stakes: 1992 Melting
Administrator's Classic: 1990 Topa Inca
Michael Roberts Handicap: 1991 Dutch Flyer

2. *Zimbabwe*

Juvenile Stakes: 1979 Gold Standard; 1980 Riboboy
Clifford Dupont Memorial Trophy: 1979 Gold Standard
Round The Course Handicap: 1976 Gondola
Sports Pool Stakes: 1977 Don Ribot

Ascot Guineas: 1979 Chintisse
Turnbull Memorial Trophy: 1980 Happy Halo

APPENDIX III: Principal Races Won in Europe

1. *UK*

2,000 Guineas: 1991 Mystiko
Oaks: 1993 Intrepidity
King George VI and Queen Elizabeth Diamond Stakes: 1988
    Mtoto; 1993 Opera House
Coronation Cup: 1993 Opera House
Eclipse Stakes: 1987 and 1988 Mtoto
Champion Stakes: 1988 Indian Skimmer
Nunthorpe Stakes: 1992 Lyric Fantasy
Hazlewood Foods Sprint Cup: 1993 Wolfhound
Juddmonte International: 1991 Terimon
Fillies Mile: 1992 Ivanka
Middle Park Stakes: 1988 Mon Tresor
Royal Lodge Stakes: 1986 Bengal Fire; 1988 High Estate
Queen Anne Stakes: 1988 Waajib; 1992 Sikeston
Challenge Stakes: 1988 Salse; 1991 Mystiko; 1993 Catrail
Yorkshire Cup: 1990 Braashee
Prince of Wales's Stakes: 1988 Mtoto
Geoffrey Freer Stakes: 1988 Top Class; 1992 and 1994
    Shambo
Lowther Stakes: 1988 Miss Demure

Sun Chariot Stakes: 1988 Indian Skimmer
Duke of York Stakes: 1992 Shalford
Queen Mary Stakes: 1992 Lyric Fantasy
Diadem Stakes: 1993 Catrail
Cork and Orrery Stakes: 1988 Posada; 1992 Shalford
Nell Gwyn Stakes: 1988 Ghariba
Earl of Sefton Stakes: 1991 Terimon
Ormonde Stakes: 1990 Braashee; 1993 and 1994 Shambo
Brigadier Gerard Stakes: 1987 Mtoto
Doncaster Cup: 1990 Al Maheb
Cherry Hinton Stakes: 1992 Sayyedati
Ribblesdale Stakes: 1992 Armarama
Falmouth Stakes: 1992 Gussy Marlowe
Musidora Stakes: 1991 Gussy Marlowe
Princess Margaret Stakes: 1990 Cloche d'Or
Molecomb Stakes: 1992 Millyant
Prestige Stakes: 1988 Life at the Top; 1992 Love of
  Silver
May Hill Stakes: 1988 Tessla
Select Stakes: 1988 Mtoto; 1991 Filia Ardross; 1993
  Knifebox
Henry II Stakes: 1993 Brier Creek
Thresher Classic Trial: 1991 Hailsham
Hungerford Stakes: 1991 Only Yours
Kiveton Park Stakes: 1988 Salse
Diomed Stakes: 1987 Lauries Warrior; 1988 Waajib
Chester Cup: 1987 Just David
European Free Handicap: 1988 Lapierre; 1991 Mystiko
Northumberland Plate: 1988 Stavordale
Queen's Vase: 1986 Stavordale

Ebor Handicap: 1987 Daarkom
Schweppes Golden Mile: 1987 Waajib
Ascot Stakes: 1990 Retouch

2. *Ireland*

2,000 Guineas: 1993 Barathea
Phoenix Champion Stakes: 1988 Indian Skimmer
Moyglare Stud Stakes: 1992 Sayyedati
Tattersalls Gold Cup: 1988 Shady Heights; 1993 George
    Augustus
Sea World International Stakes: 1992 Sikeston; 1994 Alflora
Matron Stakes: 1992 Cloud of Dust; 1993 Chanzi
Tattersalls Breeders Stakes: 1992 Mr Martini

3. *France*

Prix du Rond-Point: 1987 Waajib
Prix Dollar: 1993 Knifebox
Prix Royal Oak: 1990 Braashee
Grand Prix de Deauville: 1988 Ibn Bey
Prix du Conseil de Paris: 1992 Garden of Heaven

4. *Italy*

Premio Lydia Tesio: 1986 Dubian
Derby Italiano: 1989 Prorutori

Premio Vittoria di Capua: 1989 Just A Flutter; 1990 and
    1991 Sikeston
Premio Roma: 1991 Sikeston
Premio Presidente della Repubblica: 1991 and 1992 Sikeston
Premio Ribot: 1990 Sikeston
Premio Melton: 1994 Fred Bongusto
Premio Emilio Turati: 1994 Alflora
Gran Premio del Jockey Club e Coppa d'Oro: 1994 Lando

5. *Germany*

Ammerschlager Frankfurt-Pokal: 1991 Sir Felix
Deutscher Buchmacher Stutenpreiss von Neuss: 1991
    Palanga

6. *Turkey*

Bosphorus Trophy: 1993 Shrewd Idea

Index

More Sporting Biography from Headline

WILL CARLING

DAVID NORRIE

'This superbly written and illustrated book . . . provides a warts-and-all account that would be hard to surpass.' ROBERT ARMSTRONG, *The Guardian*

'A cracking good read about the life of England's greatest rugby captain.' TERRY GODWIN, *The People*

David Norrie's authorised biography of Will Carling has been fully updated to include England's historic victory over New Zealand in 1993, the 1994 Five Nations Championship, the end of the Geoff Cooke era and England's first tour of South Africa in ten years. Now firmly established as one of England's most popular and charismatic sporting superstars, Carling has been instrumental in raising the profile of rugby union to ever greater heights – a rare beacon of English sporting success. Carling has co-operated fully with David Norrie to ensure that this revealing and entertaining biography is the most complete portrait of him available.

NON-FICTION / BIOGRAPHY / SPORT 0 7472 4285 2

More Sporting Biography from Headline

VENABLES
THE INSIDE STORY

HARRY HARRIS and
STEVE CURRY

'Two leading football writers have presented a warts-and-all picture of Venables which praises his footballing qualities but asks serious questions about the way he has handled his business dealings.' *Guardian*

'A highly readable volume.' *Sunday Telegraph*

Hugely popular with the players and the fans, Terry Venables remains a controversial figure. Harris and Curry have built up a complete portrait of the man from Dagenham who, after a successful playing career, found his true role in football when he turned to management. Highly ambitious, he took Barcelona to the European Cup final and then moved back to Tottenham, eventually rescuing the club with Alan Sugar. But this so-called 'dream team' soon fell apart, and the mutual recriminations seemed to have tarnished his reputation so much that the England job he had always desired would again elude him. But on his appointment, the England side began to play with a style and confidence that had been lacking in the Taylor years. Harris and Curry bring the story of Venables' life right up to date and assess what the future holds for the man who looks to lead England to victory in the 1996 European Championships.

NON-FICTION / BIOGRAPHY 0 7472 4544 4

A selection of non-fiction from Headline

THE DRACULA SYNDROME	Richard Monaco & William Burt	£5.99 ☐
DEADLY JEALOUSY	Martin Fido	£5.99 ☐
WHITE COLLAR KILLERS	Frank Jones	£4.99 ☐
THE MURDER YEARBOOK 1994	Brian Lane	£5.99 ☐
THE PLAYFAIR CRICKET ANNUAL	Bill Findall	£3.99 ☐
ROD STEWART	Stafford Hildred & Tim Ewbank	£5.99 ☐
THE JACK THE RIPPER A–Z	Paul Begg, Martin Fido & Keith Skinner	£7.99 ☐
THE *DAILY EXPRESS* HOW TO WIN ON THE HORSES	Danny Hall	£4.99 ☐
COUPLE SEXUAL AWARENESS	Barry & Emily McCarthy	£5.99 ☐
GRAPEVINE; THE COMPLETE WINEBUYERS HANDBOOK	Anthony Rose & Tim Atkins	£5.99 ☐
ROBERT LOUIS STEVENSON; DREAMS OF EXILE	Ian Bell	£7.99 ☐

All Headline books are available at your local bookshop or newsagent, or can be ordered direct from the publisher. Just tick the titles you want and fill in the form below. Prices and availability subject to change without notice.

Headline Book Publishing, Cash Sales Department, Bookpoint, 39 Milton Park, Abingdon, OXON, OX14 4TD, UK. If you have a credit card you may order by telephone – 01235 400400.

Please enclose a cheque or postal order made payable to Bookpoint Ltd to the value of the cover price and allow the following for postage and packing:

UK & BFPO: £1.00 for the first book, 50p for the second book and 30p for each additional book ordered up to a maximum charge of £3.00.
OVERSEAS & EIRE: £2.00 for the first book, £1.00 for the second book and 50p for each additional book.

Name ....

Address ....

....

....

If you would prefer to pay by credit card, please complete:
Please debit my Visa/Access/Diner's Card/American Express (delete as applicable) card no:

Signature .... Expiry Date ....